St LUKES
OLD STREET
OLD STREET
OLD ST. ROAD
E C
FARRINGDON STREET
VIADUCT
NEW BRIDGE STREET
ALDERSGATE STREET
CHEAPSIDE
CANNON STREET
L O N D O
HIGH STREET SHOREDITCH
LONDON BRIDGE
T H A M E S

The London Knife Book

An A-Z guide to London Cutlers

1820-1945

by

Ron Flook

Published by: Antique Knives ltd.

First published: July 2008

Published by Antique Knives Ltd.
PO BOX 3892, Farnham Common, Slough, SL1 0JS, England.
Design, photography, layout and production:
David Watson, Graphic Solutions, Farnham Common, England.

www.antique-knives.co.uk

Printed & bound in England

British Library Cataloguing in Publication Data
A catalogue record for this book is available from the British Library

ISBN 978-0-9559507-1-1

Large 18th century folder by Bernardeau who used the name BERNADO.
This knife has cow horn scales and is stamped: **BER**
NADO

A trade card for James Bernardeau, Russell Court, Drury Lane. London has, at the top an oval cartouche inscribed;

BER

NADO

over a letter **L** over a pistol. The trade card describes James Bernardeau, thus;
"Razor maker at the Pistol & L in Russell Court, in Drury Lane.
Make's & Sell's Razors, Siszors (sic), Penknives, Lancetts and all other Instruments. Also, Silver, Chiney, Ivory, Ebony handled knives & forks."

This trade card also relates the business of one; Jaques Bernardeau at the same address "Couteliere" etc., in the French language.

James Bernardeau was of Huguenot decent probably forced into exile in England. He is listed according to Southwick from 1727 to 1753. James had 3 children, one of whom died in infancy. A second son also called James does not appear to have succeeded to the business this developing down the female line when James senior died. The business was run by his wife Ann from 1753 to 1766. She left the business to her daughter Ann who by this time was herself a widow. She subsequently married a Stephen Gagnon who himself was a cutler. Stephen remained at Russell Court until 1787 when the premises were taken over by the cutler John Underwood who died in 1803.
(*Trade card from private collection*).

Contents

Dedication

This book is dedicated to my wife Margaret.

Introduction

Most of the work that has been published on the subject of Bowie and other antique knives has concentrated on the work of either American or Sheffield Cutlers, the latter holding considerable sway over the knife market from the heyday of the Bowie until well into the 1920's. Even though the American cutlers made inroads into the supremacy of firms such as Wostenholm and Rodgers in the US market, Sheffield-made knives maintained a mark of quality even after the demise of its major share in the US market.

However, less well known in the history of Bowie, folders, hunting and others knives is the part played by London. Whilst a lot of Sheffield products went to the American market much of the work of the London cutlers found a home with military personnel and adventurers heading for Britain's extensive Colonial Empire. Included in these cutlers were the surgical instrument makers who made not only superb folding scalpels etc. but also very high quality bowies and hunting knives, a fact well illustrated by some of the knives made by Weiss and the superb exhibition knife made by Evans.

In addition as the centre of the Empire on which the sun never set there were those cutlery retailers who also served the demands for practical knives. Yet it is the case that London has been virtually ignored by previous authors. Whilst a few London Knives have appeared in books on Bowie Knives and the subject has been the subject of a short article in one American Knife book no real research has been undertaken into a centre of:

(a) cutlery manufacture which rivalled Sheffield in quality if not quantity;
(b) cutlery retailing which was, probably at its height, unrivalled anywhere in the world.

In trying to rectify this situation and given that the London Cutlery Industry dates back many hundreds of years, there being records of cutlers who existed in the 12th Century, it was obviously difficult to choose an actual time span for this book. However I decided that a good starting point was just prior to the development of the Bowie i.e. 1820 and to finish at the end of World War 2 by which time the London Cutlery industry had all but disappeared. There are however a few overlaps in these dates where it helps with the history of a particular company.

In terms of its contents the book looks at cutlers and cutlery manufacturers. It is however necessary to clarify the use of the term Cutler in relation to this book. The London Trade Directories for the period list up until circa 1925 Cutlers. This encompassed those that purely sold cutlery of all kinds i.e. retailers, as well as manufacturers. In 1925 the directory has two entries - one for cutlers and one for Cutlery Manufacturers. There were also other retailers of knives who did not have themselves listed in the cutlery section of the Trade Directories. Typically some of the London Gunsmiths who without doubt sold knives, along with toolmakers, ironmongers and fancy goods dealers etc. These latter three are virtually impossible to quantify or identify and identification can only come from examples of their wares.

There are also some references within the book to surgical instrument makers who were skilled cutlers in their own right and to some sword cutlers where they are known to have made or retailed knives. For those interested in greater detail of these specialist areas reference to one of the standard works on the subject should be made.

It is worth stating that unlike some coffee table style knife books this is not a book which just illustrates mint or exhibition quality examples of knives. It is primarily a book about LONDON makers and retailers illustrated, where possible, by examples of their work. Some of the knives shown are poor examples in collecting terms but they are in many cases the only ones found by a particularly retailer or maker or exhibit certain features which compliment the book.

The format of the book is based on an A to Z listing. Where possible the history of particular firms has been expanded to give more detail and also to identify some of the family relationships. However this is not obvious in many cases. It is possible via common addresses to conclude the family relationships between some of the cutlers but in others these are not easy to establish. A typical example of this is the name of MOORE. There are 14 entries under this surname but the actual family relationship between them is far from clear. This further complicated by the fact that in the 1881 census for London there is an Alexander Moore listed as a cutler, yet no cutler of this name exist in the trade directories for this period neither can his name be linked through the census returns to the Moore's that are listed.

Information has been drawn from a number of sources. Primarily the Post Office and Trade Directories, followed by names taken from known examples, sales and auction catalogues along with previously published works.

In regard to the trade directories I adopted the approach of searching the directories in generally 5 yearly blocks though on occasion when looking to pin down a particular firm directory entries within two or three years have been used. Thus the dates quoted will generally be accurate within 5 years. However it should be noted that the directories did not start listing by trade until 1822, prior to that they were alphabetical. Noting that the 1820 directory ran to something like 230 pages picking out all the cutlers against alphabetically listed names is bound to result in some omissions. It is also interesting to note that this 1820 alphabetical listing is missing the names of some cutlers who are known to have been in operation at that time, for example Verinder.

In using the London directories as a basis of research it is worth stating that there is a lot of confusion over whether some London cutlers were actually working cutlers i.e. manufactured and produced knives etc. rather than just cutlery retailers. In some cases the directories add confusion to this problem. For example in some Directories manufacturing cutlers are identified by some form of symbol against their name but it is the case when a company is identified as a working cutler such identification is not consistent. For example in the 1855 Directory no company is specifically identified as a working cutler, yet in the 1860 Directory such companies are identified. Consequently it is very difficult to specifically identify some firms as working cutlers or not, so the list and supporting text cannot be 100% accurate. Where the data supports a company being a working cutler I have said so, but there may be some that have been missed due to lack of accurate evidence.

Though some of the more obscure names may have slipped my scrutiny, it should also be noted that I have in most cases omitted from the listings those Sheffield cutlers who had outlets in London and placed their names in the London Trade Directories. Typically many of the larger Sheffield cutlers, such as Joseph Rodgers, had London outlets. Although there were also some with Sheffield associations who did in fact start out in London but who placed some of their manufacture in Sheffield whilst also retaining manufactories in London and in general I have made mention of those with recorded London factories as some of their products could have been London-made.

Acknowledgements

The following have assisted in the preparation of this book and they receive my grateful appreciation for answering my many questions, providing items in their collections for study or for providing information from their files:
David Petty, John Pidgeon, Harry Jones, Jeff Wheeler, John Romans The Clerk of The Worshipful Company of Cutlers, The Guildhall Library, Keith Burton for providing and allowing me to use photos from his book "A Sure Defence: The Bowie Knife Book", to Bill Adams et al for allowing me to use illustrations from the Antique Bowie Knife Book, and to Bill Clausen et al for permission to use the image of the Evans knife. Buck and Ryan, and Buck and Hickman for providing me with historical background along with permission to use images of their early premises, David Stanley Auctions for permission to use the image of John Jacob Holtzappfel, Wilkinson Sword Co, along with the late John Arlett, and Robert Wilkinson Latham for information and images relating to Wilkinson Sword. Cogswell and Harrison for the gun plate on page 42. John Weiss & Son Ltd. for permission to use the images from their surgical instrument catalogue. Reed Elsevier, owners of Kelly's Directories, for permission to use images from directories of the Victorian period. Dennis Wells for use of his Thornhill catalogue.

A major vote of thanks also goes to Dave Watson of Graphic Solutions for his major assistance on photography, layout and production.

As previously mentioned I must also give due credit to those whose research and published works have formed the basis of some of my background information i.e. Elisabeth Bennion for her work on Antique Medical and Dental Instruments, Richard Bezdek's Swords and Sword makers of England and Scotland, and Leslie Southwick's excellent study on London Silver hilted swords. Both of these latter two books are particularly helpful in regard to the biographies of London's sword makers and cutlers. Also The Directory of Gold and Silversmiths and allied trades 1838 – 1915 by J Culme which provided interesting details on a number of silversmiths who were also cutlers.

Photo Credits:

Bill Adams - Plates 118, 127, 128
Keith Burton - Plates 43, 58
Bill Clausen – Plate 45

1 The Worshipful Company of Cutlers

No book on the history of London Cutlery can ignore the part played by the Cutlers Company of London. In writing this section I have drawn heavily on Girtin's "The Mark of the Sword" and less so on "The Worshipful Cutlers Company of London- A Brief History" by Dudley Hayton.
However it should be noted that with a history dating back to the 13th Century and Girtin's work running into some 448 pages, this section can only be seen a the briefest of introductions to the Company. Its aim however is to give a flavour of the Company's involvement in the cutlery trade rather than a full history of its development.

With a history of a fraternity or society possibly dating back to the late 1100s, the first reference to the Cutlers Company occurs in 1285. In about 1307 the Company sought freedom for self rule which would give them guild status and the ability to try members in their own court. The history of the Cutlers Company was however inextricably mixed up with the politics of the day and unlike other Livery Companies it failed to make much headway in the control of the trade. It eventually received its first charter in 1416 and the independence that the Charter gave them allowed them to hold lands and houses and to have greater control over the craft.

The Company prospered over the next several centuries but not without a number of problems with other Guilds such as the Armourers. However the two Companies were put on an even footing to search for deceitful blades and searches by the Companies in the 1590s resulted in 335 blades being confiscated and 648 being defaced at Cutlers hall.

Control of the craft did however continue to be difficult over the centuries and by the middle of the 18th century

the Company ceased to have any real control, with much of the cutlery trade moving to Sheffield. The Cutlers were reduced to a point where in 1737 they were one of the Companies who pleaded poverty as an excuse for not attending the Lord Mayor's Day. By 1755 the Company only numbered 33, a fall from 123 in 1722.

During this period the authorities failed to find a solution to the problem of cutlers who were not members of the Company because they preferred to work unhindered by the Company's regulations. In 1756 there was an Act of Common Council for Regulating the Company of Cutlers in London, and it gave the Company what it required i.e. legal force behind its wish to control the trade.

However, the Company's control over the trade seems to have been lost in the later half of the 18th century, as they were more interested in their lands and estates. It was not until 1819 that they further interested themselves in the trade, when they took notice of the Act to Regulate the Cutlery trade in England.

This act made it illegal to mark or sell cast cutlery with the hammer mark i.e. the mark that could only be used by those who manufactured by the hammer. The same restriction also was applied to the use of words such as LONDON MADE or LONDON, these could not be used unless the item was made in the capital or within a 20 mile radius. It is alleged that this Act was directed in part to those London Cutlers who put their own mark on Sheffield-made products, and many working cutlers based in London did not belong to the Guild so the Cutlers Company control was almost nonexistent.

Despite this Act the Cutlers Company did not or would not act to control this alleged abuse, thus in 1825 the Sheffield Cutlery trade proposed another Bill on the marking of cutlery. This Bill was however defeated after a strong defence by the Cutlers Company. It is interesting to note that this is a repeat in reverse of an attempt by London in 1624 to stop Sheffield Cutlers using London marks.

After another period of inaction in the cutlery trade the Company, in 1842, yet again turned its attention to control of the trade. At this time most of the cutlery made in the United Kingdom was made in Sheffield, including that sold by London merchants who marked Sheffield products with their name and street but omitting the word LONDON. But at this time London did still retain a major market in the manufacture of swords and surgical instruments.

In May 1842 the Company appointed a Committee to consider the by-laws of the Company and the Act of Parliament to regulate the cutlery trade. This resulted in the Company placing an advertisement in three London newspapers the text of which read:

> *Caution to Manufacturers, Dealers and Purchasers of Cutlery*
> *The Worshipful Company of Cutlers of London have reason to believe that table Knives and other Articles of Cutlery of inferior temper and quality and manufactured at a*

The present Cutlers Hall in Warwick Lane, near St Paul's Cathedral.

great distance from London are constantly sold to the Public with false marks and as being the genuine Manufacture of Cutlers resident in London and its immediate vicinity, [They] desire for the protection of the Public and as a Caution to Manufacturers and Dealers in Cutlery to make more generally known the Statute of the 59 Geo 3, cap 7 (1819) by which it is enacted that all persons who shall mark any Knives, Blades and other Articles of Cutlery, Edged Tools and hardware requiring a cutting edge with the words London or London made or any words having a similitude thereto, unless such Articles have been manufactured in the City of London or within twenty miles thereof, shall in every case forfeit all such Articles together with the sum of ten pounds for any quantity not exceeding one dozen of the Articles so marked, sold or exposed for sale, and for every quantity exceeding one dozen ten pounds for every dozen thereof : such sums to be levied and recovered with costs, as in the Act provided.

This advertisement further went on to add that persons could visit Cutlers Hall to inspect the Act and receive further information.

The Company then again lapsed back into its old interest of lands and investments. The Great Exhibition of 1851 does not seem to have stirred their interest even though some London cutlers exhibited i.e. Thornhill, Blofeld, Deane, Mechi, J & G Morton, J & R Sharpe, J Moseley and Son, William T Loy Jnr., and Joseph Buck.
Some surgical Instrument makers also exhibited, amongst them Weiss, Bigg, Evans, Coexter, Philip and Whicker, Simpson.

The next flurry of activity in relation to the trade was in 1879 when they promoted a Cutlery Exhibition and Competition. Three classes of cutlery were admitted, General,

CLASS I GENERAL CUTLERY

Blyde. J	Milton St, Sheffield	Fine Scissors and Pen Knives
Brent. T.G.G.	43 City Road, London	Razors, scissors and pocket knives
Browne, R.H.	Hackney, London	Tailor' shears and scissors
Clarke, Shirley and Co.	Eyre Lane, Sheffield	Razors, Pocket Knives and fine scissors
Cole, G.	Pine Street, Spafields, London	Table Knives
Dewsnap, EW.	St John's Square, London	Trade Knives and Table CutleryKnives
Fenton and Sons	Eyre St, Sheffield	Table Knives and general Cutlery
Gibbins and Sons	Belgrave Works, Sheffield	Fine Scissors
Gorville and Sons	159 Eyre St, Sheffield	Fine Scissors
Greenhough, J	284 Rockingham St, Sheffield	Sportsmen's Knives
Hobson and Sons	95 Arundel St, Sheffield	Fine Scissors
Herbert and Sons	West Smith, London	Butcher's, Provision and Ham Dealers Knives
Kramm	Old Street, London	Razors
Lund and Son	Fleet St, London	Hunting Knives, Wine Knives and all kinds of table and spring knife cutlery
Morton, J	39 Cheapside, London	Scissors, Razors and Pocket Knives
Mappin and Webb	Mansion House Buildings, London	Table and General Cutlery
Meyer and Meltzer	71 Great Portland St, London	Table Knives with Patent fastenings, and patent pocket scissors
Needham, J	69 Arundel St. Sheffield	Table Knives with patent handles
Revitt, F.	53 Kenyon Alley, Allen St, Sheffield	Razors
Slater Brothers	94 Scotland St, Sheffield	Scissors, Pocket Knives, and Razors
Stacy, W.K.	4 Newgate St. London	Cook's Knives and Table Cutlery`
Saynor, Cooke and Ridal	Paxton Works, Sheffield	Pruning and Budding Knives, and Scissors
Thornhill and Co.	144 New Bond St. London	Dressing Case Instruments and Fine Cutlery
Williams, T.	West Smithfield, London	Butcher's and other trade knives

CLASS II- SURGICAL CUTLERY

Ash and Sons	Golden Square, London	Dental Instruments
Bailey and Sons	16 Oxford St, London	Trusses
Collins, D.T.	20 Poland St. London	Dental Instruments
Chapman	111 Aldersgate St. London	Lancets
Durst, F.	39 Whitcombe St. London	Trusses
Evans and Wormull	31 Stamford St. London	Forceps and Eye Instruments
Hobson and Sons	95 Arundel St, Sheffield	Surgical Scissors
Khrone and Co.	Duke St. London	Dental Instruments
Meyer and Meltzer	71 Great Portland St, London	Trepanners, Flexible Forceps, Aspirators
Maw, Son and Thompson	Aldersgate St. London	Spray Distributors, Aspirators and all kinds of surgical instruments
Masters and Sons	210 New Kent Road	Artificial Limbs
Pratt, J.F.	420 Oxford St. London	Trusses

Sanders, F.H. . . . . 23 Osnaburgh St. London. . . . . Spinal Supporters, Leg Instruments

CLASS III – SWORD CUTLERY

Wilkinson and Sons . . . . . . 27 Pall Mall, London . . . . Illustrations of Sword Manufacture in every stage of preparation, from bar of steel to the polished blade, and case of regulation and presentation swords.

The one gold medal award went to Wilkinson Sword, 12 silver, and 10 bronze medals were awarded along with a number of certificates. The full list of medal winners is below:

GOLD MEDAL	SILVER MEDAL	BRONZE MEDAL
Wilkinson and Son	J. Fenton and Son, Sheffield	Mappin and Webb, London and Sheffield
	Saynor, Cooke and Ridal, Sheffield	
	T. Williams, London	
	J. Greenhough, Sheffield	
	Gorrill and Sons, Sheffield	
	H Hobson and Sons, Sheffield	
	J. Fenton and Sons, Sheffield	
	R.H. Browne, London	
	Meyer and Meltzer, London	
	F. Revitt, Sheffield	
	Masters and Sons, London	
	Khrone and Co. London	Maw, Son and Thompson, London
	J.F. Pratt, London	
	W. Bailey, London	
	C. Ash and Son, London	
	Lund and Son, London	

Surgical, and Swords. There were 92 competitors, which comprised of 54 individual artisans or apprentices, 12 Sheffield cutlers and 26 firms from London including surgical instrument makers. The list of Companies that exhibited are listed on pages 4 and 5.

It is of note that some winners won more than one medal as the exhibition and competition had a number of different categories.

As a result of the Exhibition and the associated lectures the Company decided to further develop its influence over the trade by launching an apprenticeship scheme. In addition to the Exhibition the Company also instituted a series of technical lectures which continued until 1883. When the lectures were discontinued the Company gave a sum of money to the City and Guilds of London Institute for prizes for those engaged in the cutlery trade.

By 1903 the Apprentices were all that remained of the Company's cutlery industry responsibilities. In 1911 they were invited by Sheffield to bring a case against an Italian manufacturer who was stamping his goods with a London mark. The Company decided however not to pursue the matter.

Today the Company still maintains an interest in the cutlery trade by fostering apprenticeships in the surgical instrument trade.

The frieze on Cutlers Hall depicts various aspects of the cutlers art whilst above the door is the Coat of Arms of the Company. Also of note is the Elephant emblem. This has its links in the Elephant and Castle district of south London. The Public House called the Elephant and Castle in that area was apparently built circa 1760 on the site of a smithy that had the same name and sign. The connection being the elephant ivory used for knife hilts. The Castle refers to the howdah on the back of the elephant.

2 London Cutlers & Retailers

1. Introduction

As will have been seen from the shortened history of the Cutlers Company knives had been made in London for hundreds of years. However with the rise of Sheffield as an industrial centre, with its ready access to raw materials and water power with which to turn the grindstones, much of the London cutlery industry went into decline. There did however remain some remnants of the industry in the form of some manufacturing cutlers, surgical instrument makers, and sword makers. These were supported by a large band of retailers who bought their products from Sheffield and elsewhere.

Many of the Sheffield cutlers made their name with the development of the Bowie Knife which was conceived by Rezin Bowie and made sometime prior to 1827 and which came to prominence during the now famous Vidalia Sandbar fight involving Jim Bowie. Sheffield were quick to latch onto the demand created by the Bowie Knife and they found a ready market during the mid 1800's.

This market provided something of a golden age for the Sheffield cutlers, but London was not left behind in terms of finding ready markets for not only its manufactured products but also those it retailed. Much of this 1800s period was when the British Empire was at its height, the Empire on which the sun never set. Adventurers and colonists opened up Africa, and Queen Victoria was Empress of India. During this period eminent surgeons had their surgical instruments made by top makers such a Weiss, adventurers and military men seeking a good knife also bought knives from such makers while others frequented outlets such as the Army and Navy Stores. For the London cutlery industry, be it manufacturing or retailing, this was also a golden age.

Unfortunately it was an age that couldn't last. Further pressures from Sheffield and from foreign imports and the impact of the First World War reduced both retail and manufacture. The Second World War further reduced this until by1945 when only 36 cutlers and London based Cutlery manufacturers were recorded. Compare this with the situation in 1900 when there were in the region of 130 entries.

2 Sheffield Made or London Made?

One of the major factors in the history of Sheffield and London made cutlery is the rivalry and some times contradictory information that surround the origin of some knives bearing a London address either with or without the word LONDON. So what is the position?

As both Levine and Girtin comment, by 1842 the Sheffield manufacturers made almost all the cutlery in the United Kingdom, including that sold by the London merchants who marked Sheffield products with their own name and street address but omitted the word 'London'. This also supported by Tweedale. In his book on the Sheffield Knife industry he states that:

"Sheffield firms made large quantities of knives for retailers all over the country, especially London, and were quite happy to stamp the buyer's name and mark on them. Some of the early 19th century Bowie Knives carry LONDON retailer's names and addresses, though the knives could not have been made anywhere but Sheffield."

It is thus without doubt that the vast majority of "London" knives were made in Sheffield.

The London guild i.e. the Cutlers Company rules forbade London Cutlers from selling products made outside London marked with their own trade or touch mark, however Levine comments that both Sheffield and the Dutch often counterfeited London marks. After the 1819 Act to Regulate the Cutlery Trade in England London Cutlers could use LONDON on their blades but it became illegal for anyone to use the word LONDON on a knife made outside the city.

But how valid is the argument that a knife lacking the word London must have been made outside the city? We have seen that there was some legal force behind the use of the word LONDON, but many cutlers did not belong to the Company, which in any case had little interest or power in controlling the trade.

As will be noted from the wording of the advertisement placed by the Cutlers Company in three London newspapers in 1842 the 1819 Act required the words "LONDON or LONDON MADE or any words having a similitude thereto" to be used. The word similitude means a likeness, representation or semblance, so the wording implies that the word LONDON did not specifically have to be used only some representation or semblance of the word.

Some Cutlers used the postal area of London in their address e.g. NW for North West. For example HOLTZAPPFEL sometimes only marked pieces with their name, typically the somewhat unique butterfly-style knife shown in Plate 78. It bears no indication of a City or Street. The knife design is rather unique for the period yet a number have been noted all marked in exactly the same way, yet no piece with a name other than HOLTZAPPFEL has been noted. One must ask one's self is it likely that any maker, for instance one based in Sheffield, would make such a unique knife for another company without taking advantage of the marketing opportunity to sell some with his own name? The answer is obviously NO, as the manufacture of knives made in Sheffield and marked for the London market did not prevent Sheffield from selling exactly the same knife themselves. A typical example of this is the knife generally known as The Explorer Knife (see Plate 43).

So it is possible for a LONDON made knife not to bear the word LONDON? A letter from the Clerk of the Cutlers Company throws an interesting perspective on this issue. It states that:

The requirement upon London cutlers to mark their goods with the London dagger mark and register their own marks with this Company had died out by the time of the 1819 Act and in any event only applied to those operating within the City of London and 3 miles around. The 1819 Act did not require London makers to mark their goods and there were undoubtedly knives produced in London after that time which were not readily identifiable as being London made.

So it is seems that it is possible that knives could have been made in London which do not bear the actual name in the stamping.

The one thing that is without doubt during the competitive history of Sheffield and London cutlery is the fact that London maintained its supremacy as a centre of sword-making. Besides Wilkinson many sword makers worked in London during the 1800's and early 1900's and whilst they clearly had the technical capability to make knives, those made by London sword makers are rare.

Similarly the surgical instrument makers had the technical capability to make knives but again, except for few well known makers such as Weiss, examples of knives made but such makers are rare but those that do exist are in most cases of the highest quality.

3 A-Z Listing of London Cutlers & Retailers

This chapter provides a list of London cutlers, both manufacturing and retail, and illustrates examples of their products from 1820 up until 1945. Postcard images from the Late Victorian and early 20th century period illustrating various streets where cutlers resided have also been included which show some of the changes that took place in the architecture of London during the Victorian period. Prior to this many parts of London, including those frequented by cutlers were little better than slums.

Plate 1.
A fine folder with locking main blade and pen blade. Ivory scales. Main blade is marked on the flat and small blade on the tang:

ADAMS & SON.
57 HAYMARKET

A

ABRAHAMS, ARTHUR A.
Successor to Hyman A. Abrahams and Sons, 65 and 66 Houndsditch E. and 23 and 29 Camomile St., *1908-1912*.

ABRAHAMS, BARNETT HENRY.
126 Houndsditch East *1895* then no trace until *1925*, when listed as Manufacturing Cutler at 133, 134, 135 Houndsditch.

ABRAHAMS, LEWIS.
436 Strand, *1846*.

ADAMS & SON.
A William Salkeld Adams, and Son with an address at 57 Haymarket first appeared in the *1875* directory. By *1880* the name had changed to Adams and Son with addresses at 57 Haymarket and 14 Norris Street, Haymarket. The 14 Norris Street address is not recorded with their name in the *1885*, however in the *1890* they are listed at 57 Haymarket and works 41 and 42 Marshall St. There is no trace of the firm in the *1895* directory.

ADAMS, GEORGE.
144 High Holborn. *c1806-1890*. George Adams were machine tool makers and dealers and well known for their watch and clock maker lathes and accessories. The company were taken over by Tyzack and Son.

ADDIS, WILLIAM.
98 Fleet St., *1820*. 26 Bride Lane, Fleet St., *1828-1829*.

ADDISON, S.
Working Cutler 36 Leather Lane, Holborn. *1828-1829*.

ALCOCK, GEORGE.
(Agent) 43 Queen Victoria St., 1895.

ALDERMAN, EDWIN
41 and 42 Barbican, and 16 Norton Folgate *1832-1836*. As Mrs S ALDERMAN in *1840*.

Plate 2.
Despite there being no trace of George Adams in the *1895* directories the can opener on this blade is from this era. Knife has nickel silver scales and besides the can opener has a cork screw and the main blade is marked:

GEORGE ADAMS
HIGH HOLBORN
W.C.

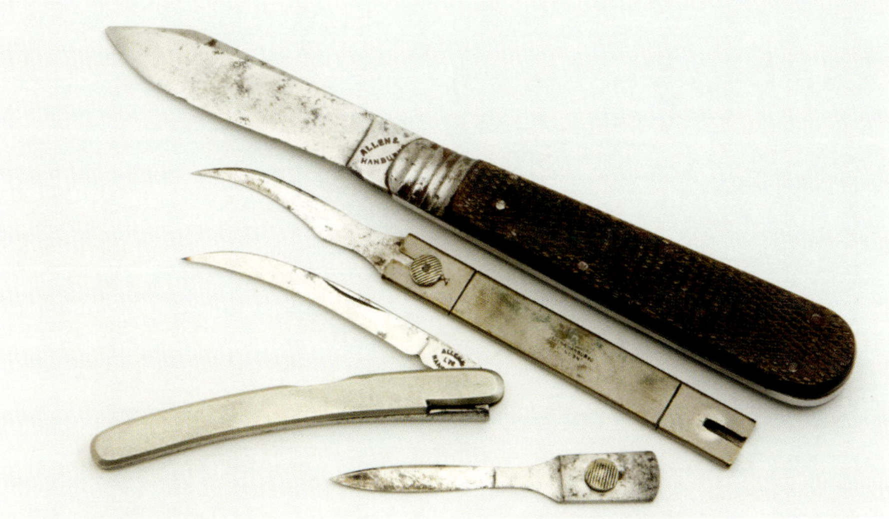

Plate 3.
(upper): Of similar form to that shown in Plate 7 this piece seems to have been constructed from the same stock but in this case the blade is fixed. The ricasso is stamped:

ALLEN &
HANBURYS

(middle): Strange military scalpel instrument that comes apart for both use and storage. The blade combination appears to be that of a Syme's Abscess and Paget's Tenotomy Knives. The piece is marked with the government broad arrow over:

ALLEN & HANBURYS
LONDON

(lower): Folding bistoury with nickel scales. Blade fitted with lock and marked on the ricasso:

ALLEN &
LTD.
HANBURYS

ALEXANDER, JOHN.
23 Clifton St. North, Finsbury, *1832*

ALLDIS, JAMES.
Manufacturing Cutler.
57 Gray's Inn Lane, *1846-1860.*
116 Gray's Inn Lane. *1866-1880*
27 Gray's Inn Lane, *1883-1895* and
1 Theobald's Rd. *1890-1895*
138 Gray's Inn Rd. *1900-1902*

ALLEN, ERNEST.
20 & 22 Parker St. Drury Lane *1915-1920* (Probably the son of James Allen see below)

ALLEN, FREDRICK WILLIAM.
1Short's Gardens, Drury Lane *1875-1900*

ALLEN, JAMES.
20 & 22 Parker St. Drury Lane *1880-1910*

ALLEN, JOHN WILLIAM.
37 Strand. Listed in *1865* as manufacturer of barrack room furniture, patent dispatch box and dressing case maker and military outfitters.

ALLEN, THOMAS.
Working Cutler. 25 New St. Cloth Fair *1823-1829.* A Thomas Allen reappears at this address *1850-1855*

ALLEN, THOMAS.
8 Green Arbour Court, Old Bailey *1832-1834*

ALLEN, WILLIAM.
6 Shire Lane *1836-1839*

ALLEN, WILLIAM.
Coal Yard, Drury Lane *1850*

ALLEN & HANBURYS.
Surgical Instrument Makers. Bennion records the history of this firm generally as follows, established in *1715* under the name of Bevan by *1774* the name had become Mildred. In *1795* the firm was titled Mildred and Allen and in *1870* the company now known as Allen and Hanburys had an address in Wigmore Street. In the late 1870's they had a factory in Bethnal Green. Taken over in *1972* by Escham Bros. and Walsh. However whilst I have not delved back into the 18th century records to confirm the early history my researches do not confirm the history as recorded by Bennion it being of note that any record of this company is curiously absent from much of the 19th century

Allen and Hanburys advertisement from 1895. (Reproduced by permission of Kelly's Directories.

directories. A William Bevan appears in the *1855* directory under Surgical Instrument Makers but is gone by *1860*. The first mention of Allen and Hanburys is in *1895* when they had an addresses at 48 Wigmore Street, 37 Lombard St. and a manufactory at Bethnal Green. The company went out of business by take over in *1972*.

AMMON, CHARLES.
45 White Street *1875*

AMOR, WILLIAM.
16 Glasshouse St. Regent St. *1885-1890*. 18 Gilbert St. Bloomsbury *1900-1910*. As AMOR W.W. Son and Co. Ltd. in *1915-1920*.

ANDERSON, WILLIAM.
Working Cutler, 24 Fleet St. *1823-1832*

ANDREWS, FREDRICK MACK.
34 Myddelton St. 1905. As second-hand cutlery 9 Chapel St., Islington. *1910-1915*

ANGLO-AMERICAN TRADING Co. Ltd.
Speciality safety razor. 12 Pindar St., Bishopsgate, *1915*

APPLEBEE, GEORGE.
14 Hatton Gardens *1822-1829*

APPLEBY, J.
Working Cutler, 4 St. John's St. Clerkenwell *1828-1839*

APPLEBY, J.
Working Cutler, 48 Banner Square, St. Luke's. *1829-1850*

APPLEBY, J JAMES.
20 Dorset Crescent, New North Road *1855-1866*. 130 East Road, City Road *1870*.

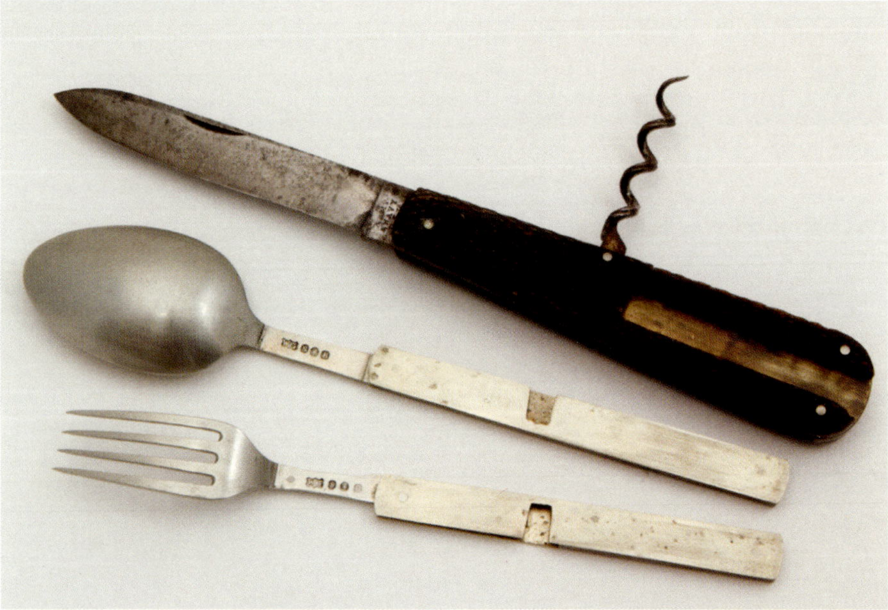

Plate 4.
Campaign/picnic knife, the hilt holds removable spoon and fork. The knife has a single blade and corkscrew with chequered ebony scales. The main blade is marked:

ARMY
& NAVY
C.S.L

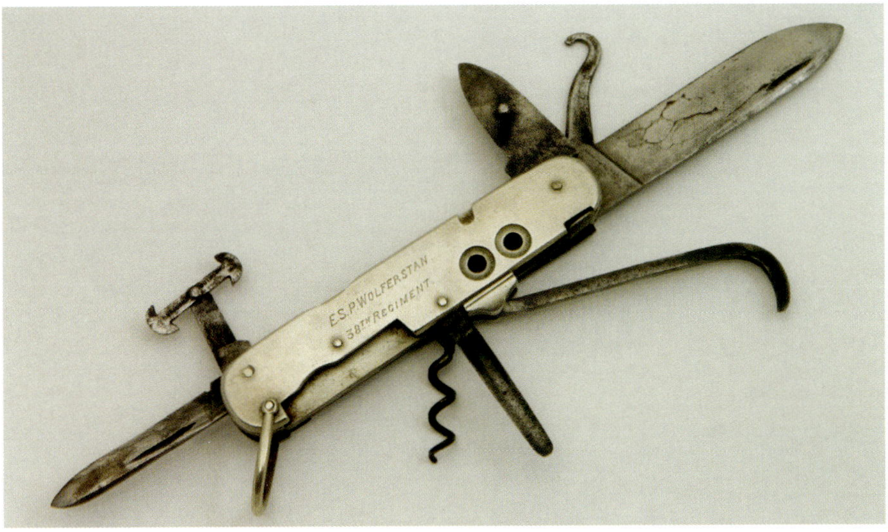

Plate 5.
All metal horseman's knife with regimental inscription to a E.S.P Wolferstan, 38th Regiment. (The Staffordshire Regiment). Wolferstan served in the line Regiment between *1881* and *1899* from then up until *1902* he served with the Militia. By a coincidence Wolferstan served in the 4th Battalion the Staffordshire Regiment at the same time as the author's great grandfather. Blades marked as previous specimen.

ARCHER, R.
3 Cummerbund St. West, Regent's Park *1846-1850*

ARDOUIN, GEORGE.
48 Banner St., St Luke's 1855

ARDOUIN, GEORGE.
299 Cambridge Rd. *1880.*
337 Bethnal Green *1885*

ARDOUIN, Mrs RACHEL.
154 Borough High St. *1895*

ARKELL, ALEXANDER.
291 Oxford St. *1875*
also at 233 Euston Rd. in *1880*

ARMITAGE J.
1 Bakers Row *1828-1832.*
2 Hampton St., Walworth Road *1836.*

ARMOUR, WILLIAM JAMES.
Cutler and tool dealer. 47 Hinchon St., Pimlico *1880*

ARMSTRONG, FRANK.
162 Fenchurch St. *1910.*

ARMY & NAVY CO-OPERATIVE SOCIETY Ltd., ARMY & NAVY C.S.L or ANCS.
Established in *1871* by a group of Army and Naval officers who

Plate 6.
A large sportsman's knife unusual in that the hoof pick is fitted with a lanyard ring. The saw blade only is marked:

ARMY
& NAVY
C.S.L

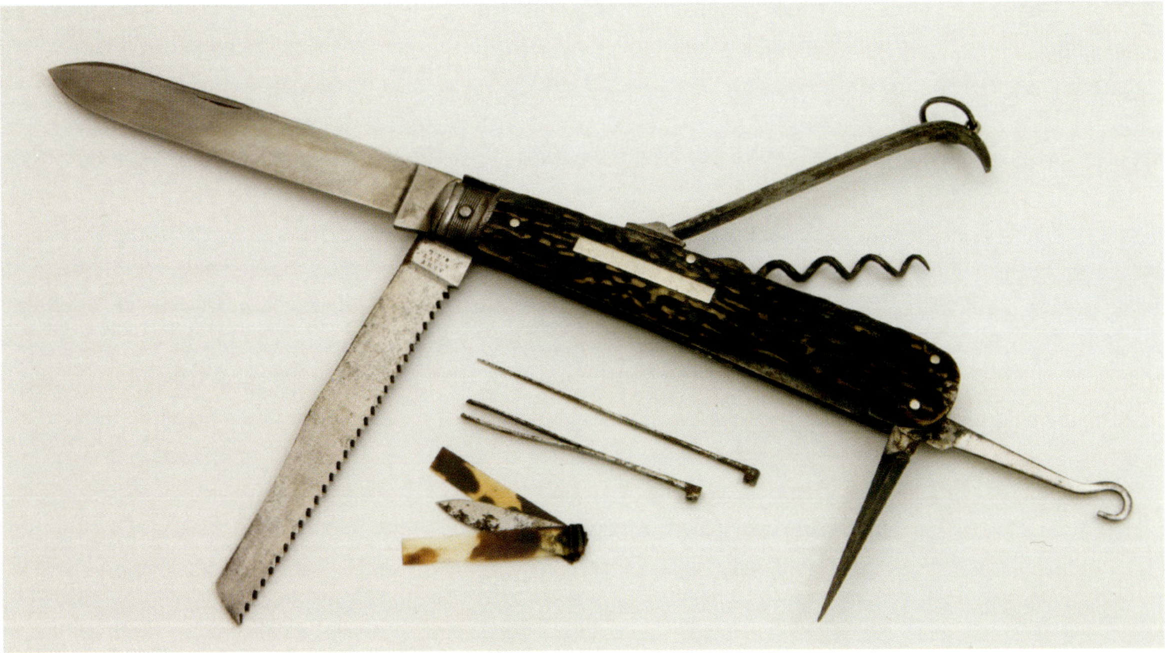

Plate 7.
(from top to bottom): This scalpel would have been part of a set, the handle being constructed so as to take a variety of different blades. The grip has ebony scales and a locking mechanism with which to hold the blades.

ARNOLD
& SONS
LONDON

Double ended folding scalpel with tortoiseshell scales. Both blades are fitted with surgical instrument locks and marked:

ARNOLD
LONDON

Scalpel marked :

ARNOLD & SON
LONDON

I do not know the pattern of this surgical/vetinary instrument but it is of the same type made by S Maw and Thompson shown in Plate 111. With nickel scales the blade is marked

ARNOLD & SONS
LONDON

Folding frame knife which may have some surgical significance given the maker but what is unknown. The frame is made from stainless steel the outer cover section being marked

ARNOLD & SONS.
LONDON

decided that wine was too expensive and that they would reduce cost by ordering it by the case at wholesale prices. Membership of the Army and Navy Co-operative Society was restricted to Officers and Noncommissioned Officers, their families and friends introduced by them. The subscription was five shillings for the first year, then half-a-crown annually. The Society acquired premises in Victoria Street London and eventually had branches in Bombay, Delhi, Calcutta and Karachi, also in Plymouth, Chatham, Aldershot and Southsea. It provided every conceivable service to its customers and its products were contained within a large cloth bound catalogue. Its co-operative status ended in *1922* when membership tickets were issued free without introduction. From a knife perspective ANCSL did not manufacture their own but bought them in from the Sheffield trade. However knives bearing their name are sought after by collectors as examples of such represent the heyday of the British Empire when an officer would have outfitted himself with a good quality knife for duty in the Colonies or even on the Western Front.

ARNOLD, ARTHUR.

90A Regent's St. *1890-1895*.
At 61A Piccadilly in *1905*.

ARNOLD & SONS.

Also listed as John and James Arnold in *1836*, and as James Arnold *1846-1850* this firm of Surgical Instrument Makers was established in *1819*. It appears to have been very much a family firm with the Arnold name being still associated with the Company in *1903* when the three partners were a Fanny Arnold, James Arnold and Edwin Arnold. The company were listed in *1897* as by appointment to HM Government as the manufacturers of surgical instruments etc. They held premises at 26, 30, 31 35, 36 West Smithfield Street E.C., 1, 2, 3, 18 and 19 Giltspur Street E.C. along with a factory at 44 Little Britain E.C. There is no record of them making any knives such as Bowies, however in *1885* they are shown as needle makers, razors makers and manufacturing cutlers.

ASH, J.
Working Cutler, 18 Plumbtree St. *1820-1823*

ASH, J.
21 Mortimer St. *1832-1839*

ASHTON, G.
16 Bleeding Hart Yard, Hatton Gardens *1855*

ASHTON, THOMAS.
Working Cutler, 133 Praed St., Paddington *1836*.

ASKINS WILLIAM CHARLES.
12 Hart St., Grosvener Square *1855*

ASPREY, CHARLES.
166 New Bond St. *1850*-present day. The well know and very high class jewellers, and one which has enjoyed a number of Royal warrants Asprey's are known to have retailed knives which bore their name. Whether or not they made the knives is open to speculation, but given the skill of their workman it is possible that they did rather than having the knives made elsewhere. Although their name only appears in the trade directories under cutlers from *1850* their history as jewellers dates back to *1781* when it was founded by a William Asprey and his son Charles. In terms of trade profession the family roots were that of ironmongers and blacksmiths. It received a Royal Warrant from Queen Victoria and has continued to receive Royal patronage right up to the present day. In more modern times has been part the Company, which owned Mappin and Webb and Garrard also a Royal Jewellers. Now operate under the name Asprey and Garrard.

Plate 8.
This strange object once opened into the star configuration and locked in that position via the screw makes an effective throwing star. Whether that was original intention is unknown. Marked:

ARNOLD
LONDON

Plate 9.
Small paper knife by Asprey with small pen blade in the hilt. Both the paper blade and the grip are stamped with silver marks of CA-GA and code marks indicate London manufacture in *1909*.

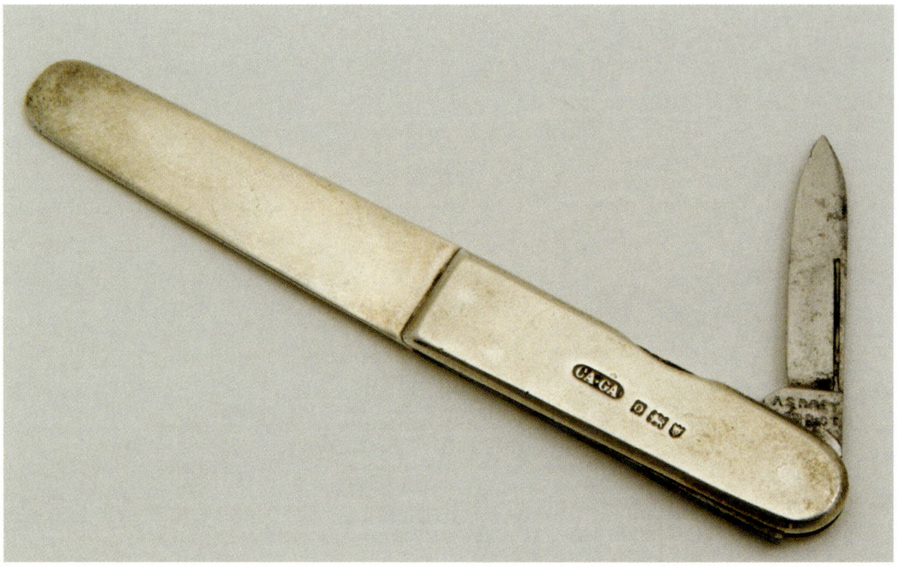

ATKINSON, WILLIAM.
22 St. George's Market *1860-1866*

ATKINSON, BENJAMIN FREDRICK.
3 Hemmings Row *1870*

AUTO-STROP SAFETY RAZOR Co. Ltd.
59A New Oxford St. Makers of the Auto-strop safety razor and "Valet" blades also the 7 o'clock safety razor. *1915-1920*

AVERY, W & T Ltd.
Butchers cutler, 11 to 17 Cowcross St. *1915*

AWDAS, FREDRICK.
11 Bath Place, Euston Rd. *1890-1905*

AWDAS, HENRY.
7 Eden St., Hampstead Rd. *1890-1895*

AWDAS, HORACE.
149 Wardour St. *1910*. In *1915* at 11 New Inn Yard, Tottenham Court Rd. as H.R. & Co. in *1920*

AYTON, WILLIAM.
169 Waterloo Road *1866-1870*

BACON, THOMAS & SON.
9 Wardrobe Place and 2 Addle Hill *1836*

BACON, THOMAS.
Working Cutler, 173 Tooley St. *1822-1832*. In *1832* known as BACON & MASON at same address.

BADDELEY J.
Working Cutler, 3 Benjamin St. West Smithfield *1828-1829*

BAINES, CATTELL & Co. Ltd.
Manufacturing Cutler, 57A Holborn Viaduct *1925-1930*. In *1940* listed at 67 and 68 Hatton Gardens.

BAKER, MARY ANNE.
Working Cutler, 186 Tooley St. *1828-1829*. Listed in *1832-1860* as Mrs. Ann Maria.

BAKER, CHARLES.
244 High Holborn. Established *1765* to circa *1894*

BAKER, THOMAS KERSLAKE.
73 Farringdon St. *1850-1866* and 1 Stonecutter St. Shoe Lane in *1860-1866*

BAKER, WALTER.
Working Cutler, 186 Tooley St., and 113 Bishopsgate *1822-1829*. Given the address and dates obviously the husband of Mary Anne Baker.

BAKER, WILLIAM.
Butcher cutler, 103 Charterhouse St. *1900*

BARBE, R. & Co.
Manufacturing Cutler, 88 Long Lane, Aldersgate *1910*

BARDLEY, H. B. & Co.
Manufacturing Cutler, 3 Finsbury Square *1920*. 20 Hatton Gardens in *1925*

BARHAM, HENRY.
Working Cutler, 18 Cloth Fair *1910-1915*

BARKER, ALBERT.
5 New Bond St. *1890*. As BARKER, ALBERT LIMITED in *1895-1910*

BARNASCONE, LEWIS.
91 Fore St. *1895*

BARNES, ARTHUR THOMAS.
4 St. John's Lane *1930-1945*

BARNES, THOMAS.
356 Caledonian Road *1870-1875*

BARNS, JOEL.
23 Gloucester St., St John St. Road. *1832*

BARNS, JOEL.
Manufacturing Cutler, 1 St. Matthias Place *1860*

BARNS, J.
25A Eyre St. Hill, Leather Lane *1855*

BARNS, JOHN.
132 Grove St., Camden Town *1855*

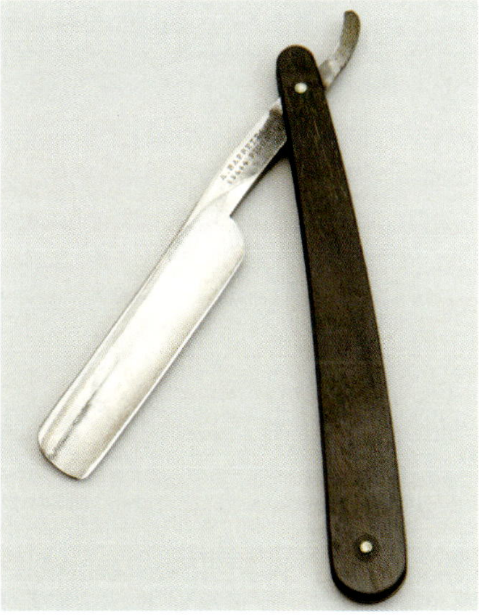

Plate 10.
Cut throat marked :
A. BARRETT & SONS
63 & 64 PICCADILLY

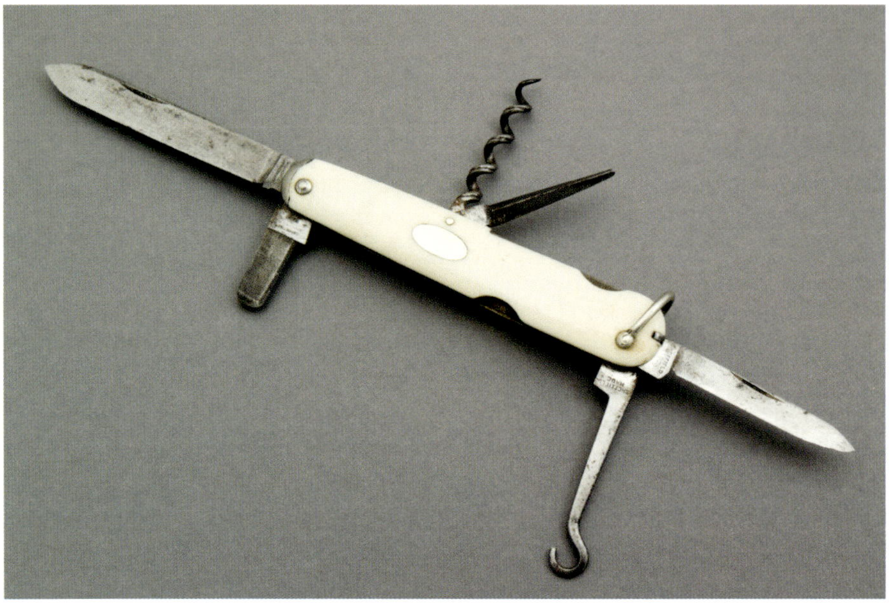

Plate 11.
Folder with ivory scales marked:
C. BARRETT & Co

BARR, GEORGE.
26 to 31 Eyre Street Hill 1910

BARRETT & SON.
1 Glendower Place, South Kensington *1910-1915*

BARRETT, A & SONS.
Andrew Barrett recorded in the *1865* directory as a brush and comb manufacturer and sponge importer with premises at 63 and 64 Piccadilly, 53 Albemarle St., 186 Oxford St., 86A Edgware Road, and 29 St. George's Place Hyde Park Corner.
The case for the razor is marked: Made in Sheffield England.

BARRETT, CHARLES.
Manufacturing Cutler, 144 Fleet St. *1895*. As CHARLES & Co. in *1900* and also at 158 Strand, *1905* also at 1 Fenchurch St. *1910* at 158 Strand and 7 New Bond St. Only at Strand in *1915-1920*. 51 Burlington Arcade *1930-1945*

BARRETT FRANCIS
144 Fleet St. 1860-1870.

BARRON, & WILSON.
436 West Strand and 7 and 8 King William St. Strand *1875-1880*.
7, 8 and 9 King William St. with works at Rose St. Soho *1885*.

BARTLETT.
A Charles Bartlett Cutler and Hardware man was recorded *1828-29* at 59 High St. The record for the name Bartlett is then blank until *1850* when a George Bartlett is listed at premises of 44 Upper Marylebone St. However his tenancy must have been short because there is no recorded for that name in *1855* listings.

BARTLETT, Mrs. MARY.
1 Cleveland St. *1865-1875*

BARTLETT, THOMAS & SON.
Falcon Hall, 17 Silver St., Wood St. EC *1860*. At 13 Little Britain in *1866-1870* (wholesaler)

BARTLETT, WILLIAM.
338 Poplar High St. *1870*

BARTON, EDWARD.
27 Hatton Gardens *1846*

BATEMAN, WILLIAM PEACE.
278 Devon's Road, Bromley *1870-1885*

Plate 12.
A dirk-style knife with Ivory hilt. This knife carries the name of either a C or G Bartlett the initial is not completely clear. The provides some difficulty is establishing exactly which Bartlett was involved or indeed if this is a London knife.

Plate 13.
Cut throat razor marked on the flat the word Eclipse, and on the tang:

BENBOW & SON
12 LITTLE BRITAIN

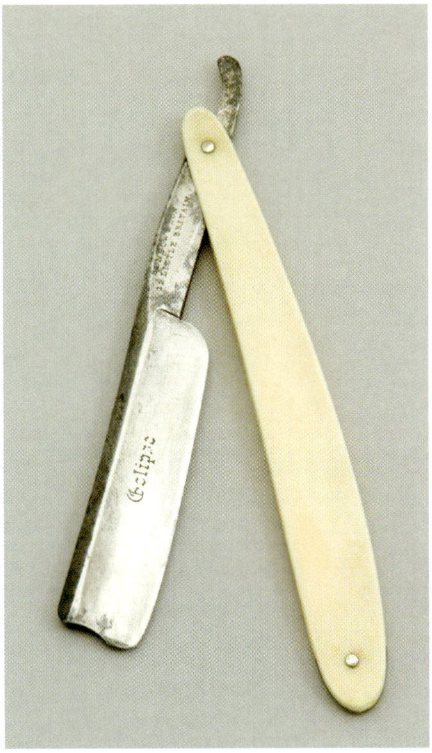

BATLEY, WILLIAM.
13 Brownlow St. *1823*

BATT, CHARLES.
11 New St., Dorset Square NW
1860

BATTEN, WILLIAM HENRY.
Working Cutler, 13 St. John's Square Clerkenwell. *1828-1829.* Church St. Hackney *1832-1836*

BAXTER, J.
3 Rose and Crown Court, Finsbury
1850

BEACH.
The name of BEACH with no street name or city noted on a small sportsman's style knife, possibly GEORGE & BENJAMIN. 176 Poplar High St. and 149 High Street, Camden Town. Listed as Ironmonger in *1865.* Though this also could be the work of another Beach who operated from Salisbury.

BEATTIE, J. & SON.
205 Regent Street *1865.* Gunsmith

BECK, JOHN.
41 Henry St., Hampstead Rd.
1875-1880

BECKER, Mrs. FREDRICK.
33 Charles St. Hatton Gardens
1900

BEDFORD, FRANCIS.
18 Queen St., Clerkenwell *1860*

BEDFORD SAFETY RAZOR Co. Ltd.
20 High Holborn *1915*

Plate 14.
Ivory scaled folder with the main and pen blades marked:

BENETFINK & CO
CHEAPSIDE

BEDINGHAM, G & Co.
108 Hatton Gardens *1920*

BEER, JAMES.
Working Cutler, 35 Rapert St., Haymarket *1832*

BELL, GEORGE.
1839 4 Queens St.

BELLES, GEORGE.
Working Cutler, 62 Paradise Row, Chelsea 1832. 5 Queens St., Chelsea
1836-1846.

BENBOW & SON.
12 LITTLE BRITAIN. In *1865* listed as Benbow and Son (late of the firm Low, Son and Benbow) wholesaler and exporter of perfumes, fancy soap manufacturer.

BENETFINK & Co.
89 & 90 Cheapside *1850-1875.* In *1880* at 107 and 108 Cheapside. As BENETFINK & FOX in *1866.* In *1885-1890* at 85, 86,89 and 90, 107 and 108 Cheapside, and 8 Honey Lane Market. *1902* 85 and 86 Cheapside no longer occupied. *1905-1920* at 107, 108 Cheapside and 8 Honey Lane Market.

BENHAM, WILLIAM
37 Assembly Row, Mile End 1855

BENHAM & SON.
50, 52 & 54, and factory 61 Wigmore St. *1870.* Also 64 Wigmore St. in *1875.* As BENHAM & SON Ltd. in *1895.* Only at 50 and 52 Wigmore St. in *1900*

BENNET, JOHN THOMAS.
156 Fenchurch St. 1832-1840

BENTS, J.
8 Long lane West Smithfield *1823*

BERONINS & Co.
4 Lloyds Avenue *1910*

BERRIDGE SHEAR Co.
67 Aldersgate St. *1902.* 85 Fore St. *1905*

BEST, FRANK & Co.
Manufacturing Cutler, 10 Dyer's Buildings *1910*

BETTRIDGE, THOMAS.
(Agent) 97 Cheapside *1866-1870*

BETTRIDGE, THOMAS.
(Wholesale) 97 Cheapside *1875.* As BETTRIDGE, JOSEPH. *1880-1885*

BEW, HENRY.
19 Newgate St. *1840*

Benetfink advertisement from 1852.
(Rperoduced b permission of Kelly's Directories).

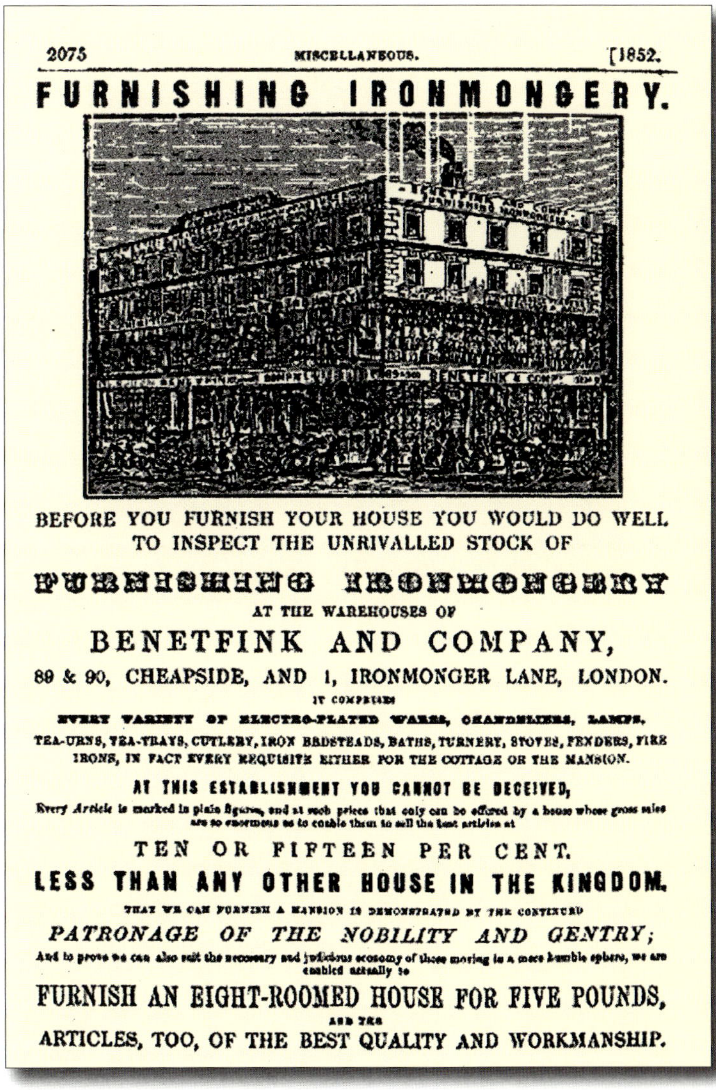

BIDGEMAN, HENRY.
Baron St. Pentonville Rd. *1875*

BIGGS, F.J.
Leadenhall Buildings sole London agent for J.J. BEAL Sheffield butchers and spear pointed knives *1885*.

BIGGS, WILLIAM.
Stratford Broadway *1846-1855*

BIGGS, WILLIAM & SONS.
122 The Grove, Stratford. *1925-1940*

BINKS, FRANCIS.
Working Cutler, 8 Long Lane *1828-1829*

BINYON, ALFRED.
40 Tavistock St. *1846*

BINYON, CHARLES.
2 Fenchurch St. *1820*. 5 Burlington Arcade *1822-1829*

BISHOP, FREDRICK.
3 Royal Exchange *1846*

BLACKWELL, CHARLES.
Cutler and Surgical Instrument Maker. 3 Bedford Court, Covent Garden. *1832-1835*. 5 Noel St., Wardour St. *1836-1850*

BLACKWELL, H.
8 Boswell Court 1832-1834

BLACKWELL, WILLIAM.
Established circa 1817. Recorded as being at 3 Bedford. Court, Covent Garden from *1835-1864*, and from *1859* until *1864* also at 9 Cranbourne Street, Leicester Square. He is variously listed as a cutler and surgical instrument maker, table knife manufacturers and manufacturing cutler. William Blackwell was succeeded by Elizabeth Blackwell, his widow. The name continued at the Bedford. Court address from *1856* until *1875* and at Cranbourne Street until *1876*. William Blackwell exhibited at both the Great Exhibition of *1851* and at the International Exhibition of *1862*.

BLAISE, LOUIS & Co.
see SAVIGNY

BLAKE, NICHOLAS TURNER.
106 London Wall *1885-1895*

BLAND, CHARLES.
39 Upper Rathbone Place *1870-1875*

BLAND, JOHN.
64 Old Street, St. Luke's. *1870*

BLAND, JOHN H.
9 Charterhouse St. *1866*

BLAND, STEPHEN
9 Norwich St., Fetter Lane *1836*. 42 Upper Rathbone Place in *1840*. 8 Percy Passage *1846-1855*, also at 7 in *1855*.

BLAND, S Snr.
7 & 8 Percy Passage *1860* only at 8 in *1866*

BLAND, STEPHEN.
49A Ferdinand St. *1875*

BLAYON, CHARLES.
5 Burlington Arcade *1832-1834*

BLEWITT, EDWARD.
Manufacturing Cutler, 69 Hatton Gardens *1880-1895*

BLOFELD, THOMAS GUEST & Co.
The fleam (in Plate 15) shows how a miss-stamping can cause confusion in trying to locate a Company. The stamping clearly looks like

BLOILLD, but no name likes this could be located. It was the address that gave the clue with a Company called Blofeld being located at 6 Middle Row.
The entry for Blofeld in the *1832* directory reads:

> *"Blofeld, Thomas Guest and Co. (and inventors of amalgamating steel and silver) 6 Middle Row, Holborn."*

In the *1836* directory they are listed as Blofeld, FG and Co. but by *1846* its back to Thomas. Listed in *1852* as cutler and razor maker, but no trace in *1855*.

BLOOMFIELD, J
10 Charles St., Drury Lane 1823

BLOOMFIELD, S.
10 Charles St., Drury Lane *1828-1832*, in *1832* also at 7 Upper King's St

BLOOMFIELD, SAMUEL & Co.
Manufacturing Cutler, 33 Charles St. Hatton Gardens *1885-1900*. 58 Compton St. *1905*. 23 Bowling Green Lane *1915-1940*

BLOXHAM, ALBERT COWLEY.
Manufacturing Cutler, 114 and 115 Holborn *1910*. *1915-1935* also at 6 and 8 Rosebery Ave.

BLOXHAM, JOHN.
103 Hatton Gardens *1895*

BLUNT, WILLIAM.
12 Hemmings Row *1832-1836*

BOCKING, WILLIAM.
378 High Holborn *1890*

BOCOCK, THOMAS WILLIAM & Co.
Manufacturing Cutler, 30 Hatton Gardens *1885*

Plate 15.
A four-bladed fleam with 3 standard fleam style blades and a lancet blade. Polished horn scales. Despite the poor stamping the three fleam blades are all marked:

BLOFELD
6 MIDDLE ROW
HOLBORN

BODEN & Co.
12 Drury Lane *1832*

BOECKER, RUDOLPH.
14 St. Mary Axe *1885-1900*

BOND, CHARLES & SON.
Toolmaker. 546 Oxford St. and 26 Bishop's Rd. Paddington *1885*

BOSWELL, HATFIELD & Co. Ltd.
Broad Street House. *1915-1920*

BOTACHAN JAMES & JOSEPH.
Cutler and Surgical Instrument Maker, 23 Worship St., Finsbury *1832*. Only as J at 35 Worship St. in *1836*. In *1840* as Joseph at 44 Worship St. Finsbury

BOTACHAN, Mrs. M.
44 Worship St. Finsbury *1846-1850*. Presumably the widow of Joseph.

BOTACHAN, JAMES.
Manufacturing Cutler, 22 Windmill St., Finsbury *1855-1860*

BOUGHTON E.
5 Wickham St., Lambeth *1832*

BOULTON, THOMAS.
280 Strand *1820-1832*.
281 Strand 1836-1840

BOWLER, WILLIAM.
30 Little Pulteney St. *1850*

BOYD, ALEXANDER & SON.
105 New Bond Street *1870-1875*

BRADBURY, JAMES.
280 Strand *1840*

BRADLY, RICHARD.
96 Bishopgate without *1846*

BRADSHAW. G.F.
Manufacturing Cutler, 64 High Holborn *1930*

BRAND, W.G.
42 Palmer St. Westminster *1930*

BRAUN, CHARLES E & Co.
Manufacturing Cutler, 37 Oxford St. *1895*. 34 and 36 Gray's Inn Road. *1900-1925*. In *1910* listed as pen and pocket knife makers.

BRAUN, EDWARD.
17 Gloucester St. *1930-1935*

BRENNAND, PEARSON.
217 High Holborn *1843-1855*. In the *1850* directory for Surgical Instrument Makers noted as (late LONG). Listed as BRENNAND, Mrs. MARY *1860-1870*. Mary was the Widow of Pearson.

BRENT, THOMAS GEORGE.
22 Windmill St., Finsbury *1870*. 43 City Rd. in *1875-1880*. 5 Tabernacle St. *1885*. 81 Long Lane in *1890-1905*

BRIAN, JOHN.
(Wholesale) 8 Great St. Andrew's St. *1822-1829*. As John and Co. *1832-1836*

BRIAN & WHITE.
Manufacturing Cutler, 8 Great St. Andrew's St., Seven Dials *1839-1920*

BRIDGEMAN, HENRY.
12 Baron St. Pentonville Rd. *1880*. In *1885* at 11 Baron St.

BRIDGEMAN, HENRY.
6 Camden Passage Islington *1880-1885*

BRIDGES, RICHARD.
90 St. Martins Lane *1820-1829*

BRIGGS, THOMAS.
A knife bearing the name and the address 27 Piccadilly has been noted and a Thomas Briggs Dressing Case Maker is noted at this address in *1840*. There is however a Thomas Briggs Surgical Instrument Maker and Cutler noted in *1852* at 4 Acton St., Grays Inn Road.

BRIMMER, JOSEPH.
Working Cutler, 21 Bowling Green Lane *1920-1930*

BRINDLE, J.G. & Co.
42 Kirby St. Hatton Gardens *1855*. At 42 Moorgate St. in *1860*

BRITTON, ARTHUR.
Manufacturing Cutler, 2A Lollard St., Lambeth *1925*

BRITTON, THOMAS.
3 Barron's Place, Lambeth *1900*

BRITTON, WILLIAM.
2A Lollard St., Lambeth *1920*

BROADBRIDGE, WALTER.
34 Carlisle St. *1935*

BROADHEAD, WILLIAM.
Working Cutler, 25 Little Pultney St. *1832-1834*

BRODIE, ARTHUR H.W.
129 Randall Avenue, Cricklewood *1935-1940*

BRODIE, ARTHUR HENRY WILLIAM.
Working Cutler, 16 Froth St. *1940*

BRODIE, JOHN & SON.
78 Seven Sisters Road *1925*. 281 Hornsey Road 1935-1945.

BRODIE, HENRY & GEORGE.
Manufacturing Cutler, 20 Whitcombe St. *1875*

BRODIE, HENRY.
36 Great Windmill St., Coventry St. Listed as both Working and Manufacturing Cutler, *1880-1930*. *1935* at 15 Broad St.

BRODIE, Mrs. M.
30 Little Pulteney St. *1846*

BRODIE, WILLIAM.
Listed as Working and Manufacturing Cutler, 30 Little Pulteney St. *1836-1870*

BROOKE, WILLIAM.
9 Tothill St., Westminster and Brooke House, King's Road, Chelsea *1846-1850*. 22 Colvill Terrace, Kings Road, Chelsea, and 8 Warwick St. Belgrave Sq. *1855*

BROOKS, JAMES.
16 Vere St., Oxford St. *1860-1875*. Additionally at 64 New Bond St. in *1875*

BROOME, EDWARD JOSEPH.
25 Stanhope St. Euston Square.*1875*

BROOMHEAD, LUKE.
21 Paternoster Row Spitalfields. *1823-1829*

BROOMHEAD, LUKE.
Working Cutler, 23 Union St. *1832-1840*. 8 Union St. *1846-1860*

BROWN, J.
2A Townshend Rd. St. John's Wood. *1855-1860*

BROWN, WILLIAM.
28 Beckford Row, Walthamstow *1828-1836*, at number 2 in *1840-1846*

BROWNE, ROBERT H.
Manufacturing Cutler and Shear Maker, 11 Paradise Place, Hackney *1880* shears maker. *1885* listed as manufacturing cutler with addresses at 386 Mare St., Hackney and 23 Chatham Place, Hackney. R.H. Browne was a member of the Cutlers Company in *1879*, he died in *1919*.

BROWNE, R.
16 Artillery St., Bishopsgate *1870*

BRUCE HALL PLATE Co.
Manufacturing Cutler, Chatham Place, Hackney *1930*

The Buck and Hickman premises at Whitechapel in 1907

BRUSTMEYER, JOHN.
Working Cutler, 18 Whitcombe St. *1875*. 42 Whitcombe St. *1880-1895*

BRYAN, JOHN.
6 Staple Inn Buildings, Holborn *1855*

BRYAN, JOHN.
24 Moreton Place, Pimlico *1860*

BUCK (BUCK & HICKMAN, BUCK & RYAN.)
Originally a family firm which developed along a number of paths and which is today still represented by what is now one of the UK's largest tool suppliers, and another that has had premises in the same general area of London for some 180 years.

The origins of the firms Buck, Buck and Hickman, and Buck and Ryan starts in the early 19th century with 3 brothers, George, Joseph and Matthew Buck who were toolmakers and dealers. The family originated in Sheffield. Mathew Buck started his business at a site near what is now Waterloo Station, whilst George operated from Tottenham Court Road and Joseph from Holborn. The development of the different branches is described below. Much of this history has been drawn from the web sites of both Buck and Hickman, and Buck and Ryan along with reference to other sources.

George Henry Buck premises circa World War I period

BUCK & HICKMAN
In 1827 Ann Buck, Mathew's daughter married a printer John Roe Hickman and they had 5 daughters and one son called John Roe Hickman born 1830.
The firm of Buck and Hickman is recorded in 1839 at 6 Church Lane, Whitechapel. John Roe senior died in 1847. It appears that John Roe junior was apprenticed to his uncle George Buck. On completion of his apprenticeship he became a partner with his uncle but this did not meet with the approval of George Buck's family and the partnership was dissolved. John then returned to Whitechapel to help his mother.
In 1859 Buck and Hickman moved to premises at 281 Whitechapel Road and are listed as saw and tool makers. By 1865 they also had premises at 1 and 2 Union St.
The firm also took over the business of William Dewsnap when it went bankrupt in 1867, though it continued to run under the name of Dewsnap and Co until 1889 when the partnership between John Roe Hickman and a James Hickman was dissolved.
John Roe junior died in 1904.

Plate 16.
The rather unusual knife bears markings which indicate military usage in India, though whether it was originally made for this purpose is unknown. The blade is very flexible, has a strengthened bolster, brass guard, stag grip with brass mounts. The sheath is of leather over wood.
The blade is marked:

BUCK & HICKMAN
281 WHITECHAPEL
RD

Along with a broad arrow ↑I mark.
Size: blade 11 inches, 15.75 inches overall.

Plate 17.
A substantial sheepsfoot blade knife with stag scales. The blade bears the name
BUCK & HICKMAN LIMD
and the date 1914.

Buck and Hickman grew rapidly opening premises in Glasgow, Manchester and Birmingham during the first 5 years of the 20th century. By WW2 they were operating from 25 different locations their Whitechapel premises being badly damaged. There were a number of take-overs and acquisition during the 70's, 80's and 90's with a number of new premises opening. There is however no longer any link with its roots in London the Company HQ being located in Coventry.

Buck and Ryan premises at 310 Euston Road circa 1920.

JOSEPH BUCK, GEORGE HENRY BUCK (BUCK & RYAN), GEORGE BUCK

The history and relationships of these branches of the family are somewhat complex. It is also of note that there is no separate trace of Mathew having his own premises.

Joseph Buck "saw, file and mechanical tool maker" is recorded at Gibson St. in 1826. In 1842 he is at 124 Newgate St and also 91 Waterloo Rd in 1852 and is still at these premises in 1865. There is then a gap in the record when another Joseph Buck (possibly a Joseph junior) appears at 56 Holborn Viaduct in 1881. In 1890's also at 220 Blackfriars. Still listed in 1915. Joseph senior appears to have died in 1884. No knives bearing either the name of Joseph Buck or the address of any of his premises have been noted.

Plate 18.
Style of knife very popular as a private purchase weapon during World War 2 but which was also available into the 1960's.

BUCK + RYAN-
CUTLERS
310.EUSTON RD.
N.W.1

Plate 19.
A very common style of bowie stamped:

BUCK & RYAN
EUSTON RD

and on the reverse:

SHEFFIELD MADE.

George Henry Buck was the son of Joseph and thus nephew to George Buck. Acquired the business of a R. Nelson Plane Maker in 1852 Nelson having a history dating back to 1823 and having occupied 122 Edgware Rd. between 1835 and 1852. George Henry is recorded from 1852 to 1867 at 122 Edgware Rd. From 1869 to 1898 the firm is listed at 261 Edgware Rd. and additionally from 1893 at 312 Euston Rd. George Henry died in 1891 and the firm then seems to have been run by his son Percy. However it was declared bankrupt in 1898 which is when it was bought by George Ryan. After World War I premises at 310 Euston Rd. were obtained and the firm styled Buck and Ryan. The firm remains in business today.

Plate 20.
Butcher Knife by BUCK. Hardwood scales possibly rosewood, blade marked:

BUCK
TOT COURT ROAD

over a heart and pipe trademark. The use of this mark is interesting. According to the Company of Cutlers in Hallamshire the mark of a heart and pipe was registered at the Sheffield Culter's Company but by a John Green in 1692! The TOT COURT ROAD stands for TOTTENHAM COURT ROAD.

Plate 21.
This knife very much in the style of a California/San Francisco skinning/hunting knife of the type made by Michael Price.
Blade is marked:

GEORGE BUCK
245 TOTTENHAM
COURT RD

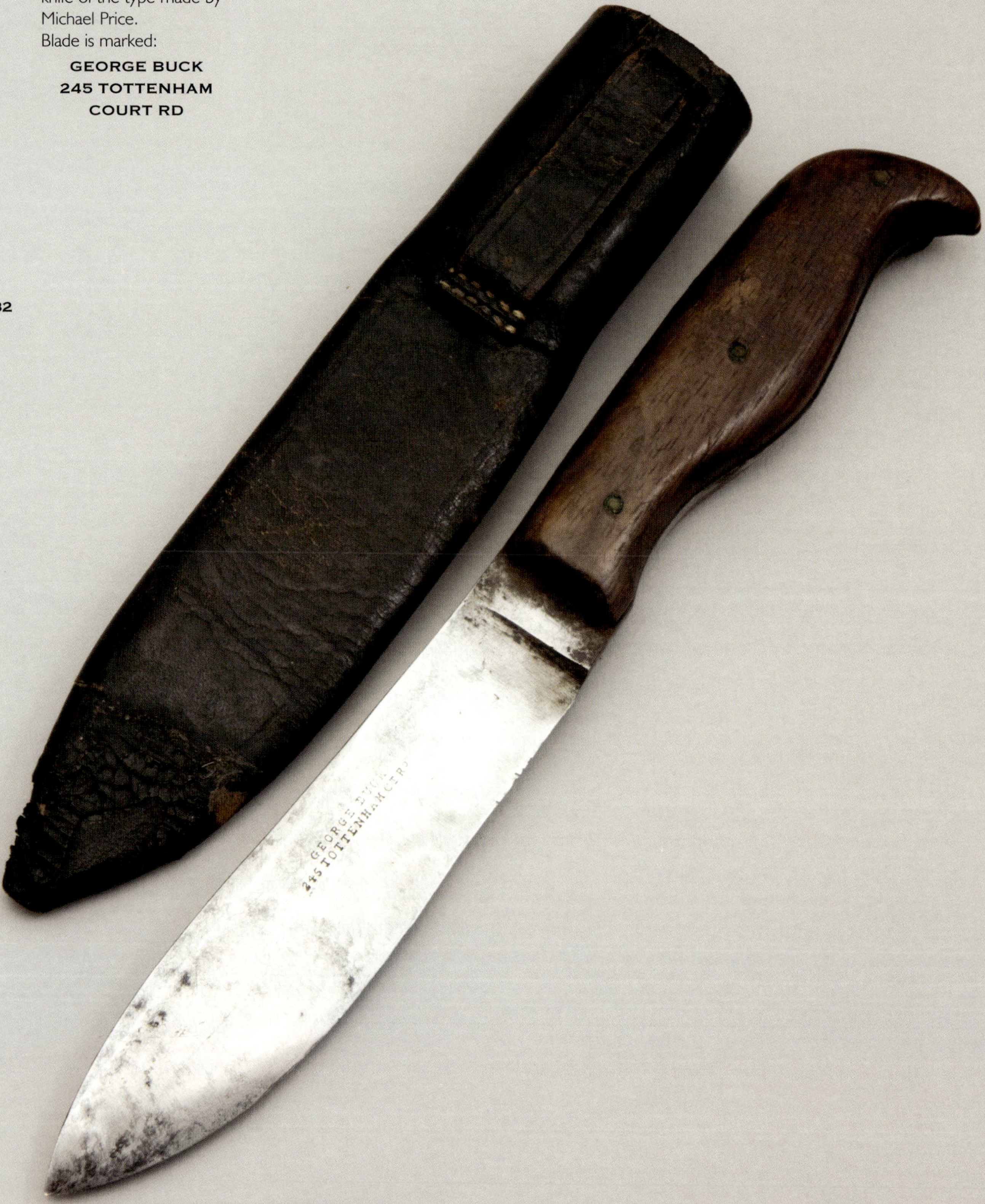

Plate 22.
Green River Knife marked:
GEORGE BUCK
245 TOTTENHAM
COURT RD

George Buck.
Most of the knives from the "Buck" lineage come from George Buck and his Tottenham Court Road premises. George Buck appears at 245 Tottenham Court Rd. in 1838 and in the 1851 census listed as Tool Warehouse employing 8 men.

In 1865 the firm also occupied premises at 245 and 247 Tottenham Court Road. George died in 1865 and the 1871 census records his wife Mary as running the firm being recorded as Tool Manufacturer employing 11 men and 2 boys. In 1901 his daughter Emma in listed as running the firm being recorded at 242 Tottenham Court Road as Toolmaker and Cutler. It is of note that despite some of the residential addresses in the census returns reflecting 245 Tottenham Court Road, the trade directories after circa 1880 list the firm at 242 Tottenham Court Road. In 1931 moved to 39 Goodge St, and in 1934 to 21 Goodge St, and an address it occupied into the post WW2 period.

BUCK & MOSELEY.
168 Strand *1920-1925. 1930* at 63 New Oxford St. Despite the use of the name Buck in this firm there does not appear to be any link to the Buck family described earlier. Though there is a link to John Moseley/Moseley and Son who are known to have occupied the 63 New Oxford St. address.

BUILIVANT, THOMAS.
Working Cutler, 1 Pierpoint Row, Islington *1836*

BULLEN, HENRY.
32 Camden Passage, Islington High St. *1890-1910*

BULLEN, WILLIAM ROBERT.
148 Clerkenwell Rd. *1905*

BULLEN, WILLIAM ROBERT.
Dominion House, Bartholomew Close *1930*

Plate 23.
A further example of a Green River Knife which bears the name of George Buck. This example has been regripped with marine ivory possibly reflecting a whaling background.

BURCHETT, JOHN.
2 Queen St., Oxford St. *1836-1839*

BURCHFIELD, WILLIAM.
Butchers Cutler, 11 West Smithfield and 20 New Newgate Market *1846-1850.*

BURLEY, JOSEPH.
18 Salisbury St. *1846-1850*

BURLEY. JOSEPH.
Working Cutler, 8 Stingo Lane Marylebone Rd. *1866-1870.* 67 York St. Bryanstone Square *1875-1915*

BURSAY, JOHN BAPTIST.
5 Lamb's Conduit St., Shadwell *1832*

BURTON, WILLIAM SAMUEL.
Manufacturing Cutler, 39 Oxford St., 1, 2 and 3 Newman St. and 4 and 5 Perry's Place *1855-1860.* William Samuel is absent from the directories for the 1870's and 1880's but reappears at 1 Newman St. in *1890.*

BURYS &Co. Ltd.
33 Gracechurch St. *1895.*

Plate 24.
A massive and unusual Camp Knife with the ricasso marked:

BUCK
TOT COURT ROAD

Rosewood scales.
Size: blade 9.75 inches long, 2.25 inches wide, 14.5 inches overall.

Plate 25.
Horseman's Knife with bone scales and the main blade marked:

CLARK
20 OLD BOND
STREET

C

CADMAN & LOCKLEY.
4 Upper East Smithfield, and 81 St George St. *1850*

CADMAN, WILLIAM.
Working Cutler. 221 High St. Shadwell. *1823-1846*. Also at 2 and 3Upper East Smithfield and 74 St George St. in *1850*. In *1860* only at 221 Shadwell High St.

CADMAN, WILLIAM & SON.
221 High St. Shadwell and 135 Poplar High St. *1866*. 121 West Ferry Rd. *1886-1895*

CAMPBELL, CHARLES.
246 Bow Common Lane *1925-1940*

CANNON, H.A. Ltd.
Manufacturing Cutler. 96 High Holborn, and 27 Cannon St. *1925*

CARPANI, CHARLES.
45 Goodge St., Tottenham Court Rd. *1866-1875*, as CHARLES CARPANI and Co. in *1880-1885* and at 25 Goodge St.

CARVALBO & Co. Ltd.
99 Fenchurch St. *1905*

CHANDLER, JOHN WILLIAM.
Working Cutler. 60 Fann St. *1930*

CHALWIN & EDWARDS.
70 High Holborn. *1895 1900 1905 1910 1915* As CI IALWIN-EDWARDS & Co. in *1920 1925*

CHANTRY, NATHANIEL.
Working Cutler 322 Oxford St. *1822*. 2 Swallow Passage, Oxford St. *1823-1832*. *1836* at 320-322 Oxford St. Only at 320 in *1840*

CHAPELL, WILLIAM.
15 St. Martin's Lane *1823*

CHAPMAN, GEORGE.
53 New King St. Deptford *1890-1895*

CHAPMAN, THOMAS.
Working Cutler. 17 Castle St. East Clerkenwell. *1836-1850*

CHAPMAN, THOMAS.
28 Charlton St., Somers town, and 28 Plough Court, Fetter Lane. *1870*. 94 Charlton St. *1875-1915*

CHAPMAN, THOMAS.
Phoenix Place, Gray's Inn Road *1880-1895*

CHAPMAN, WILLIAM HENRY.
152 and 154 Caledonian Road *1870*

CHAPPELL.
Working Cutler 10 Medway St., Horseferry Road. *1828-1829* The directories record no initial for this firm, also whilst it appears in the cutlers section of the directories it does not appear in the street directory for Medway St.

CHATTERTON, RANDALL
6 East Harding St., Shoe Lane *1832*wc

CHESTER, GEORGE.
97 Castle Rd., Kentish Town *1875 1880 1885*

CHRIS, ABRAHAM.
13 Hanbury St. *1905*

CHRIS BROTHERS.
320 Garratt Lane, Wandsworth *1935*

CHRISTY, GEORGE.
Manufacturing Cutler. 39 Great Windmill St. *1870-1880*

CHRISTY KNIFE Co.
46 Holborn Viaduct *1895. 1900* at 38 Shoe Lane

CHRISTY SAFETY RAZOR Co. Ltd.
147 Queen Victoria St. *1910-1915*

CLARIS CRUMP.
2 Union St., Borough. *1850*

CLARK, CLIFT ALEXANDER MAWER.
(KNOWN AS THE ALEXANDER CLARK MANUFACTURING Co.) Established *1890* at 138 Fenchurch St. and in *1892* manufacturing premises at Welbeck Works 29 Market Place, Oxford St. They did however move their manufacturing to Sheffield in *1900.* 188 Oxford St., 138 and 149 Fenchurch St. *1895.* 125 and 126 Fenchurch St., 8 Fenn Court. *1900-1925.*

CLARK, ALFRED.
20 Old Bond Street *1891-1899.* 33 New Bond St. *1900-1928* At some stage relocated to 7 Vigo St. Does not appear to have survived into the 1930's. Alfred Clark were dressing bag makers and silversmiths with a royal warrant in the early years of the 20th century. Are known to have supplied a Royal Presentation hunting knife for the royal visit to India in *1905/06.*

CLARK, GEORGE.
131 Waterloo Road *1844*

CLARK, THOMAS.
Cutler and Hardware man. Exeter Exchange *1820-1829*

CLARK, WILLIAM & Co.
95 & 96 London Wall EC *1860-1875*

Plate 26.
This folding Syme's Abscess knife is simply marked:
CLARKE
The quality of this piece is very high with polished horn scales.

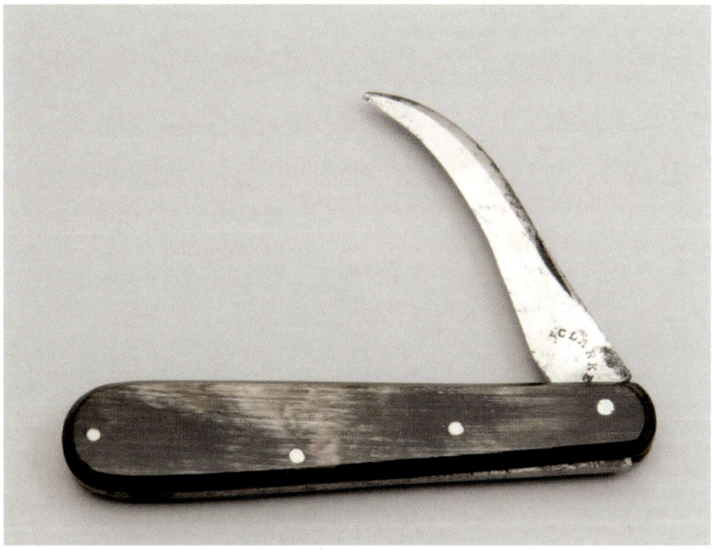

Plate 27.
All metal folder by CLEMENTS.

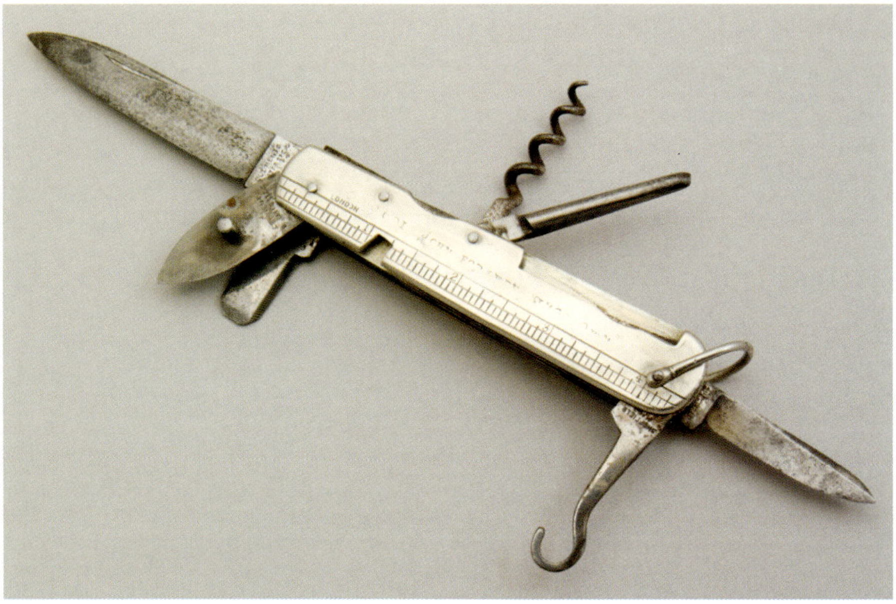

CLARK & WEATHERLEY.
Fleet Street *1820*

CLARKE.
More than likely a John Clark or Clarke. In *1846* a John Clark Surgical Instrument Maker had an address at 38 Great Windmill Street. In *1855* the address had changed to 225 Piccadilly. Around *1860* the name is recorded as Clarke. No trace after *1871*.

CLARY, WILLIAM.
6 Moscow Road, Bayswater
1870-1895

CLAUSS SHEAR Co.
34 Snow Hill. " Largest shear and scissor factory on earth" *1895-1900*

CLEGG, GEORGE DENNIS.
9 Church St., Stoke Newington
1935-1940

CLEMAK SAFETY RAZOR Co.
17 Billiter St. *1908-1920*

CLEMENTS, CHARLES JOSEPH.
Charles Clements was a prolific retailer and one who obviously had a wide range of items for sale. He is known to have sold knuckle knives during WW1, swagger sticks with concealed blades, and pocket knives. Founded between *1890* and *1895* by a Charles Joseph Clements with premises at 15B London St. Clements expanded fast as by *1900* he occupied four different premises i.e. 15B London St., 42C Old Broad St., 41 Gracechurch St., and 59 Fleet St. By *1905* he had added 45 Queen Victoria St., and 49 Moorgate St. to his list of premises. In *1908* his outlets had again expanded to include 17 Billiter St. (Note this is the same address occupied by the Clemak safety razor Co.), 42C Old Broad St., 66 Cheapside, 45 Queen Victoria St., 15B London St., 99 and 103 Strand, 41 Gracechurch St., 49 Moorgate St., and 127A High Holborn. This expansion was unaffected by the 1st. World War though some premises changed as in *1918* although London St., Gracechurch St., and Moorgate were no longer occupied 55 Kingsway, 145 Cannon St. and 79 and 79A Mark Lane had also been added to the list. However the depression years of the 1920's must have taken their toll as a number of premises were lost by *1925* with only the Old Broad St., Cheapside,

Cannon St., Strand, and 131 Fenchurch St. outlets remaining.

By the beginning of World War 2 the number of premises had reduced again i.e. 3 Victoria Colonnade, 99 Strand, 145 Cannon St., 125 Regent St., and 63 Burlington Arcade. The Company continued in business until the 1970's.

George Pearson Glen Kidston, generally always known as Glen Kidston, was born in *1899* into the wealthy Scottish family. He spent much of early life at the family estate near Hay on Wye and joined the

Plate 28.
Amputees knife marked:
CHAS
CLEMENTS

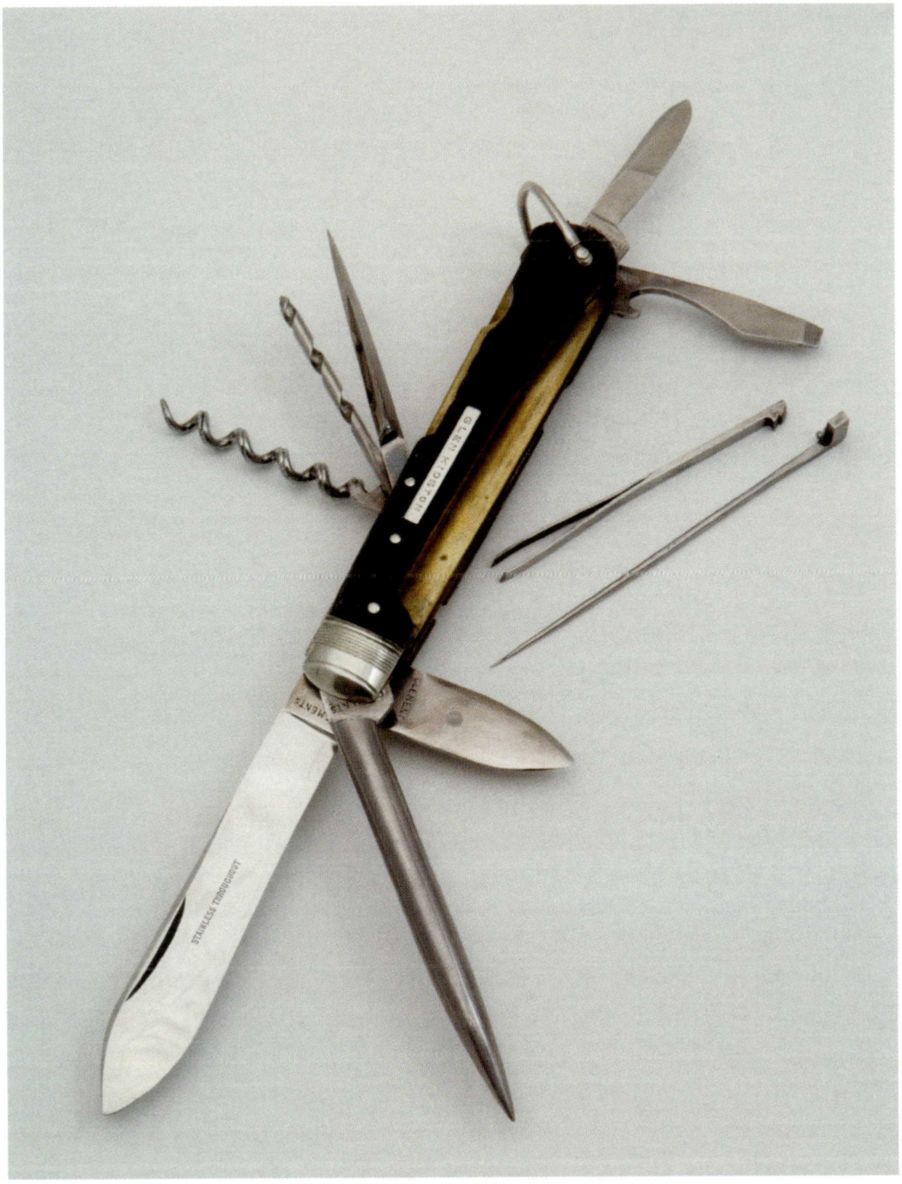

Plate 29.
Sportsman's knife with the shield engraved: to GLEN KIDSON. This knife was retailed by Clements.

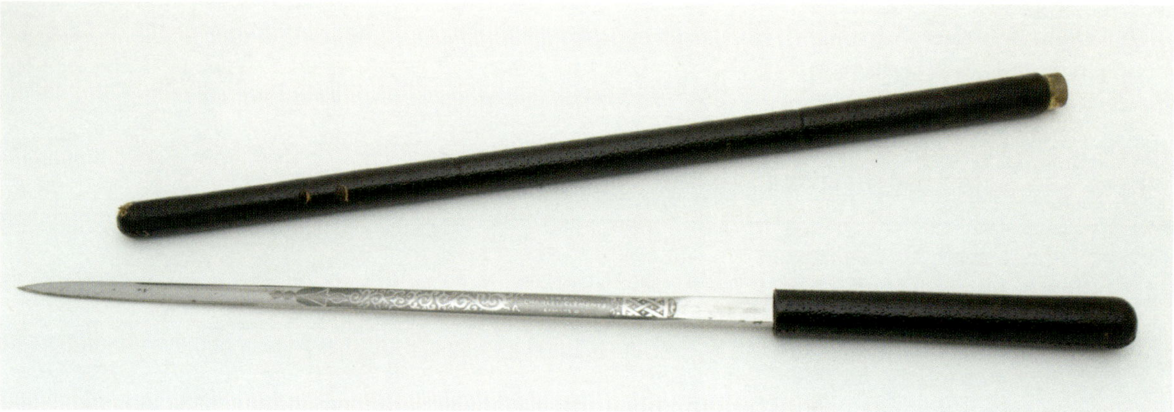

Plate 30.
Officers swagger stick with concealed blade. Blade is etched with fancy panel along with the name
LONDON CHARLES CLEMENTS LIMITED

Royal Navy as a Cadet in *1912*. In *1913* he inherited a large fortune when his father whose business interest included the Clyde Shipping Company died.
Kidston's Royal Naval record is full of praise from his senior Officers with two noting that despite being possessed of considerable private means always had the interest of the service at heart. His "free spirit" is also touched upon receiving the Admiralty's displeasure for once being convicted for dangerous driving and refusing to produce a licence, and for proceeding abroad without permission whilst on sick leave. However when he applied to leave the Royal Navy in 1928 it was noted that his retirement was a loss to the service. During his life he had been sole survivor of a plane crash in which he walked away with clothes on fire. Early in his life he had crashed a car through a wall during the 1928 Monte Carlo Rally, and had a speed boat disintegrate around him whilst doing 60mph. In 1914 as a midshipman in the Royal Navy the cruiser he was serving in was torpedoed by a German Submarine, being rescued after 2 hours in the chill waters of the North Sea by a Dutch trawler. He had sailed round the world, been the captain of a submarine, chopped three days off the record flying time from London to Cape Town and in 1930 won the Le Mans 24 hour race whilst driving for Bentley.
He died in 1931 when his plane crash in the Drakensburg Mountains of South Africa killing all on board.
Glen Kidston's knife is a most interesting multi-blade Sportsman's Knife retailed by Clements. The main blade is also marked: **SHEFFIELD MADE** but with no indication of by who. The escutcheon plate bears the inscription **GLEN KIDSTON**. The main blade is marked: **STAINLESS THROUGHOUT** and **FIRTH STAINLESS**, the springs are also marked: **STAINLESS THROUGHOUT**. Stainless steel was invented in 1912. After a hesitant start George Ibberson began using stainless steel manufactured by Thomas Firth and Sons though it wasn't an immediate success. However after the First World War it gained in popularity and demand for it began to rise.

CLEMENTS, JOSEPH.
Working Cutler. 214 Oxford St. *1832-1836*

CLIFTON, HENRY.
Working Cutler. 8 Tottenham Court Road *1828-1829*

CLIFTON, HENRY.
48 Wardour St., Soho. *1823-1829.*

Plate 31.
A high quality spear point Bowie. Note the lanyard ring at the pommel end of the hilt. The leather over wood sheath has a clip for securing the knife. The blade is marked:

COGSWELL & HARRISON
142 NEW BOND ST
& 226 STRAND

The addresses on this blade help date the knife as between 1888 and 1901.

Plate 32.
Dirk style knife with the blade etched::
COGSWELL & HARRISON LTD. GUN MAKERS LONDON

COATES, GEORGE.

(Second-hand). 9 Chapel St., Pentonville *1920.*

COGSWELL & HARRISON.

Well known London Gun makers whose origins can be traced back to *1770* when a Benjamin Cogswell started a business at 4 Bengal Place, New Kent Road, London. In *1830* he took over the business of Edward Denton of 223-224 Strand, and his son, also called Benjamin, trained as a gunsmith. In 1837 his son took an Edward Harrison into partnership. After one factory was damaged by fire the Company bought a new factory at Gillingham Street and through the period *1888* to *1901* the firm patented a number of different guns and actions. During this period the Company also maintained premises at 226 The Strand and in Bond Street. In *1917* the showrooms at 168 Piccadilly were opened and its Strand premises were sold in *1928*. In *1938* the last of the Harrisons died with the chairmanship passing to his son-in-law. In *1957* the Company was sold to the International Armament Corporation of America, a new factory was purchased and a number of take-overs completed. In *1963* the Company was bought back into British hands. This new period was one when Cogswell's secured one of its biggest orders for overseas government ammunition.

Cogswell Harrison's links with the knife trade appears to have been one of retailer. An article in Guns Review (Nov. 1970 issue) states that during WW2 the Piccadilly showrooms were kept extremely busy as the demand for pistols, holsters, and Commando Knives was so high. The knives illustrated

Gun case label of Cogswell and Harrison

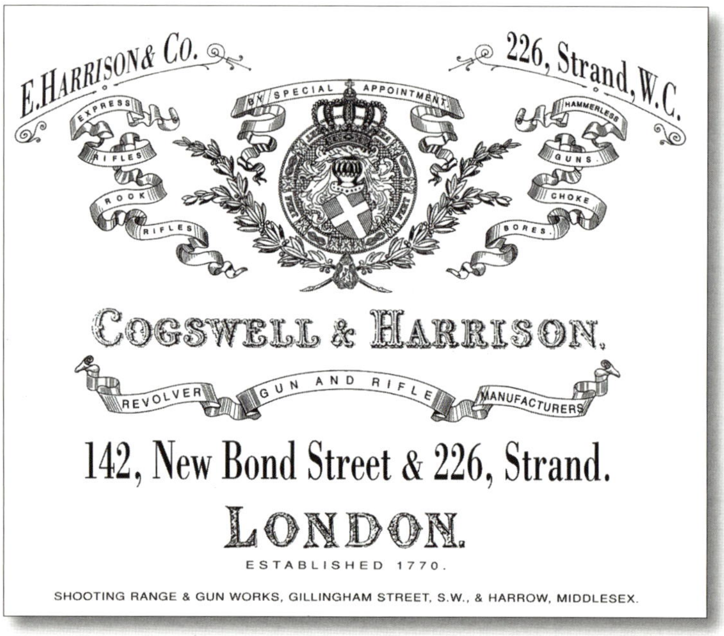

Plate 33.
This Fighting Knife is almost identical in style to the piece made by W J Waterer. This example is marked:

COGSWELL &
HARRISON LTD.
GUN MAKERS
LONDON W1

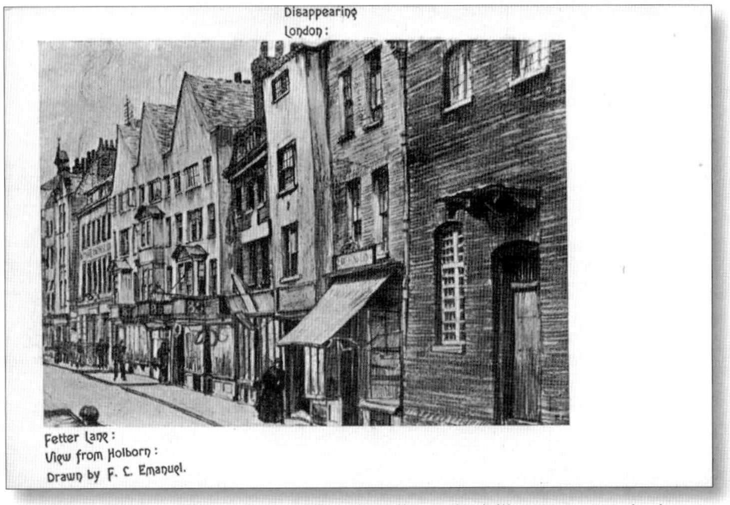

Fetter Lane from an Old Postcard

were in all probability not made by them.

COLE, GEORGE.
Manufacturing Cutler. 49 Coppice Row, Clerkenwell EC *1860*

COLE, GEORGE.
7 Wood Street, Spafields *1875*

COLE, GEORGE.
13 Pine St. Spafields *1880*

COLE, GEORGE.
50 St. John Street Road *1885-1890.* At 208 in *1895*

COLEMAN, WILLIAM.
4 Haymarket *1832-1850* (Also listed as Desk and Dressing Case Maker)

COLLETT, RICHARD.
3 Middle Row, Holborn *1836*

COLLEY, WILLIAM A Ltd.
19 and 21 Queen Victoria St. *1900*

COLLINS, D GEORGE.
Manufacturing Cutler. 96 Newgate St. *1895.* As Ltd. in 1905-1935 and at 118 Newgate St.

CONDER, W & C. E.
168 Tottenham Court Rd. *1890*

COOKE, AMBROSE.M.
115 Cheapside *1866 1870*

COOKMAN, Mrs. ELIZABETH.
50 Poplar High St. *1846 1850*

COOPER, A.W. & Co.
103 Houndsditch *1885*

COOPER BARNETT & SONS.
184 Upper Thames St. *1910*

COOPER, GODFREY CHARLES.
131 High Holborn *1890*

COOPER, JOHN.
41 St James St. *1875*

COPLEY, JAMES.
4 Drury Lane *1846*

COPLEY, JAMES.
73 Red Lion St., Clerkenwell *1875*

CORFIELD, Mrs. MARY.
10A Mount St. *1840*

CORMACK BROTHERS.
27 Ludgate Hill and Pilgrim St. *1866*

CORNOCK, W. FRANK.
62 Borough High St. *1935*

COULDEN, JOSEPH.
9 East St. Spitalfield Market. *1822-1829.* 6 Redlion Court, Spitalfields *1832-1846*

COURT, WILLIAM.
71 Brook St. *1840*

COWVAN, BERNARD & SAMUEL.
164 Fenchurch St. *1850-1870*

COWVAN, BERNARD & SAMUEL
(R. Hovenden and Sons Ltd. proprietors) 85, 89, 91. 93 and 95 City Road, and 29. 30. 31, 32 and 33 Berners St. *1900-1915*

Plate 34.
Spear point Bowie with chequered horn scales and S-shaped guard. The ricasso is marked:

CRANSWICK

on one side, and

PICCADILLY

on the other.

COX, ALFRED.
108 New Bond St. *1900*. In *1905* as and Sons and at 128 New Bond St. (late of 108 New Bond St) *1910* at 120 and 128 New Bond St. *1915-1935* only at 120 New Bond St. (see also SAVIGNY)

COX, Mrs. CELIA.
119 King St. Hammersmith *1935*

COX, Mrs. S.
8 Windsor Place, Southwark Bridge Rd. *1850*

COXETER, J & Co, J & SON, Ltd.
23 Grafton St., 4 & 6 Grafton St. *1836-1923*

CRADDOCK, GEORGE.
35 Leicester Square *1843*

CRANSWICK, THOMAS.
Thomas Cranswick of 59 Piccadilly is recorded (*1865*) as a brush and comb maker. There was some form of partnership with Cooper as in the directory entry for Thomas Cranswick it states see Cooper and Cranswick. Cooper and Cranswick are listed as brush, comb, mat, buff leather, knife board and turnery manufacturers and sponge dealers, 59 Piccadilly, and umbrella and dressing case makers 58 Piccadilly. Seems to have gone out of business circa *1885*.

CRAWFORD, J.
20 Princess St. Drury Lane *1846*

CRAWFORD, JAMES Sen.
6 High Street, Newington 1860-1890 at 95 Newington Butts.

CRAWFORD, Mrs. ELIZABETH.
95 Newington Butts *1895 1900*. In *1905-1920* as Miss Rowena at the same address. Elizabeth and Rowena would appear to be the widow and daughter of James.

CRAWFORD, JAMES Jnr.
26 Porter St. Soho *1875* probably the son of James senior.

CRESWICK & Co.
17 Craven St. *1880-1885*

CRESWICK, NATHANIEL.
(agent) 74 Hatton Gardens *1875*

CROOKES, JOHN.
Fetter lane *1822-1829*

ROOKS, JOHN.
Working Cutler. 1 Back Church Lane *1823-1829*

CROOKES, WILLIAM.
71 Brook St. *1836-1850*

CROOKES, WILLIAM.
9 Brighton Place, Waterloo Road *1860-1866*

CROSSFIELD, G.
13 Orange St. Red Lion Square *1846-1866*. At 14 Orange St. in *1870*

CROSSLEY, HENRY.
24 Back Church Lane, Commercial Road *1832*

CROWN SAFETY RAZOR Co.
10 New Union St. *1910*

CROWTHER, WILLIAM JOHN.
48 Tyres St., Lambeth *1870*

CURTIS, RICHARD.
3 Thavies Inn, Holborn (agent) *1860*

CUTTING JOHN.
268 Oxford St. *1846-1850*.
271 Oxford St. *1860-1866*

DALMAN, ROBERT.
19 Pierpoint Row, Islington *1832*. *1836* at 52 High St., Islington and 24 Marchmont St., Brunswick Square. Only at latter in *1840-1855*. 4 and 5 Marchmont St. *1860*

DALTON, THOMAS.
85 Quadrant *1852*

DAIMER, THOMAS.
33 Star Corner, Bermondsey *1870-1875*

DANIEL, WILLIAM.
125 Regent St. *1829*

DAVENPORT, WILLIAM.
Storey's Gate, Westminster *1820*. 25 Princess St. *1823*

DAVIS, DAVID S.
64 Hatton Gardens *1855*

DAVIS, JOHN.
12 Aldgate High Street *1820*.

DAVIS, J.
It is unclear if this J Davis is related to the previous Davis as there is a gap in the record but given the link with Aldgate High St. it is possible that there is. A John Davis is listed at 5 Church Row in *1829* and is a firm which had a considerable number of moves and which possibly at one stage occupied no less than 11 premises. By *1836* had moved to 88 Aldgate St. this address in *1840* is recorded as Aldgate High St. Moved again in *1846* to the Leadenhall address. An address at 39 Threadneedle St. was added in *1850* but in *1855* the firm was styled as J Davis and Son of 69 Leadenhall St., listed as razor makers. In *1860* the firm is styled as John and William Davis razor makers and manufacturing cutlers. Whilst still at the Leadenhall St. address in *1870* the firm is listed as John Charles Davis. In *1875* Trenter St. West also appears in the Directory entry but this location is

Plate 35.
Spear point bowie circa 1860, stag scales white metal guard typical of the period paste board sheath. Blade marked:
J. DAVIS
69 LEADENHALL ST

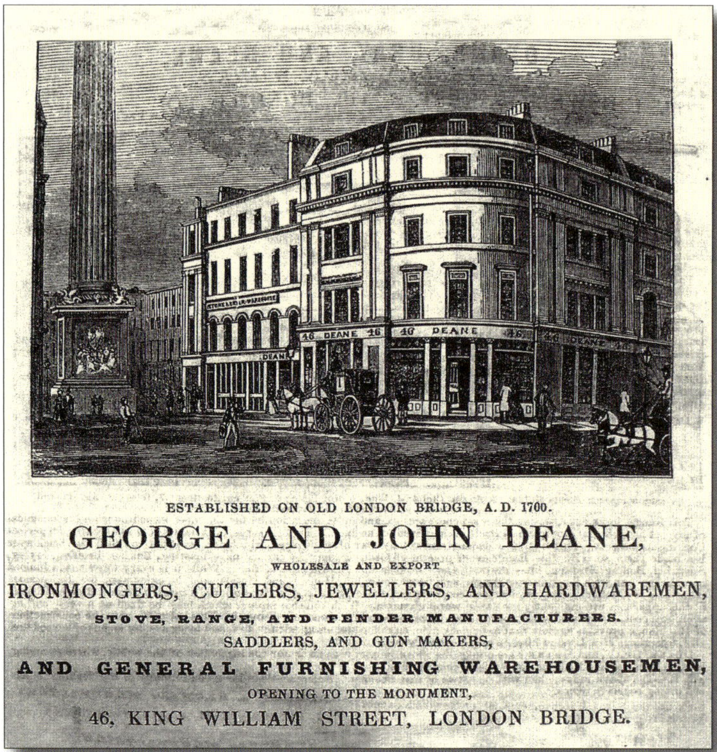

1846 advertisement for George and John Deane. These premises have like many other "cutlers" have disappeared, a large office block now stands on the site.
(Reproduced by permission of Kelly's Directories).

not recorded in *1880*. There is no record of J Davis between *1883* or *1895*.

However in the *1900* directory a J Davis and Co. Ltd. appears with addresses at 252, 253, 254, 255 and 256 Tottenham Court Road, and 12, 13, 14, 16, 17 and 18 Morwell St. Given the gap in the directory entries it is not clear if this J. Davis was linked to the early J. Davis.

DAVIS, MAURICE & Co.
82 Fore St. *1920*

DAVIS, S.
43 Wych St. *1839*

Plate 36.
A Royal Navy square point jack or rope knife marked DEANE & Co W↑D19, along with the date 1878. Interestingly this knife does not bear any markings relating to its city of origin.

DAVIS, THOMAS.
Clare Passage, Clare St. *1833*. 43 Wych St., Strand *1836*

DAVISON, GEORGE
16 Queen St. *1829*

DAY, SAMUEL.
141 Portobello Road *1875*

DAY, HENRY JAMES.
22 Pimlico Road *1885* also at 18 in *1890-1895*

DEAKIN, J.
5 Newcastle St., Strand *1822*

DEAKIN, JAMES & SONS.
14 Charterhouse St. *1895*, as Ltd. in *1900*

DEANE.
The firm developed from the business of George Deane who was a hardware man at Fish Street Hill in the mid 1780's. George and John Deane are listed as hardware man at 41 Fish St. Hill 1830 to 1832 and by 1838 are listed as gun makers at 46 King William St.

The first record for Deane as cutlers appears in The Kelly's Post Office Directory for London 1840 with a listing for George and John Deane. However, according to an advertisement in the 1846 Post Office Directory for London the firm of Deane was established in 1766 on the Old London Bridge and are described as wholesale and export Ironmongers, Cutlers, Jewellers and Hardware men, Stove Range and Fender Manufacturers, Saddlers and Gun Makers and General Furnishing Warehousemen.

They occupied 46 King William Street, London Bridge up until circa 1890, with Gun and Pistol Manufactory being at 30 King William Street, London Bridge from c1856 to 1873.

The name changed to Deane and Co. around 1851.

There were also other variations of the name including Deane and Co, around 1851, Deane, Adams and Deane (1854 to 1857) and John Deane and Son (1857 to 1872) the common link with these names being the King William St. address. In 1854 Deane, Adams and Deane are also recorded as having, premises at 1 New Weston St.

In relations to weapons there is a record that DEANE, ADAMS & DEANE received an official order to provided to the Board of Ordnance in 1853 weapons which included three Bowie knives.

DEANE, THOMAS HARRY.
104 Knightsbridge 1910-1930

DEAR, WILLIAM & SON.
Iron monger. Listed in 1900-1915 at 41 Sloane Street and Pavilion Road, but knife has been noted with a 9 Brompton Road address but no record found of when. There is also a record of them being at 14 Knightsbridge Green in *1915*.

DENISON, JOSEPH.
10 West Smithfield *1820-1836*

DENNIS, WILLIAM & Co.
17 Little Pulteney St. *1910*

DERBY, JOHN & SONS.
317 High Holborn *1910*

DEWSNAP, FRANCES.
134 Oxford St. *1820-1832*

DEWSNAP, Mrs. FRANCES.
315 Oxford St. *1840-1846*.
As Frederick Dewsnap at same address in *1850*.

DEWSNAP, H.
42 Western Exchange, Bond St. *1836*

DEWSNAP, WILLIAM.
36 High Holborn *1855-1860*

DEWSNAP, WILLIAM & Co.
57 and 58 St John's Square. The trade directories list him under Cutlers from 1885 – 1895, however is listed in the 1851 and 1861 census returns at these addresses with occupation has Table Knife Manufacturer. In the bankruptcy notice for William Dewsnap the younger of 57 St John's Square is listed as File Manufacturer. Taken over by Buck and Hickman.

DILLER, DAVID & JOHN.
5 Chandos St. *1840*

DICK, ROBERT.
93 Bishopsgate Without *1829*

DIXON, T.
Pimlico. Despite the evidence of the knife shown I have found no trace of a T.Dixon, Pimlico in the directories that would make any direct or indirect connection to the

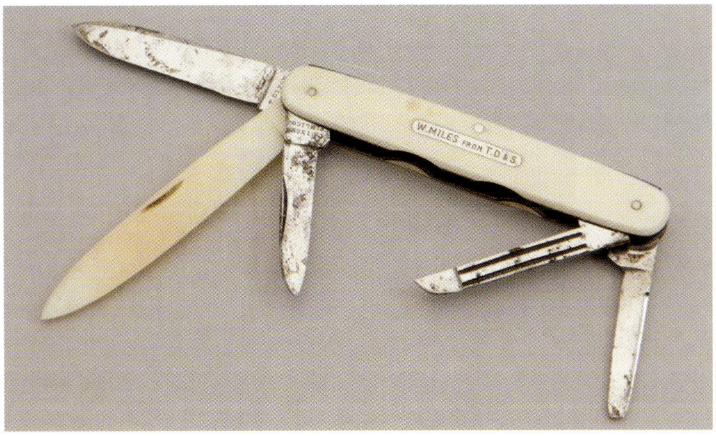

Plate 37.
The shield on this knife is engraved:
W.MILES FROM T.D & S
(possibly for T.DIXON and SON) The blade is marked:
T. DIXON
PIMLICO

Plate 38.
A typical Sheffield product marketed in London. This piece is marked: the Hunters Companion in two places on the blade which is also stamped both on the flat and on the ricasso:

J. DOBBY
95 STRAND

Plate 39.
Small cutlery handled spear point knife marked on the ricasso:

DOBBY
95 STRAND

cutlery industry. However given the engraving on the shield it is possible that this knife was a gift handed out by a T. Dixon and Son who where Auctioneers and House Agent during the *1910-1920* period and who were located in Lower Belgrave St. which is in the Pimlico area of London.

DIXON, WILLIAM

2 Tonbridge St. *1843*
also 60 Great Portland St. *1855*

DOBBY, JOHN.

John Dobby appears to be one member of a family of cutlers who first appeared in the Directories in *1829* and who were in the *1895* directory but not in any subsequent issues.

In *1829* John Dobby is recorded at 4 Blackmoor St., with a Thomas W Dobby recorded at 28 Eyre St. Hatton Gardens. Both are noted as being working cutlers. In *1832* the records show John Dobby at 20 Wych St., and Thomas W Dobby recorded at 10 Eyre St. Hill. Around *1840* these addresses had changed to 16 Wych St. for John and 54 Middleton St. for Thomas.

John in *1850* was also at 95 Strand which by *1860* had become his sole address. However in the *1860* another Dobby appears on the scene. John is still recorded at 95 Strand, a John W is at the 16 Wych St. address and a Samuel is at 1 Skinner St. In *1860* both John and John W are not noted as manufacturing cutlers and by *1870* there is no record of John.
A Thomas Dobby is now at 1 Skinner St.

In *1875* a Mrs Sarah Dobby occupies 16 Wych St., with a Francis and William recorded at 28 Charterhouse lane and 38 Skinner St. Sarah, in all likelihood the widow of John W, did not run the business for long there being no entry after *1880*. In *1883* Francis and William are styled as butchers cutlers at 103 Charterhouse St.

DOBSON, WILLIAM.

166 Strand *1820-1829*

Wych Street, Strand from an old postcard

DOBSON, JOHN.
3 Great Turnstile *1836-1840*

DOCKERY, ROBERT ALFRED.
34 Carlisle St. *1910-1930*

DODSON, J.
50 Fleet St. *1836*. In *1839* as DODSON & BATTYE

DODSON, THOMAS.
74 Newgate St. *1839*

DODSWORTH, BENJAMIN.
Mare St., Hackney *1846*

DOERKAN BROTHERS.
60 Watling St. *1870*

DONALDSON, ROBERT & Co.
47 Houndsditch *1885-1890*

DOUGHTY, Mrs. ELIZABETH.
431 Strand *1846*

DOUGHTY, WILLIAM. P
19 Strand, West End *1832*. *1836-1840* at 431 Strand.

DOWN BROTHERS.
Well known surgical instrument maker whose date of establishment is confused. Bennion states that they were established as Down Bros. Ltd. in *1874* yet there is no trace of such a firm in the *1875* directories. In *1879* a firm was known as Millikin and Down appeared at 3

Plate 40.
Folding scalpel and finger knife with tortoiseshell scales. Both blades are fitted with locks and are marked:

DOWN
LONDON

Syme's Abscess and Tenotomy Knife with nickel scales . Both blades are marked:

D.M.CO.LD FOR DOWN MEDICAL COMPANY LTD.

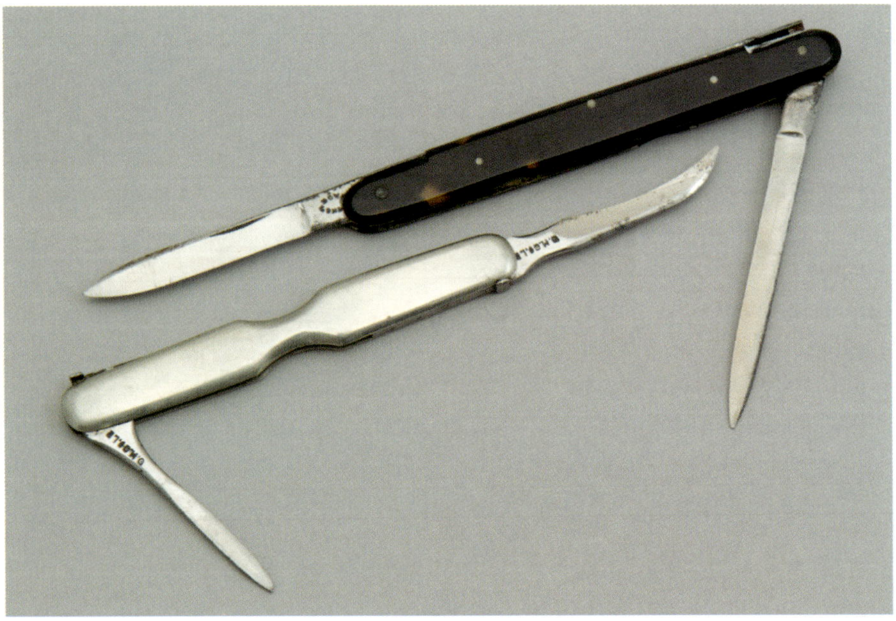

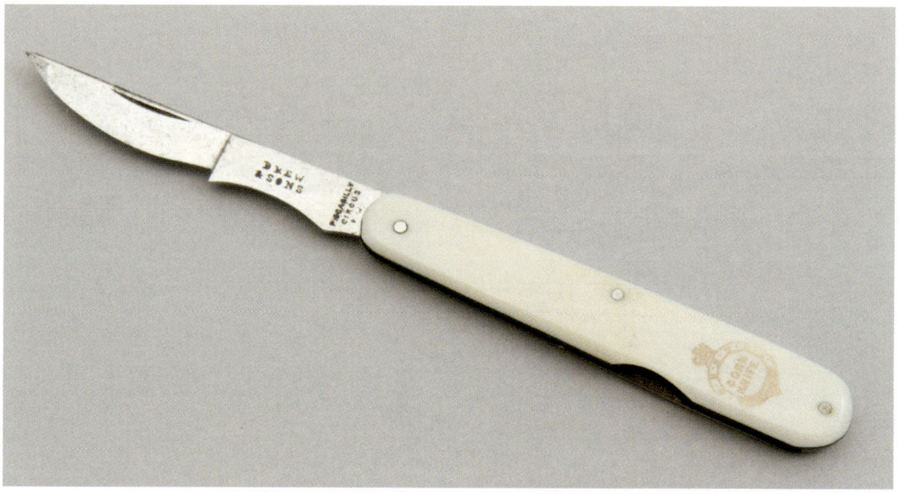

Plate 41.
Corn Knife marked:
DREW & SONS
PICCADILLY CIRCUS
W.

St. Thomas's Street. However in *1885* there is no trace of Millikin and Down but a Down Brothers is listed at the 3 St. Thomas's St. address and are described as working surgical instrument and truss makers. Now known as Down Surgical, Mitcham, Surrey incorporating Mayer and Phelps, Blyde and Gray.

Down Brothers link with knives is to all intents and purposes unknown. A knuckle duster knife stamped DOWN and dated as WWI is recorded by Gordon Hughes in his Primer of Military Knives. Whether this piece was marketed by DOWN to meet the requirements of the 1st. World War is open to speculation.

DRABBLE, CHARLES BENNETT.
14 Bridle Lane *1875-1880*

DRABBLE, SAMUEL.
Working Cutler. 35 Marylebone Lane *1832*. 1 High St., Marylebone. *1836-1880*

DRABBLE, WILLIAM.
80 Wardour St. Soho. 109 Wardour St. *1880*. As Mrs Mary in *1885-1905*

DRAKE & DAHM.
Manufacturing Cutler. 36 and 37 Upper Thames St. *1925-1930*.

DREW, J & SON.
Established in *1844*, the main business of Drew was travel goods, they are listed at various periods as portmanteau, dressing bag, luncheon and tea basket manufacturers, trunks, and leather goods manufacturers. They held

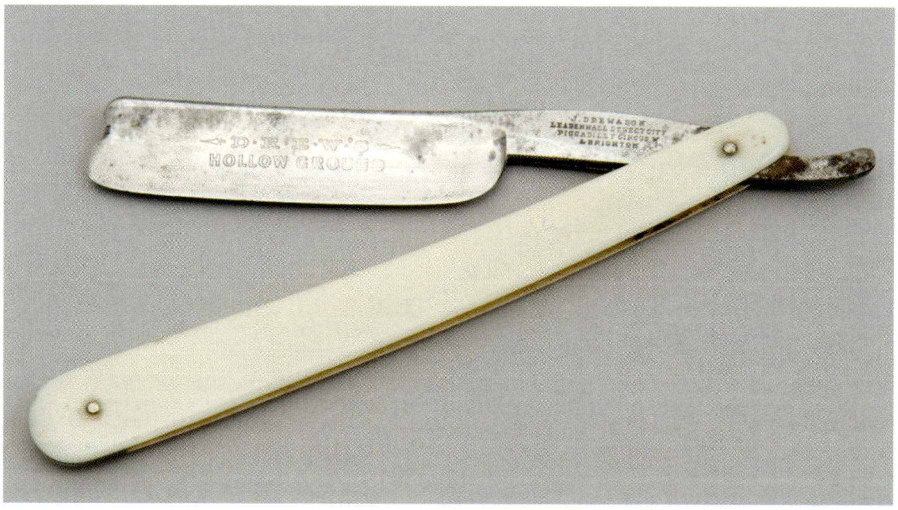

Plate 42.
Cut throat Razor marked on the flat:
DREW'S
HOLLOW GROUND
and on the tang:
J DREW & SON
LEADENHALL
STREET CITY
PICCADILLY CIRCUS
W
& BRIGHTON

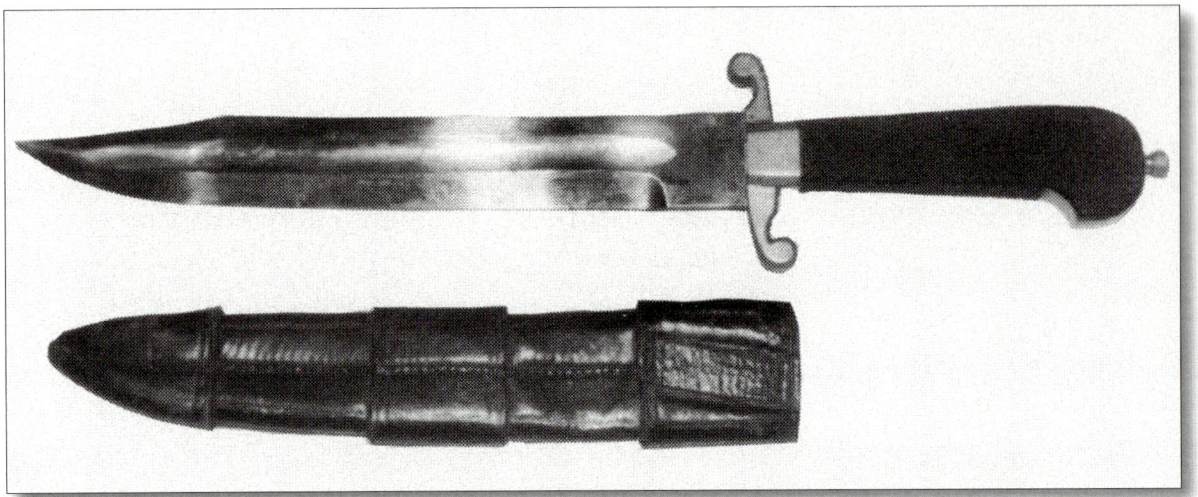

Plate 43.
The well known EXPLORER Bowie by J. Drew & Sons. (Photo courtesy of Keith Burton)

retail premises at 33, 35 and 37 Piccadilly Circus, 156 and 157 Leadenhall Street, with in *1910* Drew and Sons being recorded at the former and a Drew and Co. being recorded at the later. Their works are recorded as being at 62 Hatton Garden EC. In *1914* the firm moved to 33 Regent Street. The company converted to one of limited liability in *1928*. They exhibited at the Inventions Exhibition of *1885*. Another branch of the firm or family is also recorded as operating in Brighton. Still in business in *1930* but no record in *1935*.

DREWETT, RICHARD.
1 Spencer Place, Brixton Road *1855-1860*

DRURY, GEORGE.
32 Strand *1836*

DUDDELL THOMAS.
106 Holborn Hill *1820 -1823*

DUDLEY, CHARLES.
18 St. John's Row, St. Luke's *1855*

DUNCOMBE, ROBERT.
106 Cheapside *1870-1875*

DUNEWORTH, GEORGE.
88 Prince St. *1905*

DUNGWORTH, GEORGE.
(Butchers) 103 Charter House St. *1905*

DURHAM, JOSEPH BANKS.
261 Regent St. 1846. 456 Oxford St. *1850*

DURHAM, ROBERT.
261 Regent St. *1836-1840*

DURHAM, WILLIAM.
261 Regent St. *1832-1834*

DURROCH, WILIAM F.
2 New St. and 28 St. Thomas St. *1788-1869*

DUTTON, JOHN FRASER.
3 Athol Place, New Road *1855*

EAGLAND, CHARLES.
10 Poland St. *1826*

EAST, WILLIAM.
16 Brewer St. *1823-1839*

EAST, WILLIAM, JOHN.
91 Berwick St. Soho *1915-1930*

EDWARDS & SON.
159 and 161 Regent Street, The Cottage, New Burlington Mews. *1895-1928* Retailer. Edwards and Sons were the successors to the business of Edwards and Jones at 161 Regent Street when Jones dissolved the partnership in *1895*. The partners of Edwards and Sons who are described as stationers, dressing case and dressing bag makers were Edward Henry Edwards, Charles Alfred Edwards and John Frederick Edwards. In *1908* they also occupied 159 Regent Street and an address at The Cottage, New Burlington Mews. In *1912* the firm were styled stationers, printers, jewellers, dealers in antiques, curios and fancy goods. The firm closed in *1928* when all the stock was sold to Harrods Stores Ltd.

EDWARDS, DAVID.
166 New Bond St. *1860*

EDWARDS, HENRY.
46 Leadenhall St. *1839*

EDGEWORTH, W.
Tanners Mill, Deptford New Town *1866*

EINSLE, EDWARD.
46 St. Martin's Lane *1843-1855*

ELLERBY, ELIZABETH, WILLIAM & JOHN.
8 Ava Maria Lane *1832*, as ELLERBY, E & W in *1836*

ELLERBY, WILLIAM.
8 Ava Maria Lane *1820 –1829*. In *1820* recorded as Wholesale Sheffield Cutlery.

ELAM, ALFRED & BROS.
403 Oxford St. *1843*

ELKAN, JOHN.
138 Strand and 23 Borough High St. *1880*. In *1885* besides Strand also at 35 Liverpool St.

ELLIS, WILLIAM.
3 Thanet Place *1843*

ELTON, J & Co. Ltd.
110 Cannon St. *1920*

EMMERTON, THOMAS.
Working Cutler. 10 Red Lion St., Clerkenwell *1836*

EMMERTON, THOMAS GEORGE.
Working Cutler 11 Pearl Crescent *1836*.

EMMETT, Mrs. ELIZABETH.
27 Holborn Hill *1846*

EMMETT, THOMAS.
27 Holborn Hill and 31 Great Sutton St. *1832*, only at Holborn Hill in *1836-1840*.

ENGSTRUM, JOHN.
47 Bolingbroke Road, Kensington *1900*

ERNST, GUSTAV.
19 Calthorpe St. and 80 Charlotte St. *1860's*

EVANS & Co.
A number of Evans appear as cutlers during the mid to late 1800's. This Evans however appears to commence in *1783* with

Plate 44.
(*top*): Folding gum lancet with tortoiseshell scales and blade marked:

EVANS & CO
OLD CHANGE
LONDON

(*bottom*): Syme's Abcess and Paget's Tentonomy Knife with tortoiseshell scales, brass liners and surgical instrument locks on both blades.
Blades are marked:

EVANS & CO
31 STAMFORD ST
LONDON

a David Evans Surgical Instrument Maker. In the records for *1820* they are listed as John Evans and Co, Surgical Instrument Makers but had a considerable number of moves and occupied a number of premises. *1822* they appear as Evans and Co, Old Change Street. In *1832* the company is listed as John Evans and Co. John Evans was Master of the Cutler's Company in *1845*. Around *1855* their address had changed to 12 Old Fish St. and *1860* they are recorded at this address and also at 22½ Church St. Sometime between *1860* and *1870* the name changed Evans and Stephens of 6 Dowgate Hill and at 31½ Stamford St. This partnership did not last long as by *1875* they were styled Evans and Wormull of 31 Stamford St. In *1890* the are listed as Evans and Wormull by Appointment to the Army and Indian Government.

Evans and Wormull whilst listed in *1930* are not listed in *1935*.

The Wormull branch of this partnership seems to come from a Arthur Wormull who is listed as a surgical instrument maker in the *1850* directory as Arthur Wormull Jnr. of 182 Union St. In *1870* he is listed at 31 Stamford St. whilst a George Wormull is listed at 45 Union St. Once the amalgamation with Evans had taken place both these individual Wormull entries disappear from the record.

EVANS, DANIEL.
53 Snowfields 1829

EVANS, EVAN.
27 Fish St. Hill 1860-1890

EVANS, HENRY Jnr.
32 Holloway Rd. 1905

EVANS, ROBERT.
12 Cross St., Blackfriars Rd. *1860-1885*

EVANS, THOMAS.
27 Fish St. Hill *1895*

EVERETT, FRANK C & Co.
Manufacturing Cutler. 36 Camomile St. *1925*. *1930-1935* listed as merchants at 7 Vandy St.

EVERILL, PHILIP & WHICKER.
67 St James St. *1836-1846* see Savigny

EVERILL & MASON.
Cutler and Surgical Instrument Maker. 67 St James St. *1820-1823*.

Plate 45.
Presentation bowie marked:

EVANS & CO
12 OLD FISH ST
LONDON

(Image courtesy of Bill Claussen et al).

Plate 46.
Amputation Knife which clearly shows the ability of London surgical instrumnet makers to make substantial knives. This piece has an un-chequered ebony grip and the ricasso is marked:

EVANS & CO
12 OLD FISH ST
LONDON

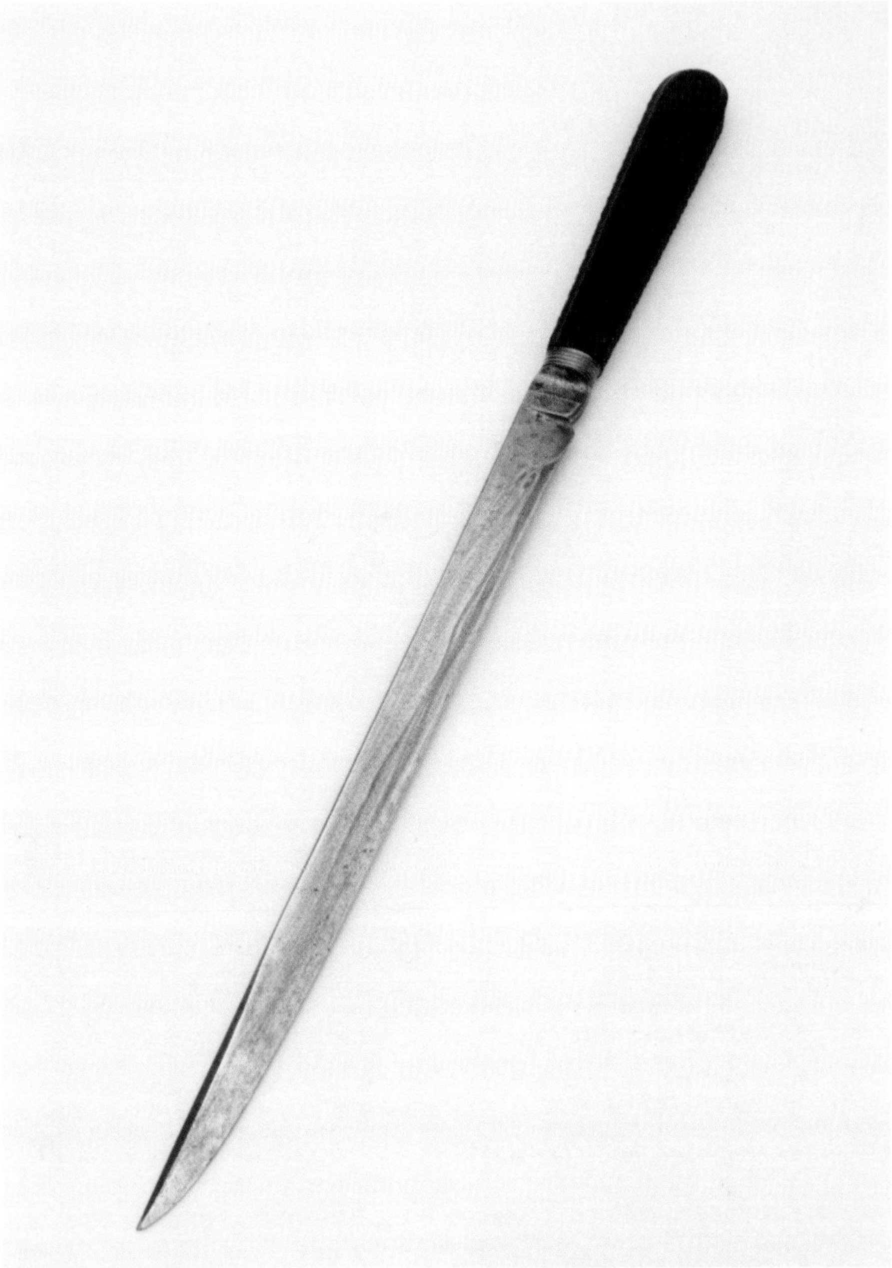

Plate 47.
All metal scalpel marked:

EVANS &
WORMULL

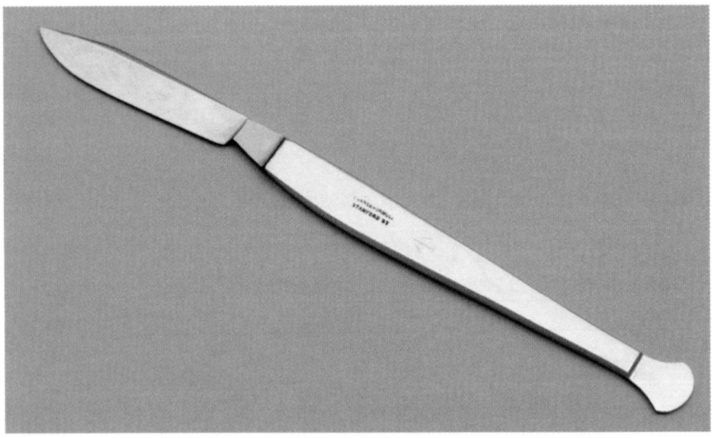

EWING, WILLIAM.

1 Drury Lane *1820-1823*. At 41 Hart St. in *1829*.

EYRE, ALBERT EDWARD.

42 College Place, Chelsea *1905-1910*

EYRE, GEORGE.

Working Cutler. 14 North St. Sloane Square *1890*. Also in *1890* as EYRE, Mrs. AMELIA.
Working Cutler. 14 North St. Sloane Square *1890*. Probably the widow of George.

EYRE, HARRY.

15 Norfolk terrace, Bayswater *1870*

FABER, J.
Working Cutler. 3 Union Terrace, Commercial Road *1836*

FAIRBAIRNS, WILLIAM.
12 Crosby Hall Chambers, Bishopsgate St. within. *1875*. *1880-1895* as William and Sons at 65 St. Mary Axe.

FARMER, JOSEPH.
32 Tavistock Street, Covent Garden *1820*

FARQUHARSON, JAMES & SONS.
Manufacturing Cutler. 61 and 62 Houndsditch *1910-1925*

FARRANT, JOHN.
48 Burlington Arcade *1846*

FARTHING & THORNHILL.
144 New Bond St. *1890-1895* see THORNHILL

FAULKNER, JOHN.
62 St. Martin's le Grand *1860*

FAVELL, R & Co.
Bucknall St. New Oxford St. *1880*

FELLA, GEORGE.
7 Eden St., Hampstead Rd. *1890*

FELLA, GEORGE CARL.
33 Mortimer Market *1930-1940*

FELLA, LEONHART.
34 & 35 Mortimer Market, Tottenham Court Rd. *1900*. In *1905* also at 295 Bethnal Green Rd. *1910* to *1915* at Pancras St., Tottenham Court Road.

FELLA, L.
(Established *1883*) 97 Charlotte St. *1910*.

FENN, JOSEPH.
Joseph Fenn appears to have traded for a relatively short period i.e. from *1845* to around *1883*. Though there is an indication in British Planemakers from *1700* that the firm existed in *1826*. Joseph

Plate 48.
A substantial pruning and cutting hatchet with back edge designed for splitting wood. Stag scales and pouch type leather sheath. The blade is marked:

FENN
105 NEWGATE ST

Size: blade 6.5 inches, 12 inches overall.

Plate 49.
This large double-edged side or hunting knife dating was illustrated in Fredrick Wilkinson's book Swords and Daggers and attributed to being circa 1850. The knife has stag grip, large steel guard and double edged blade. The sheath is of leather over wood with nickel silver mounts. The blade is just marked:

FENN

Size: blade 12 inches,
17 inches overall.

Fenn is recorded at 105 Newgate St. in *1846*, in *1860* 106 Newgate St. was added to his address, *1870* at 104 and 106. A Fenn and Co is listed in *1875* at 10 Railway Approach, London Bridge and by *1880* this had become Fenn and Co Ltd. of the same address, there is however no trace in *1883*. None of the directory entries under Cutler has any indicator that Fenn was a working cutler but the *1855* directory does list him under Tool makers and Dealers with a note indicating that the Company were also file cutters. Thus he is very likely to have had the ability to make the substantial piece illustrated.

FENWICK, WILLIAM.
(butchers) 29 Red Lion St. Clerkenwell *1866-1870*

FERGUSON, DANIEL.
21 Giltspur St. *1846-1850* and 34 West Smithfield in *1855*.

FERGUSON, DAVID & SON, JOHN & Co.
Working Cutler and Surgical Instrument Maker. 14 Castle St., 44 West Smithfield, 21 Giltspur St. *1822-1869*

FERGUSON, JOHN & Co.
21 Giltspur St. and 34 West Smithfield *1860*

FERRARI BROTHERS.
133 High St. Harlenden *1935*

FERRARI, S & SONS.
10A Archer St. *1940-1945*

FERRERS, GEORGE.
10 Red Lion St. *1820-1823*

FIELD, ALFRED &Co.
35 Cock Lane, Snow Hill *1900*

FIELD.
Willow Brook Road, Peckham. This name is something of a mystery. Enquiries with the local

Plate 50.
Knife by the mysterious FIELD of Willow Brook Rd.

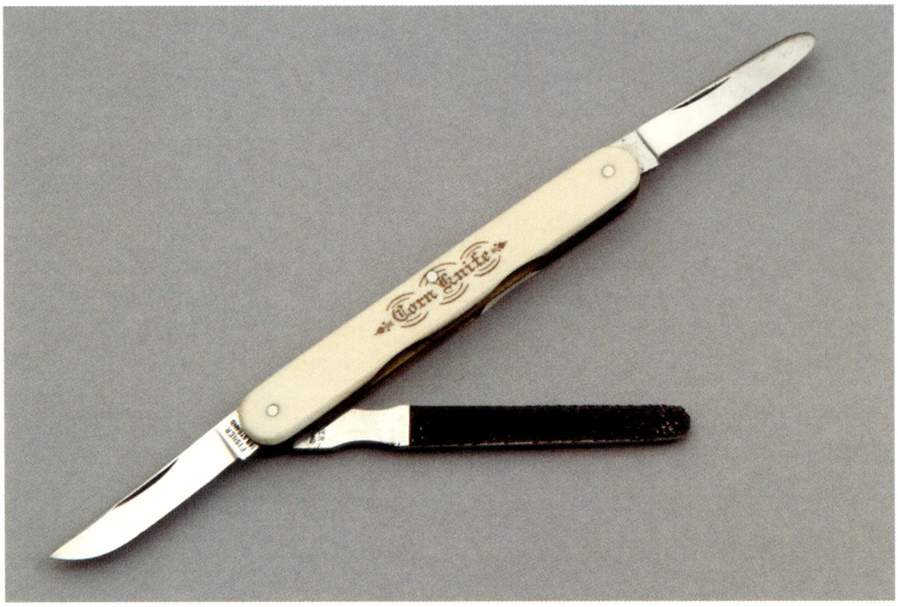

Plate 51.
A wonderful and unusual corn knife spoilt by rounding at the tip of one blade. The blades retain all original polish and comprise of two pen blades and a corn file. The scales are celluloid marked:

CORN KNIFE.

This knife was retailed by Samuel Fisher.

studies library for the Peckham area have found no trace of such a name in the London Suburban Directories between *1860* and *1923*. Whilst they may well have existed outside of this date the knife shown has stylistic similarities to a Shakespear Knife which would have clearly been a knife to be found during this period. Further checks of the directories to either side of these dates has failed to reveal any information.

FINLAY, GEORGE.
4 Castle St., Strand *1829*

FINNIGANS Ltd.
18, 19, 20 New Bond St., and Coach and Horses Yard, Old Burlington St., works 6 to 10 Lexington St. *1920*

FISCHER BROTHERS.
86 Leadenhall St. *1890-1895*

FISHER, Jnr.
Surgical Instrument Maker 185 Ratcliffe Highway *1820-1823*

FISHER, J.
Surgical Instrument Maker.
6 Nassau Place *1832*

FISHER, J.
Working Cutler. 3 Union Terrace *1839*

FISHER, JAMES.
7 Cannon St. Rd. *1846*

FISHER, JOHN & JAMES.
34 Wapping St., 7 Cannon St. Rd. *1805-1843*

FISHER, SAMUEL & SON.
Operated circa *1880* to *1910*. Address was 188 Strand and only a few variations occurred in the company name being known as Samuel Fisher and Son, Samuel Fisher and S Fisher Ltd.

FORTNUM & MASON.
With a history dating back to 1707 the firm of Fortnum and Mason are generally associated with the luxury food trade and for much of its early life had very close associations with the Royal family and in providing for Officer's food requirements during the Peninsular and Crimean Wars. By the end of the 1900's they undertook a full service to their clientele providing food, wines, flowers, table requisites and decorations, complete with chefs,

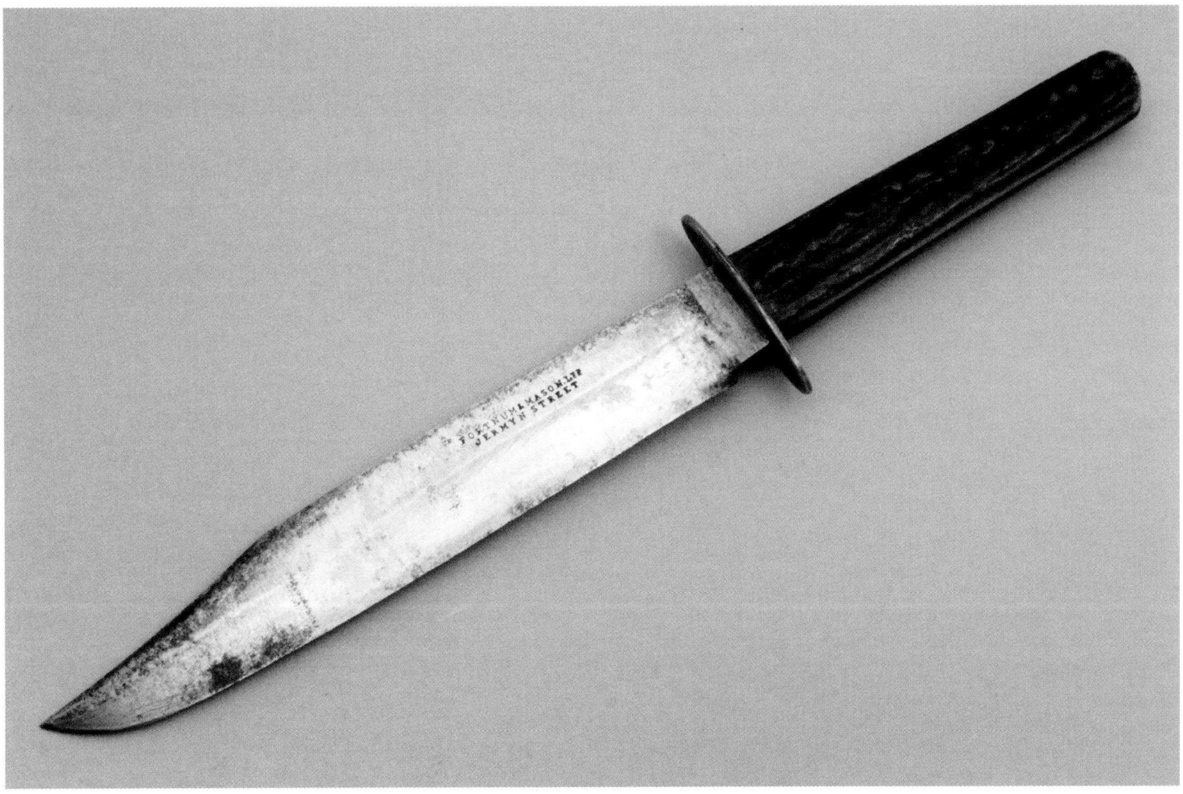

Plate 52.
A typical Sheffield product of the type sold by many retailers. The blade is marked:
FORTNUM & MASON LTD. JERMYN STREET

butlers and footmen. In 1908 a new department to cater for the needs of camping and other equipment of expeditions and cruises to all parts of the world. The firm is still in business today.

FOSTER, WILLIAM.
349 Oxford St. *1860-1866*

FOWLE, FREDRICK.
25 Balls Pond Rd. *1880-1905*

FOWLE, JOHN ALFRED.
41 Bell St., Edgware Rd. *1866 -1890*

FOWLE, JOHN ALFRED.
41 Bell St., Edgware Rd. and 163 High Road, Kilburn *1915*

FOWLE, WILLIAM ERNEST DANIEL.
41 Bell St., Edgware Rd. *1930-1940.* 18 Bell St. *1945*

FOWLE, Mrs. MARY.
41 Bell St., Edgware Rd. *1895 -1910*

FOSTER, WILLIAM ERNEST DANIEL.
41 Bell St., Edgware Rd. *1920-1925*

FOTHERGILL, CHRIS.
7 Bartholomew Close *1829*

FRANKLAND, CHARLES G.
335 High Holborn *1920-1940*

FRENCH, DAVID.
Working Cutler. 24 St. Andrews Road. *1832 -1846*

FRENCH, W.
7 Goldsmith's Row, Hackney Rd. *1866*

FRITH, THOMAS.
Hatton Gardens, *1822*

FRY, MARRIAN & WELLS.
8 Mincing Lane *1900-1905*

FULLILOVE
A family of cutlers with entries in the trade directories as shown below along with notes on their

relationship. Two other family members were cutler but whom do not have their own entries in the trade directories i.e. Robert (son of George) listed in the *1871* census as a cutler at 13 James St. and Charles (son of James) listed in the *1881* census as a cutler [Many thanks to my friend John Pidgeon for the family history information]

FULLILOVE, CHARLES (HENRY?).
54 Kings St., Seven Dials 1836-1846. The son of Thomas.

FULLILOVE, CHARLES HENRY.
13 James St., Covent Garden *1855-1866.*

FULLILOVE, GEORGE R.
14 East St., Walworth Road *1850-1866*, at 36 in *1870-1890.* The son of Charles Henry

FULLILOVE, Mrs. H.
13 James St., Covent Garden *1870.* Harriet Fullilove the wife of Charles Henry.

FULLILOVE, J.H.
Bradley's Buildings Pentonville N. *1860.* James Henry also the son of Charles Henry.

FULLILOVE, THOMAS.
Cutler. 25 Broad St. *1822-1829*

FULLILOVE, THOMAS.
Working Cutler. 3 Tower St., Seven Dials *1832*

FULLER, JOHN.
239 Whitechapel Rd. *1832-1860*

FURGUSON, DANIEL.
21 Giltspur St. *1839*

GABRIEL, CHRIS.

Working Cutler. 8 Castle St. Clerkenwell *1829*

GALLIENNE, RICHARD.

Working Cutler. 71 Goswell St. *1836-1860.* At 138 Goswell Road in *1870*

GALLIENNE, Mrs. ANNE.

138 Goswell Road *1875.* Presumably the widow of Richard

GAMAGE, A.W. Ltd.

118, 121, & 125 to 129 HOLBORN, and Nos. 1a, 2a, 3a, 4a, 1to 8 Leather Lane, London.
The well known London Department store of A. W. Gamage Ltd., generally known as Gamage's existed between *1878* and *1972.* Like many of its competitors such as Harrods, Army and Navy Stores it did not make its own knives but retailed those made by the Sheffield cutlers. An illustration in the *1905* edition of the Gamage catalogue shows a range of pocket knives along with two Bowies. Close examination of the original illustrations indicate makers such as George Butler, Singleton and Priestman, Thomas Turner, and Saynor

GARDEN, R.S.

The Checklist of Tradesmen which is listed in The London Gun Trade *1850-1920* shows a Robert Spring Garden of 29 Piccadilly as Gun and

Gamage's Store in Holborn circa *1907*

Plate 53.
This double edged Bowie knife was made by George Butler. The knife bears the **BUTLER** name on one side of the blade and **GAMAGE** on the other. This style of knife is of the type shown in the 1905 catalogue and in a 1930's catalogue of George Butler products.

Plate 54.
Horseman's knife marked:

R.S. GARDEN
29 PICCADILLY

With stag scales the blade has a butterfly/surgical instrument lock. The grip would have contained the usual array of implements but only the probe and tweezers now remain. Unusual in that it is complete with its leather carry case.

Pistol Maker as well as sword cutler operating between *1861* and *1877*. The *1865* directory actually list him as gun and pistol maker and sword manufacturer.

GARDNER, JOSEPH.
Working Cutler. 80 Watling St. *1829-1840*. In *1850* at 3 Sermon Lane.

GARDNER & SONS.
451, 454 and 63 Strand, 4 and 5 Duncannon St. and James St. *1870-1875*

GARLICK, J.
2 Benjamin St., Clerkenwell *1870*

GAUNTLETT, HARRY.
2 Temple St., Whitefriars *1875-1880*

GAY, WILLIAM & SON.
Manufacturing Cutler and razor makers. 113 High Holborn also agent for Rodgers and Sons cutlery

Plate 55.
A very fine Bowie with an address that indicates that it was made between 1861 and 1877. The pistol grip has chequered ebony scales with brass liners. The blade is etched:

R.S.GARDEN
29 PICCADILLY
LONDON

1875-1890, also at 92 Regent's St. in *1890*. *1895* only at 92 Regent St. In *1900* at 113 High Holborn and 93 Regent's St. *1905-1920* at 93 Regent St.

GAZARD, GEORGE.
55 Upper Gloucester Place. *1890-1900*

GAZARD, GEORGE.
96A Cleveland St. *1920*

GAZARD, JAMES.
96 Bishopsgate St. without *1836*

GECK, AUGUST THEODOR.
1 Scott's Yard, Bush Lane *1880*

GEHR, FREDRICK
5 Gibson St., Waterloo Road *1832* in *1836* as 5 Gibson St. Lambeth

GEORGE, GEORGE.
20 Crescent St., Euston Square *1836-1846*, also at 15 Park Terrace in *1846*. *1850-1855* at 15 Park Terrace and 5 Palace Row. Only at Park Terrace in *1860*.

GEORGE, G & SON.
217 & 218 High St., Camden Town, and 1 Wellington St., Camden Town *1870-1880*

GERARD, ALPHONSE.
Manufacturing Cutler. 21 Jewin Crescent. *1885*

GIBBENS, JOSEPH & SONS.
21 Warwick Lane *1900*

GILBERT, EBENEZER THOMAS.
48 Newington Causeway *1836-1850*

GILBERT, R.
48 Newington Causeway *1840*

GILKES, JOSEPH.
25 Commercial Road *1822-1829*

GILL, JOHN.
9 Colonnade, Brunswick Square. It is not clear from the Cutlers section of the directories if this Gill was a working cutler or a retailer, however any knife with his name and this address on it must be

Plate 56.
A locking dirk of a pattern seen with several retailers marks and thus almost certainly a Sheffield product. This example is marked:

GAY & SON
HOLBORN

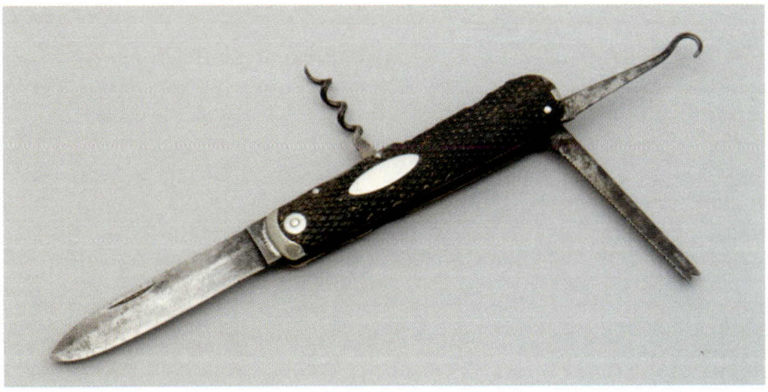

Plate 57.
Knife which has fish hook disgorger blade. Locking main blade, corkscrew, button hook, with probe, folding ruler and tweezers. The scissors and an awl blade are missing. Main blade marked:

J. GIBBENS
& SONS

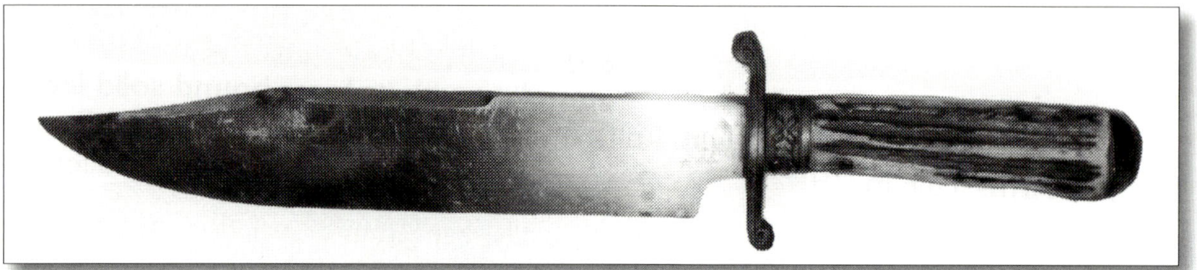

Plate 58.
Bowie by J. Gill
(Photo courtesy of Keith Burton)

Plate 59.
A hunting knife with the grip containing button hook, corkscrew, tweezers, probe, and fleam. The grips are of worked black horn and the blade has file work on the back edge which extends on the tang. The blade is marked:

GILLES
LONDON AND
UXBRIDGE

rare because he only existed at the Colonnade for a very short time between *1842* and *1849*. There is being no appearance of his name either before or after these dates. However a John Gill of 45 Salisbury Square is listed as a Surgical Instrument Maker in *1825* and a knife is illustrated by Burton which is marked: 'J. Gill, Percy Street', and dated to circa *1860*. There is no clear evidence to link these 3 nor has any trace been found of the latter John Gill even though there is a Percy St. in London.

GILL, GEORGE & SON.

36 Whetstone Park, Kingsway. *1925*

GILLES, WILLIAM.

William Gilles was born in Sheffield in *1821*. In *1841* both he and his elder brother James are recorded as Pen Knife Cutlers and two younger brothers Thomas and Fredrick as Apprentice Cutlers. William is still recorded in the Sheffield in *1851* however by *1855* he had moved to the London area where he established businesses in both London and Uxbridge. Uxbridge remaining his home until his death in *1904*. The census returns recorded him living at the High Street Uxbridge.

Gilles occupied a number of London premises but also had a very intermittent appearance in the trade directories. In *1855* was listed at 22 Oakley Street, Lambeth, is missing from *1860* directory but appears in *1870-71*, *1875* and *1880* at 52 Paddington St. In *1905* is at High St., Marylebone but no trace after *1910*.

From the census records it would appear from circa *1865* that the London business was looked after by William's son, also named William

who was born in Sheffield in *1846*. He is listed as living in Uxbridge in *1861* but in *1871* is recorded as living at 52 Paddington St. where his occupation is listed as cutler. By *1881* his address is High St. Marylebone which despite the lack of entries in the trade directories would appear to indicate operation from this address through the *1881-1905* period.

The younger William died in *1903*.

GILLHAM, THOMAS.

Manufacturing Cutler 77 Kensington High St. Manufactory 12 and 14 Ball St. *1875*

GLADWIN, S.

24 Ely Place *1920*, as Gladwin Ltd. in *1925*

GOLDSMITHS & SILVERSMITHS Co. Ltd.

112 Regent St. and 47, 48 and 49 Warwick St. *1910-1920*.

GOODBEBERE, GEORGE THOMAS.

(Wholesale) 9 Wellclose Square and 143 Shoreditch *1836*

GOODWIN, Mrs. RUTH.

19 Porter St., Soho *1846*. Presumably the widow of Samuel.

GOODWIN, SAMUEL.

Working Cutler. 19 Porter St., Soho *1832*

GOODWIN, SAMUEL.

13 Little Newport St. *1850-1880*. Possibly the son of Samuel above.

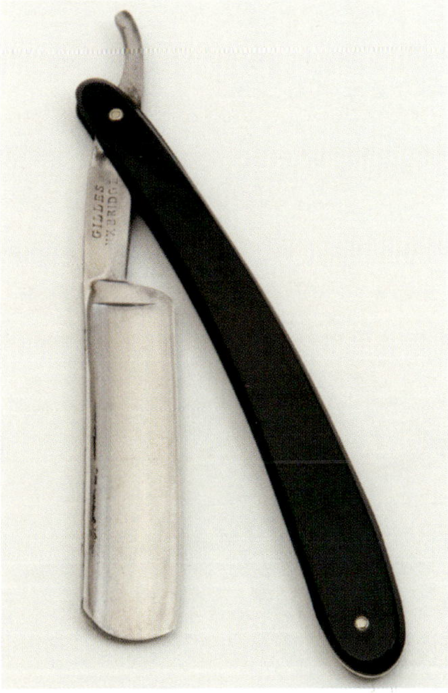

Plate 60.
The two dirk knives shown are both simply marked **GILLES** on one side and **LONDON** on the other. The larger of the two has a 5-inch blade and is 9" overall. The scales are of horn. This smaller piece which retains all original polish has ivory scales, it has a 4-inch blade and is 8" overall. The cross-guard are of identical shape on each example and both knives have chevron-work to the tangs.

Plate 61.
A cut throat razor reflecting Gilles Uxbridge connection being marked on the tang:

GILLES
UXBRIDGE

GOULD & VERINDER.
Working Cutler. 79 St. Paul's Churchyard *1820* (see also Verinder)

GRAY, GEORGE EDWARD.
Working Cutler. 26 to 31 Eyre St. Hill *1915-1935*. As GRAY & BRAY in *1920*.

GREEN, FRANCIS.
31 Drury Lane *1836*

GREEN & GREEN Ltd.
31 Hatton Gardens *1900*

GREEN, J.
Working Cutler. 27 Great St. Andrew's St. *1823-1832*.

GREEN, J.
13 Upper York St. *1839*

GREEN, J.W.
7 St. Peter's Alley, Cornhill *1840*.
17 Gough St. *1846*

GREEN, JOHN.
Working Cutler. 31 Drury Lane, *1820-1832*

GREEN, JOHN.
15 Ave Maria Lane *1820-1823*

GREEN, JOSEPH.
19 Black Lion Yard. *1920*

Plate 62.
All metal knife with main and pen blades, corkscrew and unusual can opener. The scales are marked in script 'W Rose'. The inside of the can opener blade is marked with a crowned harp this being the mark of both Wingfield, Rowbotham and Co. and Thomas Turner, Turner having acquired the mark when they took over the former in1898. Main and pen blades marked:
GREGG
27 SLOANE SQUARE

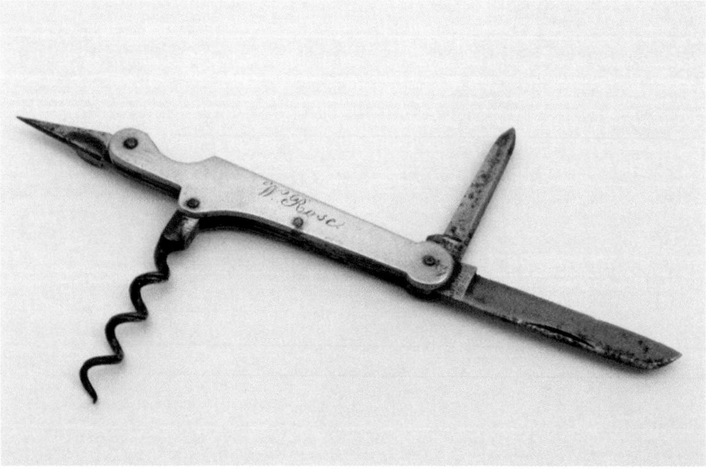

GREENE, HENRY & SON.
16 & 17 King William St., 19 Nicholas Lane, 155 Cannon St., 138 Regent St. *1870-1875*

GREENWOOD, JOHN & SONS.
34 Farringdon Rd. *1895*.
16 Clerkenwell Close *1900*.

GREER.
With a history going back to the mid 1700's this family of working cutlers played a prominent role in the Cutlers Company. John was a Master of the Company in *1813*, his son Charles master in *1852*. Frederick was Stewards for the Lord Mayors dinner in *1851* though his name is not separately recorded in the trade directories even though when he became a freeman his address was given as 44 Newgate St. A Robert Greer is also noted as being made free of the Cutlers Company in *1846* but like Frederick there is no separate listing for him in the Trade Directories.

GREER, JOHN.
Ave Maria Lane *1820*

GREER, CHARLES.
56 Newgate St. *1820-1832*.
At 44 Newgate St. *1836-1850*

GREER, CHARLES & SON.
44 Newgate St. *1855*

GREER, CHARLES & JAMES.
79 Newgate St. *1860*.

GREER, JAMES.
90 Newgate St. *1866*. 23 and 90 Newgate St. in *1870*

GREGG, JAMES.
50 Tothill St., Westminster in *1850*.
27 Sloane Square *1866-1945*
James Gregg is listed as a working

cutler for most of the listed entries between *1866* and *1885*, but in the *1883* he is listed as a razor maker. However the knife shown in *Plate 62* was retailed by them has it has Sheffield made blades. In *1910* recorded as James Gregg and Co.

GRIEBEL, HENRY.
3 Crown St., Walworth Road *1860*

GRICE, JOHN, GRICE, & FULLER.
239 Whitechapel Rd. est.*1800-1832*

GRUBB, GEORGE.
6 Feathers Court, Drury Lane *1829*

GRUBB, GEORGE & Co.
Working Cutler. 39 Cowcross St. *1836*

GUNNER, JOHN.
Working Cutler 129 Church St., Bethnal Green 1832-1870

GURNER'S CUTLERY.
31 Aldermans Hill *1925-1958*.
Located in the north part of London at Palmers Green this firm had some strange entries in the telephone directories for the period and it is of note that despite terming themselves Cutlers they have no entry in the trade directories under that heading. In *1926* their address is shown as Radio Dept.
31 Aldermans Hill. In the 1940s and 50's the entry reads *Dog Outfitters and Cutlers*.

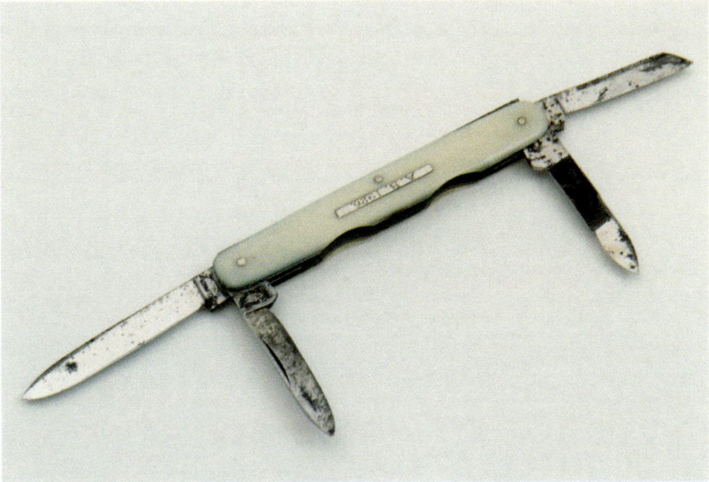

Plate 63.
Four piece pocket knife with the shield marked: 'A.B. 1926'. All four blades are marked:
GURNER
PALMERS GREEN

HAGUE, WILLIAM.
Working Cutler. 11 London Road *1823-1829*

HAGUE, JOHN.
57 Banner St., St Luke's *1875-1885*, in *1905* at Bowling Green Lane

HALCROW, EDWIN.
154 Borough High St. *1890*

HALES, HENRY.
4 Manor Row *1820-1829*

HALL, CHRISTOPHER CHARLES.
24 and 124 New Oxford St. *1915*

HALL, JAMES.
Manufacturing Cutler. 87 London Road *1846-1866*.

HALL, Mrs. JANE.
87 London Road *1870 -1875* widow of James.

HALL, JAMES.
76 Islington High St. *1880-1935*

HALL, JAMES.
3 Camden Passage, Islington High St. *1940*

HALL, JOHN.
Working Cutler. 51 London Road *1832-1836*

HALL, JOHN.
Working Cutler. 31 Old St., St Luke's *1832-1846*

HALL, JOHN.
52 Rafford's Buildings Islington *1846-1866*. 39 High St. *1870-1875*

HALL, ROBERT.
Tailors Cutler. 53 Bath St., City Road *1850-1860*, also at 54 in *1870*

HALL, ROBERT.
Cutler and shears maker. Plummer's Cotton Mills, Golden Lane *1846-1850*

HALL, SAMUEL.
5 Crown St., Finsbury *1846*

HALLAM, FREDRICK HYMAN.
74 Lisson Grove North *1855-1860*

HALSTAFF, WILLIAM & Co.
228 Regent St. *1840*

HAMILTON, ADAM.
68 Newgate *1820-1822*, 17 Aldgate within. *1832*. In *1836* at 73 Hatton Gardens and listed as agent for J Rodgers and Sons

HAMILTON, WILLIAM.
Butchers Cutler.
18 Clothfair *1880-1900*.
51 Long Lane. *1905-1915*.

HAMMOCK, CHARLES.
53 Chiswell St. *1829*

HAMPTON & SONS.
Manufacturing Cutler. 8, 9, and 10 Pall Mall East, .2, 4 and 6 Whitcombe St. Works at Belvedere Rd. *1890-1895*

HANCOCK, CHARLES.
Working Cutler. 22 Lower St., Islington *1823-1829*

HANCOCK, W.T. & Co.
308 High Holborn *1895*

HARDING, G & SONS.
Manufacturing Cutler, pen and pocket knife maker, razor maker. 25, 27, 31 to 51, 36 and 38 Long Lane, and 19 Tabard St. *1905-1910*

HARDY, MISS ELIZABETH.
12 Three Colt St. Limehouse.
1890-1905

HARDY, EPHRAIM.
Working Cutler. 3 and 9 Tudor Road *1900-1905*. 26 Lamb Lane Hackney *1910-1935*

HARDY, JOSEPH.
10 Jubilee Place, Commercial Rd. *1866*

HARDY, RICHARD.
314 New North Rd. *1895-1905*

HARDY, THOMAS.
Working Cutler. 11 Cambridge Road *1836*, at 70 Three Colt St., Limehouse *1846* and at 25 in *1850-1866*. As Hardy, T Sen. in *1870-1885*

HARDY, THOMAS.
22A Palace Place, Well St., Hackney *1855*

HARFORD, J.
Working Cutler. 10 Charles St., Westminster Road 1836. No trace for several years when reappears *1866-1870*

HARRIS, SAMUEL.
55A Houndsditch *1870-1875*. At 154 and 155 *1880-1890*, also at 3 Aldermansbury postern *1895*. Only at 154 and 155 Houndsditch *1900-1905*

HARRISON, RIDDLE & Co.
Butchers Cutler 77 Charterhouse St. *1885*, and 55 Long Lane *1890-1900*. *1905-1925* only at 77 Charterhouse St.

HARRODS.
Brompton Road, Knightsbridge. *1834*-Present. The well known London Department store of Harrods had its origins with an East End grocer Charles Henry Harrod started business in Stepney. In *1849* he moved to the Knightsbridge area where he took over a small shop on the site of the present store. The business grew rapidly and by *1880* was selling not only groceries but medicines, perfumes etc. The store burnt to the ground in *1883* but was quickly rebuilt. Harrods like all the major department stores did not make its own knives but sold those made by others typically the piece shown.

HART & LEVY.
27 Houndsditch *1855*

HASLEHURST, HENRY.
17 Hereford Place *1860*

HASLIP, JOSEPH.
1 Gray's Inn Passage *1832*

HASLIP, HENRY.
18 High Holborn *1840*.
11 Southampton Row, Russell Sq. *1846*

Plate 64.
This knife was made by George Butler for Harrods their mark appearing on one ricasso whilst the other is stamped

HARRODS
BROMPTON ROAD
S.W.

Plate 65.
Unusual kukri-style knife by HILL & SON. The blade has the etched panel:

GRAHAM

GAUNTLETT

size: Blade 14.5 inches, 20 inches overall.

HATFIELD, AARON.

Working Cutler. 2 Falcon Court, Fleet St. *1823*

HATRICK & Co.

A Jason L Hatrick appeared as a wholesaler of instruments, ligatures and dressing shortly after *1900* with an address at 82 Turnmill St. By *1905* the address had changed to 70 St. John St. Circa *1910* the firm had become James L Hatrick and Co Ltd. of 70 and 72 St. John St. who besides being a wholesaler is also recorded as a surgical instrument maker. By *1940* the company name had changed to James L Hatrick (London) Ltd. of 58 Britton St. Still listed in business in *1960* at 170 Archway Road.

HATTERSLEY, ROBERT.

Working Cutler. 4 South Melton St. *1823*

HAVEMANN, CHARLES.

Working Cutler. 44 White lion St. Norton Folgate *1910*

HAWARD, GEORGE WILLIAM.

133 Hampstead Road *1885*

HAWKINS, GEORGE.

69 Oxford St. *1840*

HAWKINS, SAMUEL.

6 Kings St. *1829-1832*

HAWKSLEY, GEORGE.

A George Hawksley is listed at 74 Strand between *1832* and *1840* but he is not listed in *1846* or thereafter.

HAWKESLEY, THOMAS.

Surgical Instrument Maker. Thomas Paton Hawkesley of 4 Blenheim St. is listed as a surgical instrument maker in *1870*. In *1875* he was listed at 300 Oxford St. and Sedley Place, Oxford St. going under the trade description of "bougie, catheter, truss, orthopaedic, ophthalmoscope and physiological instrument maker". It is not clear if there is any link between George and Thomas but it is very likely that they were father and son. Also listed as HAWKSLEY, THOMAS & SON Ltd. 357 Oxford Street *1865-1925*. Note the variation in spelling of the surname.

HAWKSWORTH, EYRE & Co Ltd.

25 Bouverie St., Fleet St. *1875*

HAWTHORN, FREDRICK.

Gibbon Rd, Nunhead *1940*

HAYCROFT & SON.

45 Deptford Broadway *1890*

HAYES, SAMUEL FORD.

56 Brompton Road. *1905-1920*

HAYMAN & BENJAMIN.

3 to 6 Camomile St. *1885*

HAYWARD, RICHARD. E.

21 Bouverie St. *1840-1855*.
50 Long Acre *1860-1880*

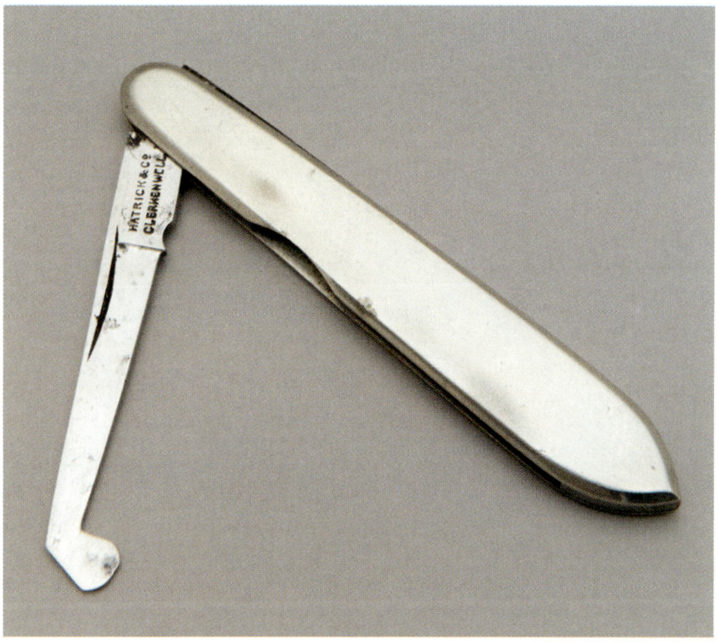

Plate 66.
All metal Gum Lancet marked:
HATRICK & Co
CLERKENWELL
It is interesting to note there is no street address - just an area, but the company's address was located in the Clerkenwell area of London.

Plate 67
Sheffield made product retailed by Hayes, blade marked:

S F HAYES
56 BROMPTON RD.
SW

HAYWOOD, JOSEPH & Co.
56 Holborn Viaduct *1885-1895*

HEBERLEIN, B.C. & Co.
107 and 109 Gray's Inn Road *1910*

HEINISCH, ROCHNS.
115 Cheapside *1870*

HEMS, BENJAMIN.
49 Blackman St. *1840*

HEMS, HENRY.
39 Hedge Row, Islington *1850*

HEMS, WILLIAM & BENJAMIN.
49 Blackman St. *1839*

HEMS, WILLIAM AND SON.
Working Cutler. 37 High St. Whitechapel *1820-1832*. In *1836* as Hems and Son at 39 and 142 High St., Whitechapel, at 39 only in *1840*, also at 142 in *1846*. *1850-1866* listed at 39 Whitechapel High St. and 23 Aldgate.

HEMMINGS, AUGUSTUS F.
45 Chiswell St. *1843*

HENDRY, WILLIAM T.
71 Cannon St. West *1860*

HENNIG & Co.
Operated for only about 15 years from *1890* to circa *1905* at 26 Coventry St. being described as razor makers.

HENTSCH, FREDRICK CHARLES.
Operated Between *1826 –1894* from a variety of addresses i.e. 18 Dukes Court, 25 Bartlett Building, and 49 Greek Street.

HERBERT & SONS.
Butchers Cutler. William A. Herbert was master of the Cutlers Company in *1912*. Occupied a number of addresses over various periods: - 6 and 7 West Smithfield, 319 Gray's Inn Road, and 47 St. George St. *1885-1910*, *1905-1910* also at 321 Grays Inn Road. By *1915* George

St. address dropped. *1920-1925* at 6 and 7 West Smithfield and 206 Goswell Road, *1925* also at 41 Theobald's Road and 24 and 25 Cowcross St. *1930-1945* at 6 and 7 West Smithfield and 204 and 206 Goswell Road.

In the *1881* census William Herbert is recorded at 319 Gray's Inn Road and listed as a Scale Maker Employing 4 Men 3 Boys.

HERBERT, T & SONS.
Butchers Cutler. 319 and 321 Gray's Inn Rd. *1895-1900*. T.Herbert was Master of the Cutlers Company in *1938*. Thomas was the son of W.A. Herbert

HERBERT, EDWARD.
12 Cross St. Blackfriars *1890*

HERBERT, JOHN.
Working Cutler. 39 Cross St., Islington 1829-1836. At 135 Upper

Plate 68.
Large 8 blade folder with the main and saw blades marked:

HENNIG & CO
26 COVENTRY ST

Plate: 69.
Skinning Knife marked:

HERBERT & SONS
WEST SMITHFIELD

along with WARRENTED in a circle, and a trade mark which has not been identified.

Plate 70.
White metal bodied pocket knife with main blade, can opener button hook corkscrew, file blade and wine/champagne foil blade. Complete with its leather carrying pouch. The main blade is marked:

HILL
LONDON

however the foil blade and file are marked with the name and address of PRIEST 515 OXFORD ST. The main blade shows no signs of having been replaced which raises the issue of whether or not there was some link between HILL and PRIEST.

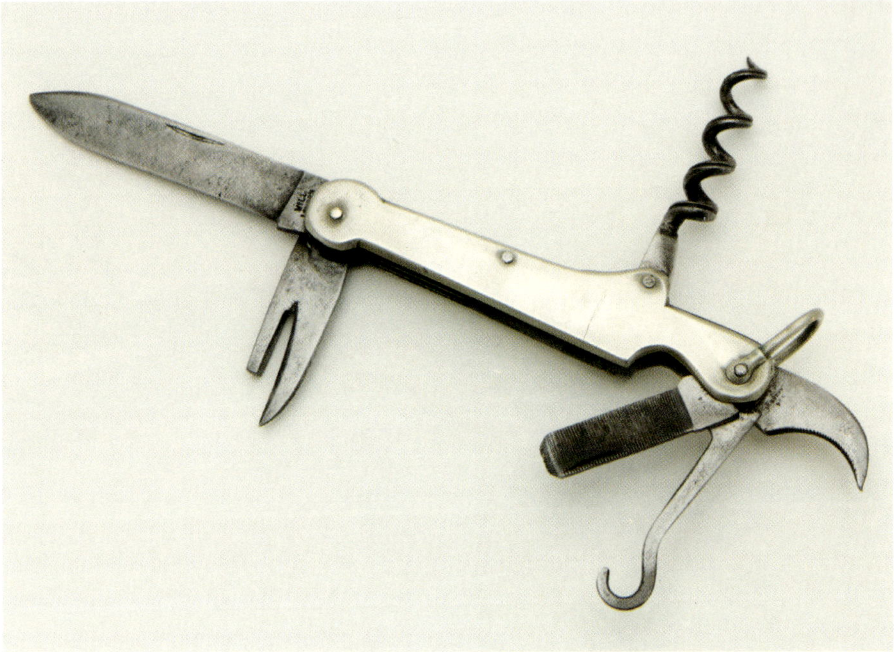

Plate 71.
Lock back folder with corkscrew, button hook, punch and small pen blade. Chequered scales. All blades are marked:

T. HILL
4 HAYMARKET

Plate 72.
A highly unusual folder in the style of a Spanish knife with the main blade marked:

HILL & SON
4 HAYMARKET
LONDON

Plate 73.
A very unusual and small knife with the blade stamped:

HILL & SON
LONDON

The blade is only *3 inches* in length and the overall length of the knife is 6 inches and is stamped on the reverse side of the blade with a 16 the significance of which is unknown. The scales are of hallmarked silver stamped with London marks for 1892.

St. *1840-1855*. *1860* at 164 Upper St. In *1875-1880* at 67 Cross St. Islington in *1880* also at 65. *1885-1895* at 50 Cross St.

HERMANN, FRANK.
2 Hoxsan St. *1885-1895*

HERMITAGE, EDWARD W.
Butchers. 2 Middle St. *1925*. As Henry Hermitage in *1930-1940* at same address.

HIBBITTS, PERCY.
46 Marchmont St. *1900*

HIGGINS, FRANCIS & SON.
9 Newman St., and 3 and 4 Newman yard *1890-1905*

HIGHAM, Mrs. PRISCILLA.
48 Jermyn St. *1843*

HILL & SON.
A Thomas Hill, of 4 Haymarket is listed in the Cutlers section of the *1855* Post Office Directory as Desk and dressing case manufacturers thus at this stage he must have been a cutlery retailer. However in the *1880* directory he is listed as Hill and Son and described as a working cutler. In *1885* his addresses are 4 Haymarket, and Sage's Buildings 80 Gray's Inn Road. In *1887* the Gray's Inn address in dropped from the entry and in *1890* the entry reads Thomas Hill and Son. At this point they still occupy the Haymarket site and are still listed as working cutlers. In *1895* they are additionally listed as razor makers. At sometime between *1895* and *1900* the name changed to Edwin Hill and Son. The *1910* directory list 3 Hill's, Edwin and Son at 4 Haymarket manufacturing cutler and razor makers, Edwin S. Hill and Co. of 23 Old Bond St., and a James Hill and Co. Ltd. 100A Queen Victoria St. and 2 Lambeth Hill. There is no trace of James Hill in *1912*, and Edwin S Hill does not appear in the *1930* directory. Edwin Hill and Son are still at the Haymarket in *1945* but not in *1950*.

Plate 74.
Folder marked:

HILL & SON
4 HAYMARKET

The white metal scales are marked with ruler divisions on one side and on the other

W STEVENSON
FROM RUTLAND
JAN 1911

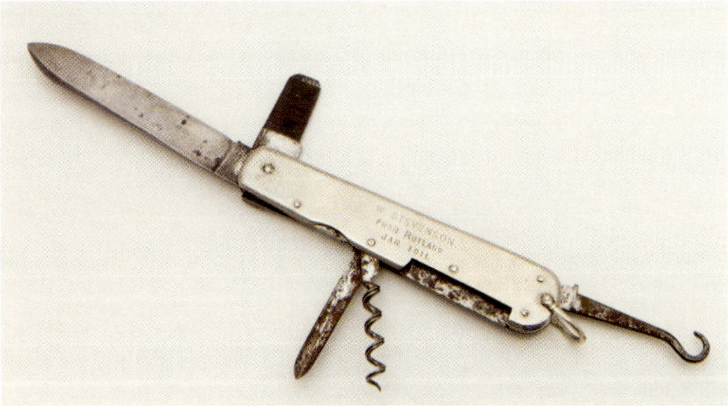

Plate 75.
This knife is of a very unusual shape and has been attributed by some collectors as being of San Francisco in style. The knife has chequered ivory scales and is stamped on the ricasso:

HILL
4 HAYMARKET
LONDON

Hill and Son are responsible for a relatively well known spear point Bowie which bears the etched motto 'Death to Traitors', and which appeared in the Butterfield and Butterfield auction of the Berryman and Schreiner collections. This piece been attributed as being circa *1860*, the motto being generally one that is associated with the American Civil war period. However this attributed date is some 20 years too early, as Hill and Son did not adopt this title until circa *1880* and this must cast doubt on the authenticity of the etch.

HILLS, HENRY J.
46 Kings Street. *1820-1853*. Also known as Monson Hills.

HINDE, HAROLD.
9 Newbury St. *1935*

HINDMARSH, ALEXIA.
87A Cowcross St. *1875* also at Blackhorse Yard, Aldersgate St. in *1880*, in *1885* at 118 Aldersgate St. and 20 St. John's Rd., Hoxton. In *1890* at 37 Old St.

HINDMARSH, FREDRICK.
37 Old St. *1895*

HINDMARSH, JOHN.
35A Beech St. Barbican *1900-1925*. 48 Old St. *1930-1945*

HIRST, ERNEST.
35 Charles St. Hatton Gardens *1900*. 19 D'Arblay St. Soho. *1910*

HOBSON, HENRY & SONS
1845-1930. Generally attributed as a Sheffield company the history of this firm illustrates the inter-linking of the London and Sheffield trade. Both Henry Hobson and George Hobson were involved in this firm and both had residential addresses in London or its surrounds. The business was established by Henry Hobson in

1845 with its London Branch being listed at 68 and 69 Houndsditch. The firm later named George Hobson and Sons registered London silver marks in around *1894* whilst occupying premises at 67. 68, 69 and 88 Houndsditch. During this period the firm also occupied premises in Sheffield with their factory being at 92 Queens Street Sheffield being listed as *manufacturing cutlers, electroplaters and foreign importers.* Knives bearing the name Henry Hobson and Son have been noted however these curiously lack any city mark. Maybe this was a clever way of getting around the laws on the marking of knives.

HOGG & JOHNSON.
71 Houndsditch (wholesale and export) *1860-1880*

HOLBORN CUTLERY Co.
5 Furnival St. *1905*

HOLBORN SURGICAL INSTRUMENT Co. Ltd.
Founded circa *1905* as Holborn Surgical Instrument Co Ltd., 26 Thavies Inn and listed in *1908* as Manufacturers of high class instruments, sterilizers, and aseptic furniture. Contractor to the War Office, Indian Government.

In *1915* their address is recorded

Plate 76.
Lock knife which is just marked:

HENRY HOBSON & SON

Plate 77.
Castrating knife with the blade marked:

HOLBORN Co HOLBORN CIRCUS

John Jacob Holtzapffel circa 1800 (Courtesy of David Stanley Auctions)

as 26 Thavies Inn, Holborn Circus and the entry in the directory also indicates that they were awarded Grand Prix and Gold medal at the *1913* International Congress of Medicine London. They had also expanded their list of clientele as their entry also reads:

Contractors to the war Office, Honourable Council of India, the Crown Agents for the Colonies, the Egyptian Government and leading hospitals in the United Kingdom and Colonies.

If their entries in the directories are any guide they did not appear to add veterinary instruments to their range until sometime between *1925* and *1930*.

In *1945* their address was 26 Ely Place and by *1950* it was Cubbon House, Charterhouse St. Were still in business in *1960*.

HOLDEN, WILLIAM LLOYD.
12 Finsbury Pavement 1855

HOLDEN, WILLIAM LLOYD & SON.
12 Finsbury Pavement *1870* just as HOLDEN, WILLIAM in *1875-1880*

HOLLAND, WILLIAM PETER.
203 and 205 Newington Butts *1866*

HOLLAND & ALDRIDGE BROTHERS.
203 and 205 Newington Butts *1870*

HOLLER A. E. & Co.
39 Monkwell St. *1870*. 1 Wood St., Cripplegate in *1875*

HOLLER, F.W.
Manufacturing Cutler. 5 Love Lane, Wood St. *1870*. 6 Love Lane, Aldermansbury *1875-1885*. 5 London Wall Avenue *1890-1895*.

HOLTZAPFFEL & Co.
Started by a John Jacob Holtzapffel, who came to England in *1792* from the Alsace and set up business in London in *1794* specialising in the manufacture of turning lathes. In *1829* the firm was known Holtzapffel and Deyerlein 64 Charing Cross Rd. though this appears to have been a short-lived

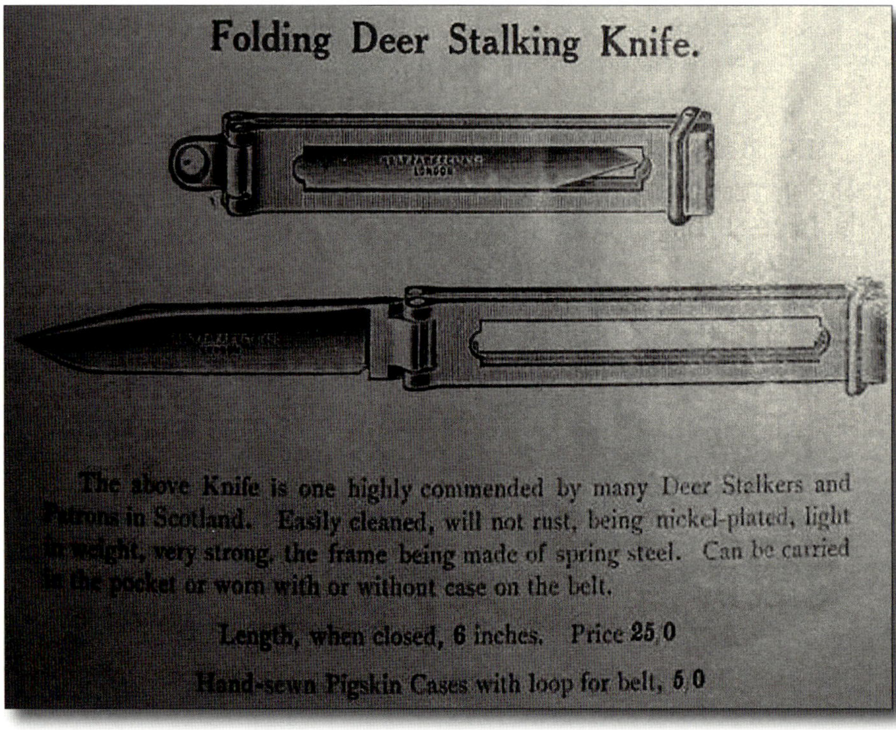

Illustration from the 1923 Holtszapffel Catalogue

Plate 78.
Four examples of this folding knife marked just 'HOLTZAPFFEL & Co.' have been noted. They seem to date from around the World War I period though they are also shown in a 1923 dated catalogue. Each of the examples noted have been nickel plated and marked:

HOLTZAPFFEL & CO

name as in *1836* the firm is listed as John Jacob and Charles Holtzapffel. Even though the firm held this name in *1836* John Jacob had actually died in *1835,* being succeeded by his son Charles who died in *1847.* His son John Jacob (the second) was an infant at the time and his widow carried on until John Jacob took over. He died in *1897.* Firm then carried on under a nephew George William Holtzapffel Budd till *1924* when his son Col. G.H. Budd took over. All engineering activity ceased in *1928* but they remained recorded as cutlers in *1930.* There does appear to have been a short-lived partnership after this date under the name Walkers and Holtzapffel (Retail) Ltd. 61 Baker St. an address which is still recorded against their name in *1935.*

In their history they occupied a number of premises, 64 Charing Cross under the name John Jacob and Charles Holtzapffel, 64 Charing Cross and 127 Long

Plate 79.
A superb set of campaign cutlery by HOLTZAPFFEL with the handles bearing the crest of the Duff family of Fetteresso Castle, Stonehaven, Kincardineshire. These date from around the mid to late 1800's and could have belonged to either The Rt. Hon Sir Robert William Duff who was a Commander in the Royal Navy or to his son who was a Major in the Royal Field Artillery.

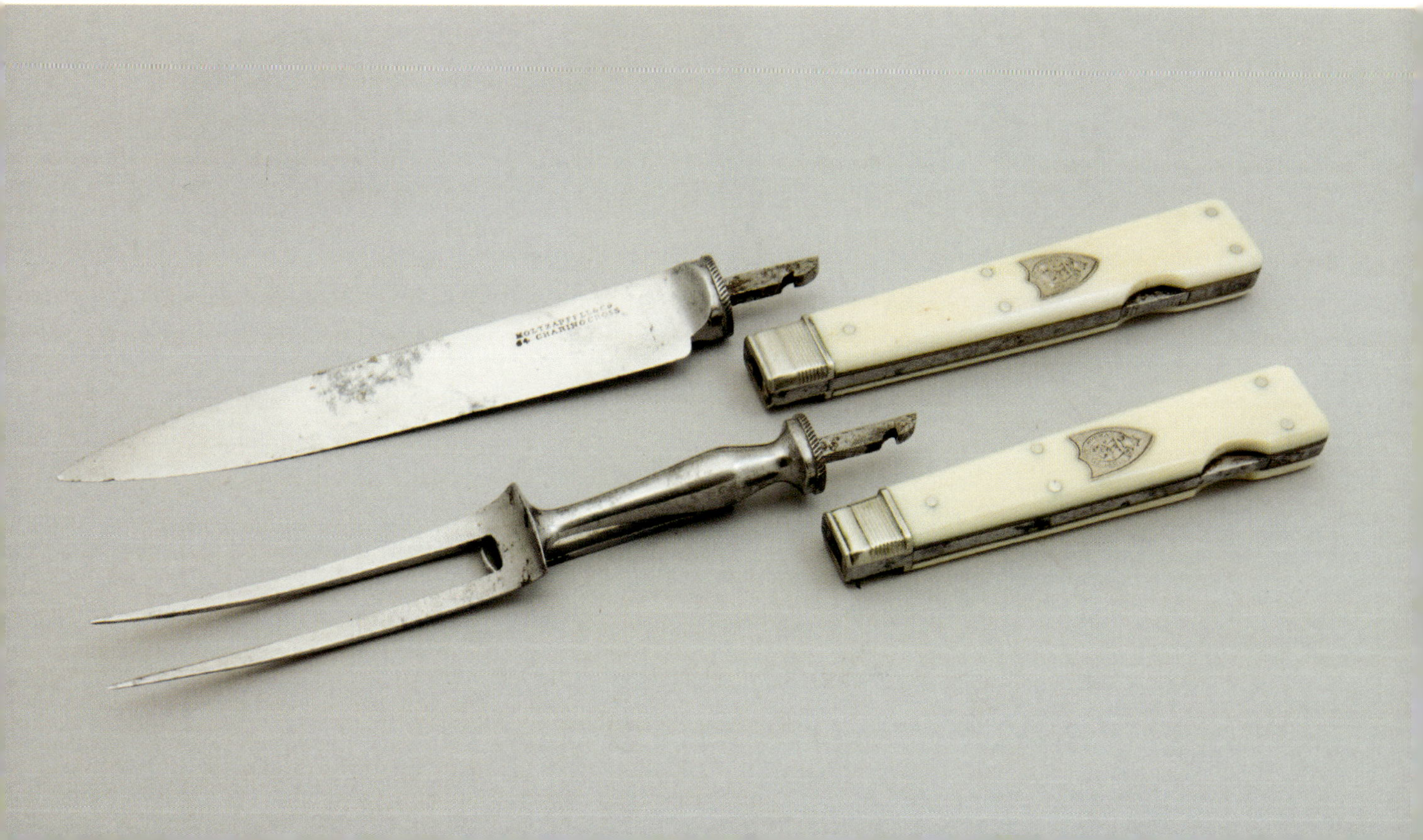

Plate 80.
These very unusual pieces were in at least two cases designed for use as a reversible lance head mounted in the end of a walking stick as shown. Two of the pieces have solid hilts whilst the third has a hollow hilt and is unmarked. The solid hilt versions are marked:

HOLTZAPFFEL & CO
LONDON

Acre as Holtzapffel and Co., 64 Charing Cross and Sharples Hall St. Their long association with the Charing Cross address is reflected by the entry in the *1910* directory of Holtzapffel and Co. 53 Haymarket (late of 64 Charing Cross) and Sharples Hall St. There was also a short association with 79 Wigmore St. in the early 1930's. The firm continued in business into the *1960's* but was a shadow of it former self. During the company's history they made Bowies, folding and hunting knives along with tomahawks and engineering equipment. The company also retailed knives, at least one folding Bowie marked: 'HOLTZAPFFEL & Co. COCKSPUR STREET' and 'Sheffield Made' has been noted. They occupied these premises between *1904* and *1906*.

HOOKER, T.A.
57A Holborn Viaduct *1935*

HOOKHAM, ALFRED R.H.
Working Cutler. 82 Railway Arches, Galena Rd., Hammersmith *1935-1940*

HOOKHAM, HENRY.
13 Greek St., Soho *1910-1915.*
17 Denmark Place in 1920

HOOLE, GEORGE.
61 Great Saffron Hill *1822-1823*

HOOLE, RICHARD.
85 Westside off Fleet Market. *1820*

HOOLE, RICHARD.
13 Margaret St. *1832* (Listed as cutler and ivory cutter)

HOOLE, STEPHEN.
Working Cutler. 41 St. John St. *1822-1829*

Plate 81.
Spear point bowie possibly made for HOLTZAPFFEL, though this is not possible to confirm as part of the ricasso marking has been erased. Chequered horn scales, note the offset guard. The markings on the ricasso that are visible are:

HOLTZAPFFEL & Co
64

which would indicate that the address would read 64 Charing Cross

86 *Plate 82.*
This piece is simply marked:
HOLTZAPFFEL & Co.

Plate 83.
This Bowie is marked:

HOLTZAPFFEL
& Co
LONDON

Note the similarity in design of the cross-guard to that shown in *Plate 82*.

Plate 84.
A billhook which has rosewood scales secured by three steel rivets with brass washers and a cleaver blade. The tang of this piece is tapered indicating a high standard of manufacture. Heavy duty sheath with side opening. The blade is marked:

HOLTZAPFFEL & Co
LONDON
6

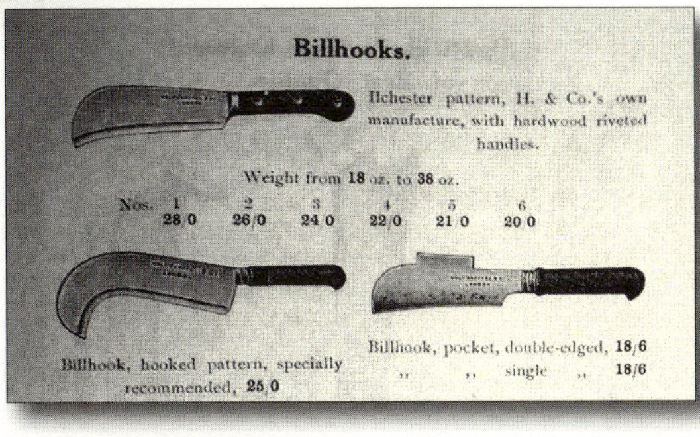

Billhooks.

Ilchester pattern, H. & Co.'s own manufacture, with hardwood riveted handles.

Weight from **18** oz. to **38** oz.

Nos.	1	2	3	4	5	6
	28/0	26/0	24/0	22/0	21/0	20/0

Billhook, hooked pattern, specially recommended, **25/0**

Billhook, pocket, double-edged, **18/6**
,, ,, single ,, **18/6**

Illustration from the 1923 Catalogue

Plate 85.
A full size kukri with black horn scales and white metal mounts to the base of the grip. One of the mounts is engraved:

G.R ROUGIER
M.C.O.T.C. 1918

G. R. Rougier was born in Odessa in 1900. He attended Marlborough College from 1915 to 1918, the M C O T C standing for Marlborough College Officer Training Corps. He subsequently had a distinguished law career and was married to Georgette Heyer the historical novelist.

The blade of the Kukri is marked:

HOLTZAPFFEL & Co
LONDON

And the reverse of the scabbard belt loop is stamped

HOLTZAPFFEL & Co
LONDON
53 HAYMARKET

Size: blade 11 inches, 15.5 inches overall.

Plate 86.
Small kukri style knife marked on the blade:

HOLTZAPFFEL & Co
LONDON
6

Has a sturdy pouch type sheath. The pommel of this knife is engraved:

HCP 60TH RIFLES

Size: blade 8 inches, 12.25 inches overall.

Plate 87.
A similar kukri with blade marked:

HOLTZAPFFEL & Co
LONDON
2

The reverse of the scabbard belt loop is marked with the firm's name.
Size: blade 7.5 inches, 12 inches overall.
Kipling's son Jack is recorded as taking a Holtzapffel kukri to the WW1 trenches.

Plate 88.
With marine ivory scales hunting knife similar in style to some Californian knives.
The piece is accompanied by a pouch style sheath.
The blade is marked:

HOLTZAPFFEL & Co
LONDON

Plate 89.
Folding bowie which whilst Sheffield made was marketed by Holtzappfel.
The ricasso being marked:

HOLTZAPFFEL & Co
53 HAYMARKET

The scabbard belt loop is stamped

HOLTZAPFFEL & Co
LONDON
53 HAYMARKET

HOPPE & Co.
Manufacturing Cutler razor maker, pen and pocket knife manufacturer. 25 Jewin Crescent *1890. 1895-1915* at 151 Aldersgate St. 3 Featherstone Buildings *1925*

HOPPER, CHARLES & SONS.
167 Camberwell Road. *1925-1945*

HORNE, WILLIAM.
114 Ratcliffe Highway *1832*

HORTON, J. (LONDON) Ltd.
Lombard House, Little Britain *1935*

HOUGHTON & Co. (London) Ltd.
31 Royal Exchange *1945*

HOUSE, A.T. & Co.
170 Falcon Rd. Battersea *1935-1945*

HOUSE, JOSEPH.
20 Little Windmill St. *1866-1880.* In *1885* at 30 Little Windmill St. and 38 Glasshouse St. *1890* at 38 Glasshouse St. and 21 Lexington St. *1895-1910* only at 2 Lexington St.

HOUSE BROTHERS.
2 Lexington St. *1915-1925.* 9 Brewer St. in *1930-1940.* 52 Brewer St. *1945*

HOVEDEN, R & SONS.
Manufacturing Cutler and razor maker. 31 and 32 Berners St. 93 and 95 City Road, 1, 2 and 3 Cowper St., and Park Place *1885. 1890-1900* at 31 and 32 Berners St. 93 and 95 City Road. In *1905* at 85, 89, 91, 93 and 95 City Rd. and 29 to 33 Berners St. *1910-1930*

HOWARD, JAMES.
498 Kingland Road *1870*

HOWARD, WALTER.
498 Kingland Road *1875*

HOWES, J.
38 Kinnerton St. *1930*

HUBBARD, JOHN.
22 King St. *1866*

HUBBARD, JOHN.
3 Cain Place, Kentish Town *1875*

HUDSON, GEORGE LEWIS.
152 Fenchurch St. *1870*

HUDSON KNIFE Co.
84 Fairholt Rd. *1895*

HUGHES, FRANCIS & Co.
247 High Holborn *1843*

HUGHES, RICHARD. HUGH.
Atlas Works 96 Hatton Garden and 6, 7 and 8 Robin Hood Yard, Leather Lane *1870-1890*

HUNNKIN, GEORGE.
293 Euston Road *1900-1905*

HUNT, GEORGE J.
10 Bishopsgate St. within *1900*

HUNT, JOSEPH.
13 Fenchurch St. *1832.* Wholesale and retail cutler.

HUNTER, MASON & Co.
44 Webberrow, Blackfriars *1843*

HUTTON, WILLIAM & SONS Ltd.
Manufacturing Cutler. 7 Farringdon Rd. *1895-1905*

HYAM, DAVID & Co.
58, 59 and 60 Houndsditch.

HYDE BROTHERS 32 Southampton St. *1840*

INFIELDS Ltd.

Listed as Manufacturer and Importer. 174 Aldersgate St. Appear in the directories circa *1927* continued in business into the post war years.

INTERNATIONAL DISTRIBUTING Co. Ltd.

("Every Ready" safety razors) 6 and 7 Stonecutter St. 1915

ISAACS, LEWIS.

94 St. George St. 1860

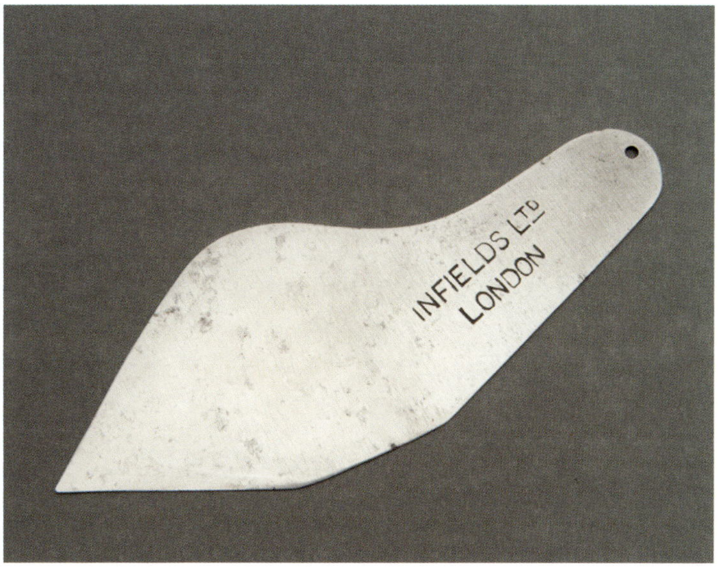

Plate 90.
Furriers Knife.

JACK, WILLIAM.
118 Culford Road *1875*

JACKSON, J.
Working Cutler. 30 Bell Yard, Lincoln's Inn *1823-1824*

JACKSON, MONTAGUE L.
18 Bartlett's Buildings. *1925*

JAMES, DAVID MORGAN.
18A Lower St., Islington *1860*, at 58 Essex Rd, Islington *1866-1875*

JAMES, J.U. & SONS Ltd.
Manufacturing Cutler. 226 Bishopsgate *1935-1940*

JAMESON, CALEB.
71 Houndsitch *1870-1885* as Caleb Jameson and Co *1890-1895*.

JAMESON & Co.
Proprietors of the Autocrat razor. 71 Houndsitch *1905*. *1910-1925*. In *1930* listed as JAMESON & CO (London) Ltd. *1935* also at 19 and 21 Wilson St. As JAMESON & CO (Tools) Ltd. at 23 Wilson St. *1940 -1945*

JAY, RICHARD ATTENBOROUGH & Co. Ltd.
Speciality reliable guaranteed stainless steel table and cheese knives. 142 and 144 Oxford St. *1910-1945*

JENKINS, THOMAS HERBERT.
15 Henry St. Deptford. *1885*

JENKINS & RINGROSE.
Manufacturing Cutler 30 Ely Place *1930*

JENKINS & TIMM.
96 Newgate St. *1895*

JENNER & KNEWSTUB.
A Fredrick Jenner and Fabian James Knewstub trading as Jenner and Knewstub are listed from *1857* at 33 St James Street SW and from *1862* at this address and 66 Jermyn Street, St. James SW. They are described as dressing case makers, stationers, cutlers etc. and also as jewellers, watchmakers. They are also recorded as having wide range of stock of fancy goods. The firm was absorbed by A Webster and Co in

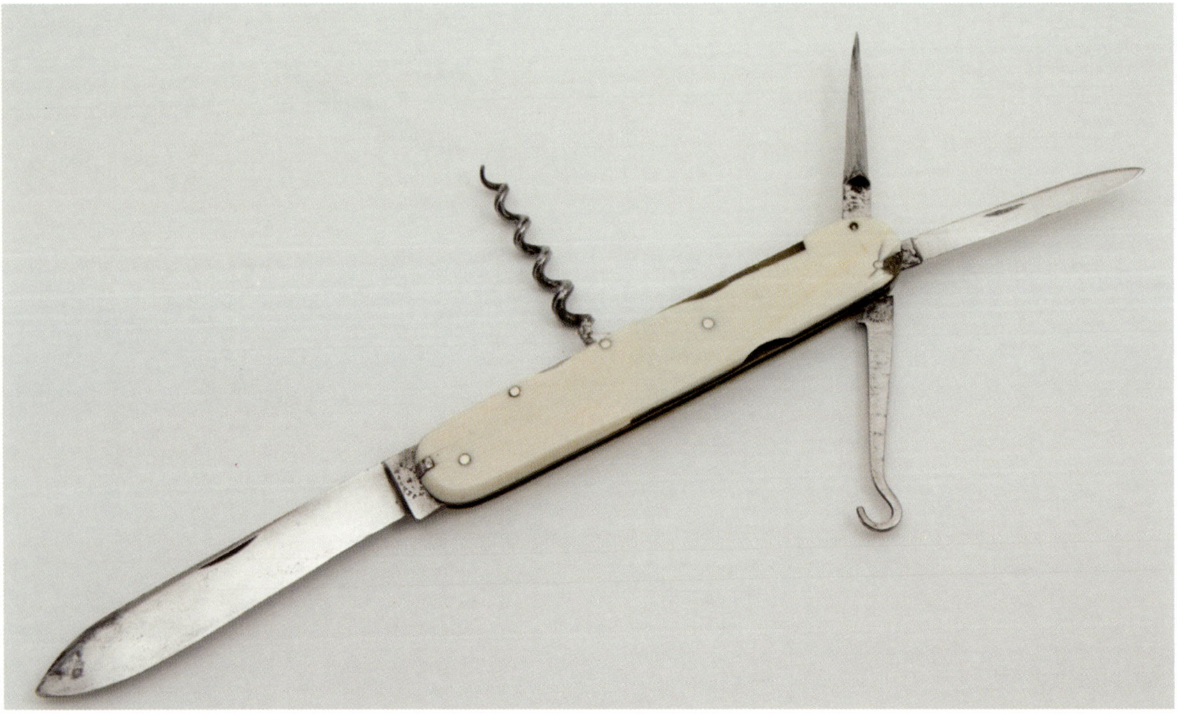

Plate 91.
A superb Ivory scaled folding knife with locking main blade, secondary pen blade, corkscrew, button hook, awl and probe and tweezers contained in the grip. The main blade is marked on one side JENNER & KNEWSTUB in an arc and on the other with their 33 St James St. address.

1890. They exhibited at the London *1862* Exhibition and at the *1878* Paris Exhibition.

JEWESSON & BEATIE.
Working Cutler. 137 Fenchurch St., and Town Head St. *1832-1836*

JEWESSON, & SON.
Working Cutler. 25 Cullum St. 1829

JOHNS, RICHARD. JOSEPH & Co.
(Agent) 121 Newgate St. *1900*

JOHNSON, WALKER & TOLHURST Ltd.
80 Aldersgate St. and 21 Conduit St. *1915*

JOHNSON, THOMAS.
39 Stanhope St. *1839*

JOHNSTONE, WILLIAM.
Cutler and Surgical Instrument Maker. 6 Lisle St. *1836-1839*

JONES, GEORGE.
Working Cutler. 22 Union St. *1885-1900* also at 20 Union St. *1905-1930*

JONES, T.
45 Joiner's St. *1829*

St James St. from old postcard

JONES, THOMAS.
Working Cutler and Razor Makers. 9 Finsbury Place *1823-1860*

JONES, THOMAS.
41 St James St.reet *1880. 1885.* Two prize medals Paris Exhibition *1878*

JONES, THOMAS & SONS.
Dominion House, Bartholomew Close. *1935-1940*

JOPLING, THOMAS.
9 Feathers Court *1829*

KAMMERLING, CARL & Co.
13 Tottenham St. *1935*

KEARNS, JOHN.
425 Oxford St. *1836-1866*

KEILY, EDWARD WILLIAM.
22 Windmill Lets, Finsbury *1866*

KEITH, WILLIAM.
10 Victoria Road *1846*. 2 Shaftesbury Terrace in *1850*

KELLY, ALBION WILLIAM.
Working Cutler. 9 Tachbrook St. Pimlico *1930*

KENDALL, JARVIS KELSON & Co.
(agents) 1 King Edward. St., Newgate St. *1866*

KENNARD, WILLIAM & Co.
57 Little Britain *1895-1930*

KEYWORTH, CHARLES.
77 Scalter St. Bethnal Green *1870*

KEYWORTH, Mrs. CHARLOTTE.
4 Leather Lane *1866*

KEYWORTH, GEORGE.
Manufacturing Cutler. 19 York St. Westminster *1846-1855*. 5 Dorset Place, Pall Mall *1860-1870*

KEYWORTH, JAMES.
Working Cutler. 4 Leather Lane *1836-1860*

KIDERLEN, GEORGE WILLIAM.
Manufacturing Cutler and agent for ERNs razors pocket knives and scissors. 26 and 27 Milton St. *1895-1910*

KIDSTONE, W & Co.
18 Bishopgate St. *1850*

KIERAN, WILLIAM ARTHUR.
133 Regent St. *1900*

KING, JOHN W. LAPIDARY Co. Ltd.
Manufacturing Cutler 1 Albermarle St. *1930-1935*

KINGABY, WILLIAM HENRY.
Hornsey Rd. *1870*

KINGSBURY, B.J.
165 New Bond St. *1822 -1823*

KINGSBURY, THOMAS.
Razor Cutler. 165 New Bond St. *1832-1836*, at 106 in *1840*. 152 Regent St. *1846*. 9 New Bond St. *1850-1880*

KIRK, JOHN E & P.
Manufacturing Cutler. 5 Water Lane, Great Tower St. *1910-1915*

KNIGHT, WILLIAM.
17 Albert Terrace, Nottinghill Place *1890*. At 45 Pembridge Rd. in *1895*

KNOWLES, J.
41 Bell St., Edgware Road *1855-1860*

KNOX, ALBERT WILLIAM & Co.
(Agents) 28 Eldon St. Finsbury *1900*. 5 Tabernacle St. *1905*

KNOX, HENRY AUGUSTUS. & Co.
30 Houndsditch *1875-1885*, in *1890* at 59 and 60 also at 58 in *1895*.

KOHL, PAUL.
Manufacturing Cutler. 30 and 31 Newgate St. *1925*

KOOYSTRA, JUSTIN.
Working Cutler and Surgical Instrument Maker. 69 Oxford. St. *1820-1836*

KRAMM, CHARLES.
267 Old Street *1880-1885*, at 267 Old St., and Smither's Mill Cross St. in *1890*. Only at 267 Old St. *1895-1915*

KROHNE, CHARLES WILLIAM.
44 Great Dover St. *1860*

KROHNE, & SESEMAN.
8 Duke St., 241 Whitechapel *1860-1926*. Bought by A. Cox in *1926*

KROPP MANUFACTURING Co.
Manufacturing Cutler 51 and 52 Frith St., and 8 Bateman St., Soho *1905*. Also at 11 Bateman St. *1910-1920*. *1925* only at Firth St. *1930-1945* at 51 and 52 Frith St., and 34 and 35 Dean St. Soho. See also OSBORNE, GARRETT & Co.

LAMB, HENRY.
47 Clement's Rd. Bermondsey *1915*

LAMB, HENRY T & Co.
31 St. John's Square, Clerkenwell. Circa *1880-1945*. Henry T Lamb and Co were listed as Masonic Jewellers. The firm survived on into the *1960s*. There is no apparent connection with the Henry Lamb listed above.

LAMBERT & BLABER.
Manufacturing Cutler. 26 and 27 Hatton Gardens *1940-1945*

LANCASTER, CHARLES.
Gunsmith. This firm was started in *1847* as Charles William Lancaster with an address in *1850* of 151 New Bond Street, an address which was retained up until *1881*. For the period *1861* to around *1881* they also occupied 2 Little Bruton St. From *1855* to *1861* Charles was in company with a Alfred Williams, more than likely his brother however Alfred split from Charles in *1862* to occupy his own premises though for a period in the 1900's they occupied together an 11 Panton St.

LANG, ROBERT Jnr.
Manufacturing Cutler and factor 16 Lensden Place, Golden Lane *1925-1930*

LANGLEY, F.
214 Queen's Rd. Peckham *1935-1940*

LANGLEY, RUBEN.
Working cutler. 4 Hornsbay Place, Hornsbay St. Old Kent Road *1895*

LAUNDY, SAM, JOSEPH, & SON.
9 St. Thomas's St. *1783-1843*

LAVY, CHARLES & Co.
Manufacturing Cutler. 23 Ropemaker St. *1915-1925*

LAWRENCE, GEORGE.
9 New Bond St. *1840*

LEADBEATER, GEORGE.
17 Charlotte Terrace, New City, Lambeth *1829*

LECOULTRE RAZOR Co.
34 Paternoster Row *1910*

LEDDELL, HENRY & Co.
24 High Holborn *1866-1875*. 19 and 20 Cowcross St. *1880*

LEHMANN, MAURICE.
61 Commercial Rd. East. *1900-1905*. 132 Back Church Lane. *1910*

LEONARD, JOHN.
14 Bridge St., Lambeth *1832*

LESLIE RAZOR Co.
Razor Makers. Regent House, Kingsway *1915*

LESLIE, SIDNEY.
61 Upper St. Islington *1875-1885*

LEUCHARS & SON.
Originally founded in *1794* by a James Leuchars trading as a perfumier and hairdresser. Occupied 38 Piccadilly in *1820* but not listed in the cutlers section of the directory until *1880* when they were recorded at 28 and 29 and 31 Gerrard. St. Soho. *1885* at 38 and 39 Piccadilly and 31 Gerrard. St. Soho. *1890-1900* at 38 and 39 Piccadilly and Sherwood St.

LEVIN, MOSES LEWIN.
1 Bevis Marks *1855-1860*

Plate 92.
A Masonic dagger etched on one side with the masonic symbol of a square and compass, and on the other:

H LAMB
ST. JOHN'S
SQ^{RE}
CLERKENWELL
LONDON

Size: blade 9 inches, 14 inches overall.

Plate 93.
An very large double edged Bowie with chequered ebony grip which is fitted with a "clamshell" style pommel piece, nickel silver guard with integral bolster. The blade is marked:

CHARLES
LANCASTER
151
NEW BOND ST
W

Size: blade 11 inches, 17 inches overall.

Plate 94.
BALDOCK KNIFE SPEAR

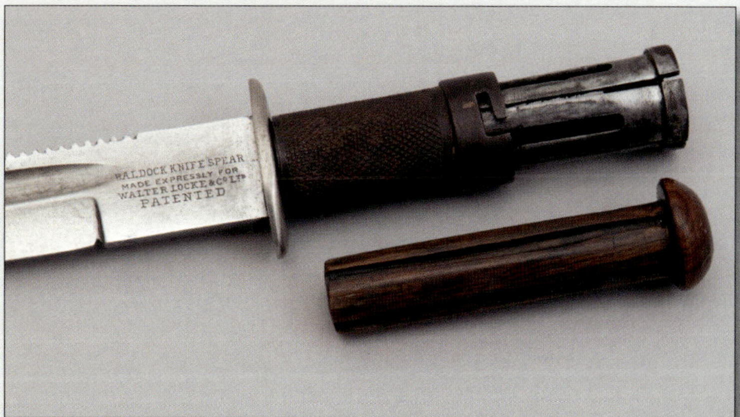

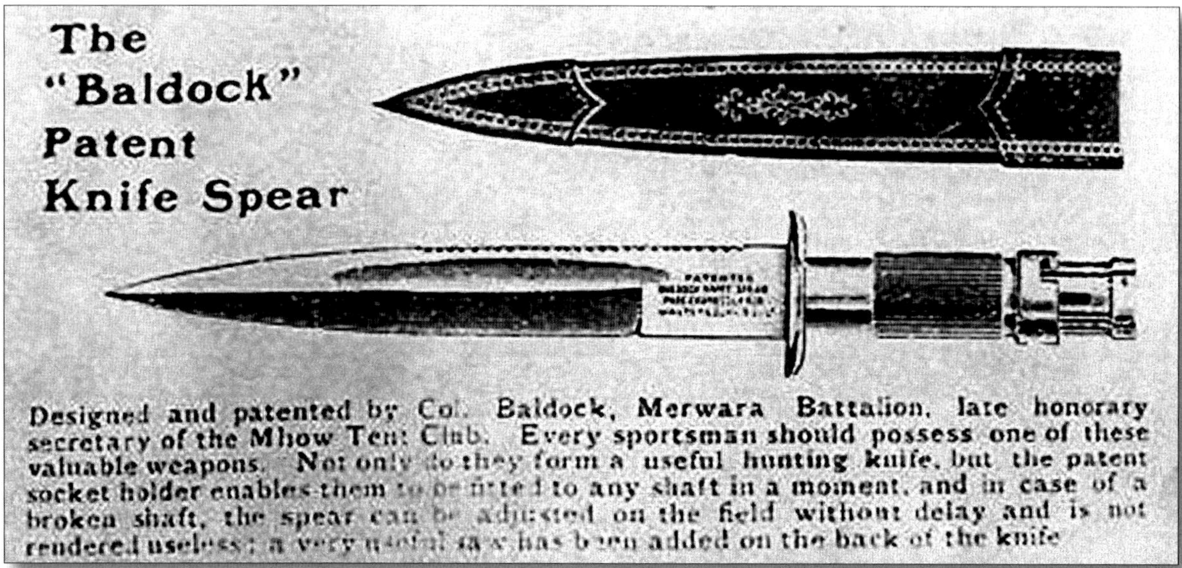

Extract from a Locke catalogue showing the Baldock Knife Spear.

LIGHT. EDWARD.
15A Lime St. *1885*

LIGHT. EDWARD.
22 Fenchurch St. and 45A Jewin St. *1890*

LINGS, WILLIAM.
51 Aldersgate St. *1832-1834*

LINGS, WILLIAM.
1 Jewin St. *1846-1860*

LILLEY, SARAH.
30 Holborn Row Lincoln's Inn Field *1823-1829*

LITTLE, JOSEPH.
476 and 478 Kingsland Rd. *1880-1885*. Only at 478 in *1890*

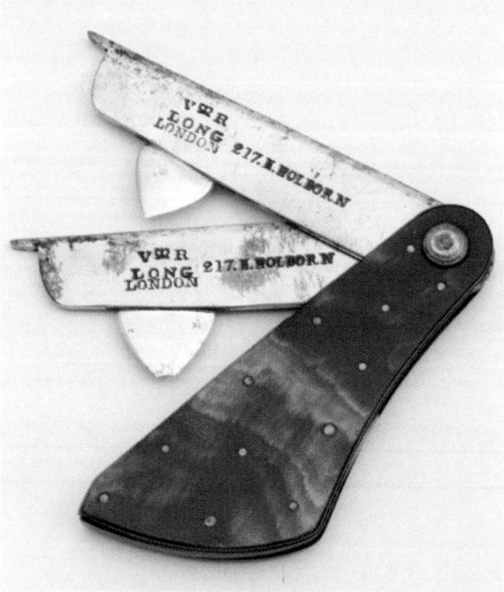

Plate 95.
Sturdy two-bladed fleam which is rather unusual most are 3 blades by LONG. Horn scales with brass liners birds eye rivet and pin work consisting of 12 pins. Both blades marked with:

V (CROWN) R
LONG
217 H HOLBORN
LONDON

LLOYD, WILLIAM.
9 St. Andrew's Hill *1829*

LOCKE, WALTER & Co Ltd.
Gunsmith. *1892- c1920*. 391 Strand. In knife terms primarily known as the outlet for the BALDOCK KNIFE SPEAR which was patented in *1902* by Major Charles Blair Baldock. Locke also had premises in India which was probably the destination of the bulk of the knife spears.

LOCKLEY & CADMAN.
81 St. George St. *1860*

LOCKLEY, Mrs. ELIZABETH.
81 St. George St. *1870*. 222 St. George St. *1875-1890*

LOCKLEY, JAMES.
7 Norway Place, Hackney *1855-1860*. 226 Hackney Road *1866-1880*

LOCKLEY, JESSE.
83 Upper East Smithfield *1855*. 81 St. George St. *1860-1866*

LOOKER.
42 Leadenhall St. *1704-1855*. Founded by James Looker around *1704*, he was the father of a

Thomas, James (II), William and Henry. The son of William a Henry Looker who was a Master of the Cutlers Company in *1815* and *1833*. His son Henry William (II) continued at his fathers address until circa 1855. Henry William the elder is recorded as dying in *1861*.

LONDON CUTLERY COMPANY.
Manufacturing Cutler. 31 Newman St. *1900-1905*

LONDON & COUNTY WAREHOUSE Co.
168 St. John Street Road *1895*

LONDON PLATE & MANUFACTURING Co.
Manufacturing Cutler. 181 and 183 Well St. Hackney *1930*

LONDON & SHEFFIELD CUTLERY Co.
(Thomas Elliot manager) 31A King William St. *1866*

LONDON SILVERSMITHS Co.
Manufacturing Cutler. 55 Holborn Viaduct *1925*

LONG, RICHARD.
In *1820* Richard Long was located at 217 High Holborn as a surgical and veterinary instrument maker. In *1823* he had royal appointment to his Majesty, his majesty being George IV (reigned *1820-1830*). By *1832* the entry becomes Mary Long (veterinary instrument maker) to the King but of course by this time Queen Victoria was on the throne. Mary seems to have remained as the head of the firm until about *1866* a date by which instead of being recorded under Surgical Instrument maker she is listed under cutlers. A Joseph Long, presumably her son, is listed at 21 Coventry St. in *1860* does not seem to have remained in business long as there is no trace after *1870*.

LORBERG.
A Charles Henry and a George Lorberg are listed as cutlers and there are entries for Charles as a surgical instrument maker in *1850*, *1855* and *1860*. Charles Henry is listed in *1850* at 5 Brompton Road, in *1870* the address is 46 Brompton

Plate 96.
A hunting axe marked:
G (CROWN) R
LONG
on the head. The piece has stag scales with a fold out saw in the shaft. The shaft bears the same marking as the head along with:
217 H HOLBORN.

Plate 97.
Spear point bowie circa 1860 marked with a crown above the name **LORBERG**.

Road. In *1880* the name changes to that of Charles Henry and George of 46 Brompton Road and 59 Kensington High St. By *1885* they have added 38 Kensington High St. to their premises.
In *1890* the firm seems to split with Charles Henry being recorded at 59 Kensington High St. whilst George is at the Brompton Road address.
In *1895* Charles also occupies an address at 6 Station Buildings. By *1910* however Charles is at a completely new address of 185 Kensington High St. Both branches did however survive the 1st. World War but there is no record. of George by *1925*.
Charles remained in business until at least *1935* but does not appear in the *1940* entry for cutler.

Plate 98.
Cut throat razor with decorated scales probably made from Bakelite or similar material. The tang is marked:

LUND
57 CORNHILL

LOWCOCK
Family of cutlers and razor makers founded in *1622* and which existed until circa *1880*

LOWCOCK, GEORGE.
Working Cutler and razor maker. 8 Ball Alley, Lombard. St. *1820-1836*. 38 Cornhill *1839-1850*. As George and Co. *1855-1875*. Just. as Lowcock and Co. in *1880*.

LOVE & HARVEY.
31 Hatton Gardens *1885*

LOY, RICHARD.
17 Dartmouth St. *1822*. As William and Richard in *1823*, and then reverts to just Richard in *1829*.

LOY, THOMAS.
67 Long Lane, Smithfield *1850*

LOY, WILLIAM.
Working Cutler. 24 Kings St. *1829-1846*, 39 Chapel St. *1855-1866*

Plate 99.
A multi-blade folder with finely chequered horn scales, brass liners and file work to the back springs. The knife has 10 blades along with the scissors, tweezers, probe and fly tying pliers. The oval shield is engraved:

J HORN
NOV 15TH 1886

The ricasso is marked:

LUND
CORNHILL

LOY, WILLIAM.
2 Myddleton Terrace *1860*

LUDLAM, J.
Working Cutler. 1 Bowling St. *1832-1850*

LUNA SAFETY RAZOR Co. Ltd.
51 and 52 Barbican *1910 1915*

LUND.
Established in *1796*. By *1820* Thomas Lund is listed as cutler and writing desk maker at 56 and 57 Cornhill and as an importer of altering stones. A William Lund appears circa *1836* as manufacturers of dressing cases, fine cutlery and real drilled eyed needles at 24

Plate 100.
This magnificent folder with ivory scales is in the Spanish form. Blade marked:

LUND
CORNHILL

Plate 101.
This Bowie with stag grip which also has an ivory collar is marked:

LUND
CORNHILL
LONDON

Plate 102.
Folding Bowie marked on the ricasso:

LUND
CORNHILL

Fleet Street. Apparently by *1852* these two businesses had been amalgamated under the name of William Lund. However it is interesting to note that in the *1840* directory only Thomas appears under Cutlers whilst William appears under Desk and Dressing case makers but with a notation that he is a cutler. When William died in *1872* the firm passed to Charles Lund with addresses at 57 Cornhill, and 23 and 24 Fleet Street an address which they no longer occupied in *1901*. In *1897* they are listed as cutlers, travelling bag, desk, dressing case and pocket book makers and ivory turners. In the same period they are listed as the manufacturers of a variety of patented implements such as Lund's gravitating decanting machines, Lund's patent durable double fold umbrellas. In *1903* Charles disposed of his interest in the company to a William Gibson and Edwin Routley trading under the William Lund name at 56 and 57 Cornhill, and 20 Red Lion Street,

Plate 103
Stag grip Bowie with the blade marked:

LUND
CORNHILL
LONDON

Clerkenwell. Routley retired in *1905*. By 1913 Lund were listed as cutlery manufacturers, goldsmiths, silversmiths, jewellers, watch and clock makers, ivory and tortoiseshell workers, dressing bag and case makers, purses, fancy leather goods etc. at their Cornhill address and at Leadenhall Buildings.

Throughout the *1850* to *1883* the directory notations list them under cutlers as Needle, razor and Desk and Dressing case makers. However in *1885* they are additionally identified as working cutlers and they are so identified up until *1920*. The firm subsequently traded as a jewellers from circa *1937* to *1964* at 54 Old Broad Street.

LUXTON, RALPH.

26 Moorgate St. *1910*

LYNCH, JAMES.

29 Platt Terrace, Old St. *1860*

Plate 104
Folder with the main blade and can opener marked:

LUND
OLD BROAD ST
E.C

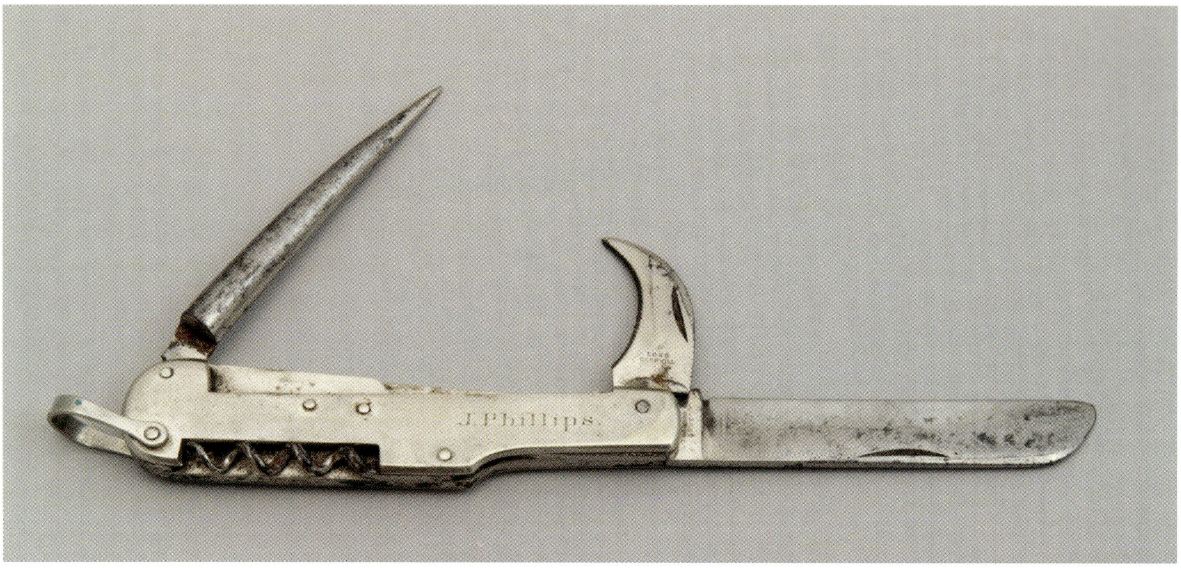

Plate 105.
An all metal consisting of main sheepsfoot blade, marlin spike, corkscrew and foil cutter. Main blade and foil cutter are marked:

LUND
CORNHILL.

Plate 106.
A marine ivory-hilted hunting knife with blade stamped:

LUND
24 FLEET ST
LONDON

McBEATH, ALEXANDER.
11 Ryder's Court *1832*

McCARTHY, WILLIAM JOHNSON.
50 Barbican *1855*

McLELLAN, WILLIAM.
3 Twiner St. *1805-1852*

MAASSEN & CARTER.
Butchers Cutler 19 Clothfair *1910*

MAASSEN, CARTER & SAMUEL Ltd.
Butchers Cutler. 51, 52 and 53 Long Lane *1910 –1925*. As MAASSEN, CARTER & Co Ltd. *1930-1945*

MACDANIEL, CHARLES.
Manufacturing Cutler and razor maker. 343 Oxford St. *1820-1866*. As MACDANIEL, & Co 343 Oxford St. *1870*, then as MACDANIEL, & Co. (MORTON) *1875-1885*. In *1890* at 233 Oxford St.

MACKENZIE, SAMUEL HENRY.
162 Fenchurch St. *1920-1930*

MACHIN, GEORGE.
Working Cutler. 76 Leadenhall St. *1820-1839*

MACMILLAN & ARTHUR.
Manufacturing Cutler. 1 to 4 Giltspur St. *1925*

MACNAMARA, JOSEPH.
95 Strand *1870-1875*

MALLARDS Ltd.
Manufacturing Cutler. 59 and 60 Holborn Viaduct *1930*

MALLESON, H.
Working Cutler.
9 Great Titchfield St. *1822*

MANCHEE, PETER.
59 Poplar High St. *1860*

MAPLE & Co. Ltd.
141 to 149 Tottenham Court Rd, 248 and 253 to 279 Euston Rd., 8 to 44 Grafton St., factories at Beaumont Place, Midford Place and William St., Hampstead. *1895*. In 1900-1905 at 141 to 150 Tottenham Court Rd. 248, 251, 253 to 279 Euston Rd, 8 to 44 Grafton St., 143 to 157 Gower St. factories at Beaumont Place, Highgate Rd., and William St., Hampstead. *1920*

MAPPIN, JOHN.
Cutler and Surgical Instrument Maker. 10 Hill St. *1823*

MAPPIN, J.
Working Cutler. 29 Vauxhall Walk, Lambeth *1832* There is no apparent link between this J. Mappin and the Mappin and Webb lineage.

MAPPIN & WEBB.
1774 to the present day. Despite its strong Sheffield links and origins at least one knife marked Mappin and Webb and London Made has been noted.

A somewhat confused history because of the Mappin name being used by different branches. Appears to have been founded by a Sheffield silversmith,

Plate 107.
Small pen knife with two pen and one quill blade. All blades are stamped:
S.H.MACKENZIE
162 FENCHURCH ST

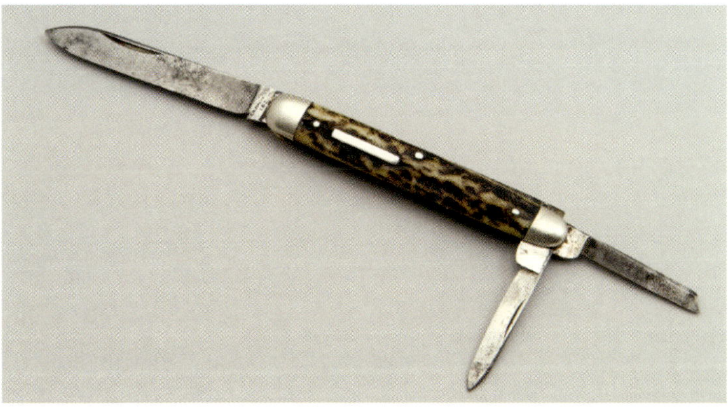

Cheapside from old postcard

Jonathan Mappin in *1774*. Mappin Brothers was founded in *1810* by Joseph Mappin. In *1858* upon his retirement from Mappin Brothers John Mappin invited his brother-in-law George Webb to join the business forming the early association of Mappin and Webb. but initially trading under the name Mappin and Co. The actual Mappin and Webb name not appearing until *1863* and one which grew out of the confusion which arose over the names Mappin Brothers and Mappin and Co. which led to Mappin and Co. adopting the Mappin and Webb name. The firms links to cutlery were created by Joseph Mappin who traded with another partner as Arundel and Mappin manufacturers of pen knives, spring, sporting and table knives and razors. Mappin Brothers also absorbed the cutlers William Sampson and Sons in *1845*. Mappin and Webb eventually absorbed Mappin Brothers in *1902*. The firm holds Royal Warrants for silversmiths to Her Majesty Queen Elizabeth II, and Silversmiths to His Royal Highness Prince Charles.

During its history operated under a number of different names and from the addresses as detailed below.

MAPPIN, BROTHERS.

Manufacturing Cutler, razor maker and dressing case maker. 67 and 68 King William St., London Bridge, 406 Euston Rd. 220 and 222 Regent St. *1870-1875*, number 220 only in *1880*, back at 220 and 222 in *1885*. In *1890* at 35 St Paul's Churchyard and 220 Regent St. In *1900* listed at 220 Regent St. and 64 Cheapside. In *1905* just at 220 Regent St. and listed as incorporated with Mappin and Webb Ltd.

MAPPIN, HALL & Co.

27 Sun St. Finsbury *1905*

[Note: There is no clear link between this firm and other of the Mappin name.]

MAPPIN, JOSEPH

(wholesale) 15 Fore St. *1846*, as Joseph and Brothers in *1850*, in *1855* at 37 Moorgate St. In *1860-1866* at 67 and 68 King William St.

MAPPIN & WEBB

(wholesale). 71 and 72 Cornhill, 76, 77 and 78 Oxford St. Manufactory Winsley St., Oxford St. *1870*. No Cornhill address in *1875* but Mansion House Buildings, Queen Victoria St. In *1880* at 76, 77 and 78 Oxford St. and 2 Queen Victoria St. *1885* manufacturing cutler, razor makers, shear & needle makers, dressing case manufacturers 158 to 162 Oxford St. and Mansion House Buildings. In *1890* at 158 to 162 Oxford St., 18 to 22 Poultry and 2 Queen Victoria St.

Plate 108
This large hunting knife, which has overall dimensions of 19.75 inches and a blade length of 13.5 inches, carries the Mappin and Webb 'TRUSTWORTHY' trade mark on the blade but is clearly marked 'LONDON MADE' on the ricasso. The piece has a stag grip with steel pommel cap, ferrule and crossguard - all of which have engraving. The guard is pierced to take the scabbard catch. The scabbard is leather over wood with silver mounts. The shield on the scabbard is engraved with the initial'MSK', along with a star over a crescent (see detail). This piece was purchased by Muhammed Sadiq Khan Nawab of Bahawalpur, from one of Walter Locke's Indian outlets. This piece was accompanied by its original receipt which, although in too poor condition to be reproduced, is dated 1906.

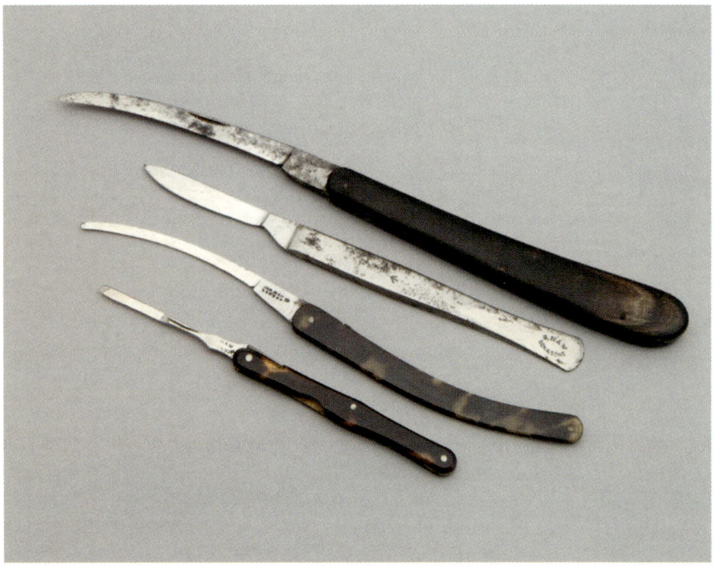

Plate 109.
Folding surgical instrument with horn scales. Blade is marked:

S MAW & SON
LONDON

This would seem to date the piece between c.1840 to c.1870.
All metal scalpel marked:

S MAW
LONDON

A folding curved bistoury with tortoiseshell scales blade marked:

J & S MAW
LONDON

along with a crown stamp.

A superb folding Tenotomy knife with tortoiseshell scales. The blade locks via a surgical instrument style lock. Blade marked:

MAW
LONDON

MAPPING, J.
8 Paradise St. *1829*

MARKHAM, EDWARD, TUTHILL & Co.
Wholesale and speciality in butcher's cutlery. 41 Clothfair *1880*, at 41 and 42 Clothfair *1885-1925*

MARR, DAVID.
27 Little Queen St. *1878*

MARRIAN, BOCOCK & Co.
Manufacturing Cutler. 39 Hatton Gardens *1880*

MARRIAN & WELLS.
Manufacturing cutler, razor maker, pen and pocket knife maker.
23 Ropemaker St. *1910-1920*

MARSDEN BROTHERS & LLOYD.
31 Snow Hill. *1895*

MARTIN.
64 Streatham High Rd. *1940*

MARTIN, ALFRED.
125 High St. and 24A Lewis Grove, Lewisham *1935*

MARTIN, RICHARD. JOSEPH.
4 Palagrave Place, Strand *1846-1850*

MARTIN, THOMAS & Co.
63 Gracech St. 1855. 22 Cannon St. in *1860*

MASCALL, JOSHUA.
Baldwin's Gardens, Leather Lane *1885*

MASON, EDWARD.
56 Gloucester St., Commercial Road *1875-1880*

MASON, RICHARD. ANTHONY.
Working Cutler. 43 Rosamond St., Clerkenwell *1832-1840*

MATTHEWMAN, BENJAMIN.
50 Myddleton St. *1890-1895*

MATTHEWS BROTHERS.
27 Carey St., Lincoln's Inn *1875-1885*. 10 New Oxford St. in *1890-1925*

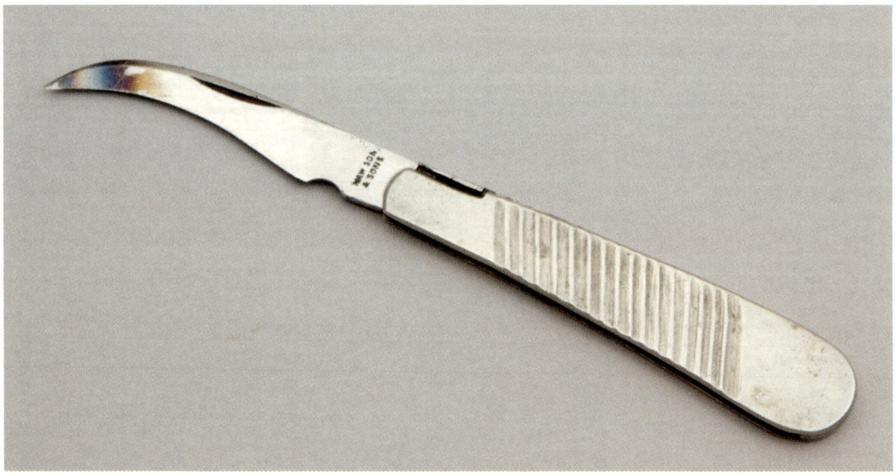

Plate 110.
Folding Syme's Abscess knife with nickel scales. Blade has surgical instrument lock and blade is marked:

MAW SON
& SONS

which would date the piece to around 1900.

MATTHEWS, ALFRED SAMUEL.
Manufacturing Cutler. 17 and 18 King's Head Court, Shoe Lane *1860-1870*, only at 17 in *1875-1905*

MATTHEWS, CHARLES AND SAMUEL.
18 Kings Head Court *1829-1832*. Listed as MATTHEWS, SAMUEL AND CHARLES. Working Cutler. 17 and 18 Kings Head Court 1836. Just a MATTHEWS, CHARLES in *1840-1855*

MATTHEWS, CHARLES ALFRED.
Cutler. 17 and 18 Kings Head Court *1870*

MATTHEWS, GEORGE HENRY.
Cutler. 8 Long Lane, Smithfield *1850*

MATTHEWS, R & SONS.
19 Kings Head Court, Shoe Lane *1822, 1823*

MATTHEWS, WILLIAM.
Cutler and Surgical Instrument Maker. 10 Portugal St. Lincoln Fields Inn *1850*

MATTHEWS, WILLIAM.
Cutler and Surgical Instrument Maker. 8 Portugal St. and 32 Carey St., Lincoln's Inn *1855-1866*

MAUGHAN, T.
Wholesaler. 10 Percival St. Clerkenwell *1820-1829*.

MAUGHAN, J.
10 Percival St. Clerkenwell *1840*

MAW.
This family of surgical instrument makers established in *1807* as Hornby and Maw of Fenchurch St. In *1822* it was recorded as George Maw, 55 Aldermansbury. Some

Plate 111.
A folding scalpel/veterinary instrument with polished horn scales and brass liners
S MAW SON & THOMPSON

Plate 112.
Amputation knife with chequered ebony grip. The ricasso is marked:

S. MAW SON
LONDON
& THOMPSON

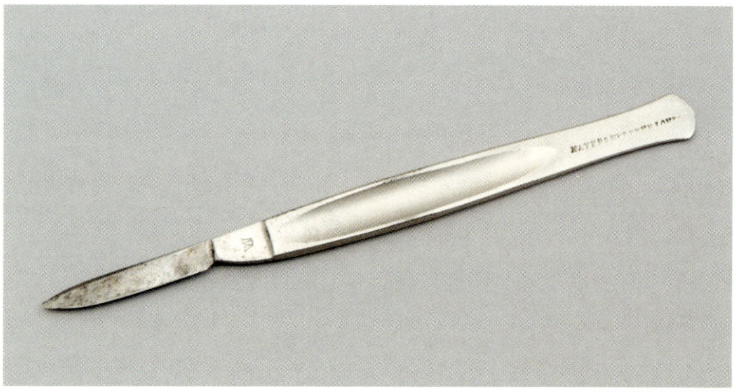

Plate 113.
All-metal scalpel by Mayer & Meltzer

10 years later they are at 54 and 55 Aldermansbury as John and Solomon and then at 11 Aldersgate St. John disappears from the name shortly thereafter as by *1840* it is recorded only as Solomon Maw. In *1870* Solomon and a Son amalgamated with a Thompson to form S Maw Son and Thompson.

It is not clear which Thompson actually amalgamated with Maw. A J Thompson Surgical Instrument Maker operated out of Great Windmill Street from about *1817* to circa *1850*. But there is no trace of him in the *1855* directory. A Charles Henry Thompson located at 49 Carnaby St. does appear in the *1860* directory as a cutler but is absent from the *1870* directory.

The S Maw Son and Thompson partnership continued up until at least *1895*, but by *1900* the name had become S Maw, Son and Sons.

MAYER, JOSEPH.
51 Great Portland St. *1866*

MAYER, JOSEPH, & MELTZER.
Surgical Instrument Maker. 51 Great Portland St., 59 Great Portland St., 71 Great Portland St. *1864-1874*

MAYNARD, SAMUEL ANDREW.
186 Toley St. *1866-1870*

MAYNARD, SAMUEL.
514 Old Ford Road, Bow. *1900*

MEACHEM, GEORGE.
45 George St., Portman Square *1860.*

MEARBECK, JOHN.
35 Hatton Gardens *1875*

Plate 114.
A 24 piece knife with tortoiseshell scales with silver pin work. This is a very high quality piece but only the small pen blade is marked:

MECHI
LONDON

Plate 115.
A magnificent Bowie by MECHI from circa 1850. Although this piece is marked:

MADE BY
MECHI
LEADENHALL ST

It was in all probability made in Sheffield.
Size: blade 11 inches, 16 inches overall.

The cover of a Mechi catalogue dating from the period 1830 to 1865 as this was the period during which he occupied the 4 Leadenhall Street address.

MECHI, JOHN JOSEPH.

Of Italian extraction John Joseph Mechi was first listed as a cutler in *1827* with an address at 130 Leadenhall Street. In 1830 he moved to number 4 Leadenhall Street. In *1855* he purchased the cutlery business of Vining's in Regent Street. In *1859* the firm was re-titled Mechi and Bazin when the latter joined as a partner. In about *1865* the Leadenhall Street premises were closed and the whole business transferred to Regent Street. Bazin died in *1865* and whilst it retained the name the company reverted to the name of Mechi by *1870*.

Plate 116.
Quill Knife with mother of pearl scales marked Mechi and Bezin.

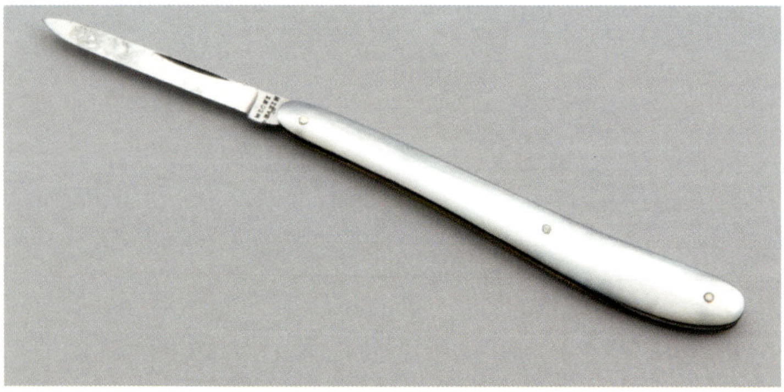

Mechi exhibited at the 1851 Great Exhibition where he displayed examples cutlery, razors, tableware, pen knives etc. Mechi and Bazin exhibited at the 1862 International Exhibition. Mechi was a man of wide interest being a member of the Society of Arts, a juror at the great Exhibition and an Alderman of the City of London.

Besides cutlery the company also advertised a wide variety of other accoutrements including his magic razor strop.

Shortly before his death in December *1880* the company was placed into liquidation.

This small catalogue list cutlery of all kinds and contains some wonderful language such as

New Married COUPLES, Families, Captains, Military and Nautical Gentlemen proceeding to India or the Colonies, will find Mechi's a very Emporium, in which they can instantly procure almost every article (except clothing and furniture) that a protracted absence from their native country renders necessary.

Mechi's Peculiar Steel Razors
Plain and Black Handles........ each £0-3-6
Ivory Superfine....................... £0-5-0
Ditto Silver Mounted............. £0-9-0
Seven-day Razors, in Cases... £1-5s to 2-10-0

The character of Mechi's razors being (during the last six years) so

well established, it may be merely necessary to remark that every razor is stamped "Exchanged, if not approved" with the addition of "Mechi's peculiar Steel", and it is most particularly requested that no gentleman who has a defective razor of Mechi's will hesitate to return it at any period of time; for loss of recommendation from such cause is of infinitely greater importance than the value of a Razor.

The frontage of Mechi's premises in Leadenhall Street. From Paget & Co. Directory of London, 1839.

MELHUISH.
Founded as Richard Mehuish Ltd., 143 Holborn between *1905* and *1908*. In the *1930's* the name changed to Richard Mehuish (London) Ltd. Still listed in *1960*. None of the directory entries identify him as a working cutler.

MERCANTILE CUTLERY Co.
Pen and pocket knife makers, razor makers. 15 King St. *1915*

MERFIELD, JASON.
111 Goswell St. *1822-1832*

MERFIELD, WILLIAM.
4 Cateaton St. *1836-1846*

MERFIELD, WILLIAM
20 Budge Row *1855*

MIDDLETON, WILLIAM & Co.
4 Edmond's Place, Shepherdess Walk, *1895*

MILLARD, GEORGE.
29 Turnmill St. Clerkenwell *1836-1839*

MILLARD BROTHERS.
123 Houndsditch *1895-1930*

MILLER HARRIS & Co.
Manufacturing Cutler. 25 Aldgate *1925*

MILLER, LEWIS.
10 Brick Lane *1925*

MILLER, LOUIS.
40 Osborne St. Whitechapel *1920*

MILLIKIN.
Surgical Instrument Maker and Cutler. Millikin appeared in the *1820* directory as John Millikin of 301 Strand. They also operated under a variety of names:

- *1829* as MILLIKIN & WRIGHT, 301 Strand
- *1836* as JOHN MILLIKIN, 301 Strand
- *1846-1855* as JOHN MILLIKIN, 161A Strand
- *1860-1870* as MILLIKIN & LAWLEY, 161A Strand

Does not appear after *1870* as a Cutler but continued as a surgical instrument maker into *1880*.

Plate 117.
Folder which from the style of the bottle-opener would appear to date from the 1930's or later. Knife has main blade, pen blade, can opener, corkscrew, punch and can opener, stag scales which carry the usual probe and tweezers. Main and pen blades marked:

MELHUISH
HOLBORN EC

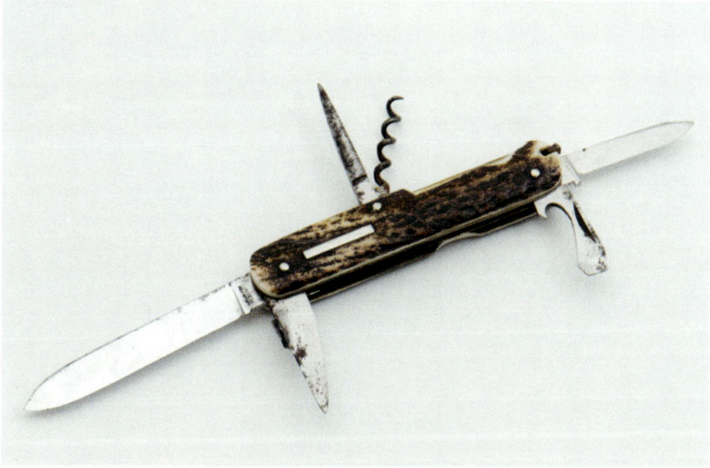

Plate 118.
Fine lock back folder by Mills of High Holborn.
(Photo courtesy of Bill Adams et al.)

MILLS, GEORGE.
Working Cutler. 166 Walmer Rd. *1910-1945*

MILLS, WILLIAM.
Gunsmith. 120 High Holborn *1825-1840*

MILNE, GEORGE.
Working Cutler. 22 Paradise St., Rotherhithe *1836*

MILNE, GEORGE.
59 Snow's Fields *1846*. 7 Star Corner in *1850*. 33 Star Corner in *1855-1866*

MILNER, JAMES.
Working Cutler. 8 Long Lane West Smithfield *1820 -1823*.

MILNER, MARK.
Working Cutler. 39 Cheapside *1832-1840*

MINTER & SONS Ltd.
St. Michael's House, Church Alley, Basinghall St. *1900-1905*

MINTRIDGE, BENJAMIN.
Butchers Cutler. 4 West Smithfield *1855*

MITCHELL, JOHN.
15 President St. *1846*

MITTON & Co.
Manufacturing Cutler. 161 Wool Exchange, Coleman St. *1918-1920*. *1925* as Mitton, Paul and Co. at 161 Wool Exchange. 157 Wool Exchange *1930*. 6 Wool Exchange (also listed under Mexeur and Cie) *1940-1945*

MONTAGUE, HENRY.
23 Piccadilly *1910-1915*

MONTAGUE, JOHN HENRY.
(Late partner of C. Wright and Co.) 101 New Bond St. *1905-1915*. 69 New Bond St. *1920-1930*

MONTFORD, WORMESLEY & Co.
Manufacturing Cutler. 78 Old Broad St. *1925*. 36 and 37 Cock Lane, Snow Hill. *1930*

MOORE, Mrs. ANN.
220 Tottenham Court Road *1850*

MOORE & SONS.
Working Cutler. 23 Titchborne St., Haymarket *1822-1823*. In *1829* as MOORE, BARBARA & SONS. *1832* as MOORE, BARBARA and in *1836* as Barbara and Son.

MOORE, JAMES.
Working Cutler. 349 Oxford St. *1822-1839. 1840-1905* at 211 Oxford St., also at 162 Fenchurch St. in *1905*. In *1910* only at 211 Oxford St.

MOORE, JOHN.
Working Cutler. 38 Queen St. *1829*

MOORE, JOSEPH.
93 Bishopsgate-without, Whitechapel *1820-1822*

MOORE, JOSEPH.
Working Cutler. 11 Hand St., Holborn *1823-1832*

MOORE, JOSEPH J.
104 High Holborn *1836-1939*. In *1839* also at 12 Red Lion Passage, Red Lion Square.

MOORE, NATHANIAL.
11 Hand St., Holborn *1820-1822*

MOORE, NATHANIAL.
Working Cutler. 213 Tottenham Court Road *1820-1929*

MOORE, STEPHEN.
31 Brown's Lane *1875*. 13 Hanbury St. Spitalfields *1880-1895*. 169 Brick Lane. *1905-1915*.

MOORE, WILLIAM.
214 Tottenham Court Road *1832*

MOORE, WILLIAM.
Working Cutler. 1 Middle Row, Knightsbridge *1832* also at 22 Titchborne St. Haymarket in *1840*. *1846-1855* only at 22 Titchborne St.

MOORE, WILLIAM.
Working Cutler and razor maker. 220 Tottenham Court Road *1840-1890*

Plate 119.
Cut throat razor with shield set into scales. Tang marked:
J. MORTON
223 OXFORD ST

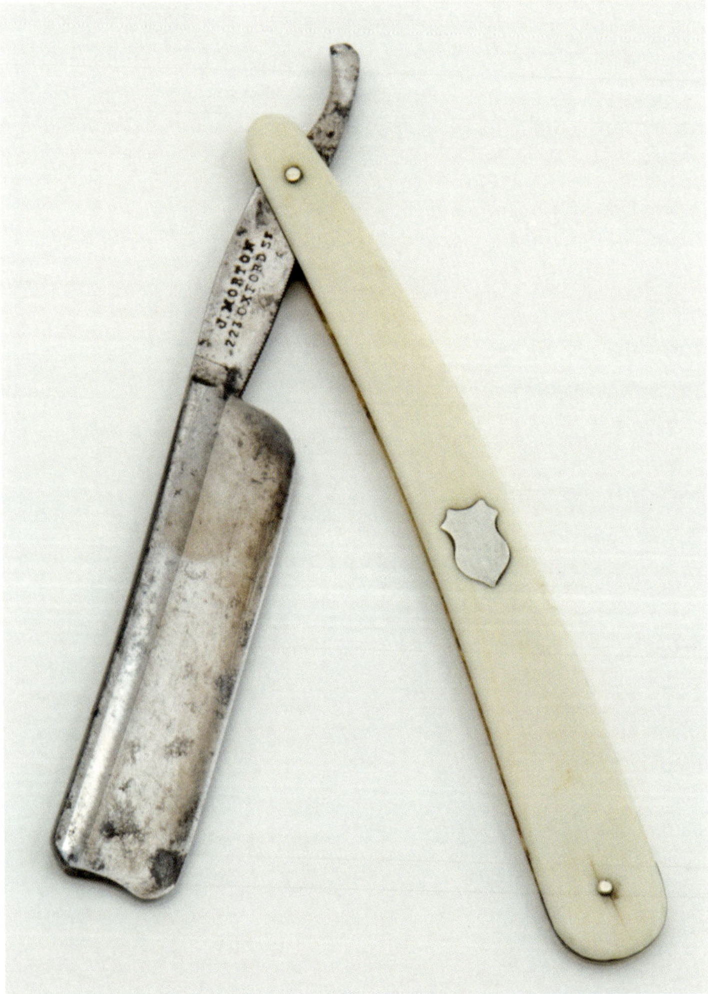

MORGAN, THOMAS.
Working Cutler. 113 Bishopgate St. without *1832*

MORING, J.
29 Garden Row, London Road *1860*

MORLEY & Co.
Manufacturing Cutler. 42 Leadenhall St. *1820 -1822*. MORLEY, JOHN & SON in *1832* and as MORLEY, JOHN *1836*.

MORLEY & THORNHILL.
144 New Bond St. *1820*

MORRELL, GEORGE.
60 and 61 Burlington Arcade *1836* but only at 61 in *1840*. Back at both 60 and 61 in *1846 1850* and in *1855* also at 164 Oxford St. As MORRELL, Mrs. SOPHIA MATILDA. 60 and 61 Burlington Arcade *1860-1870*

MORRELL, HORACE WALTON.
164 Oxford St. and 50 Burlington Arcade *1870*. *1880* as MORRELL, Mrs JANE ARUNDELL.

MORRIS, CHARLES.
9 Tachbrook St. *1920-1925*

MORRIS ROSE Ltd.
Manufacturing Cutler. 2 New Union St. *1925*

MORROW, B.A.
Manufacturing Cutler. 64 High Holborn *1930*

MORSE, ANN.
18 West Smithfield *1822 -1823*

MORTON, CHARLES & Co.
11 Upper East Smithfield *1823*, at 7 Upper East Smithfield in *1829*

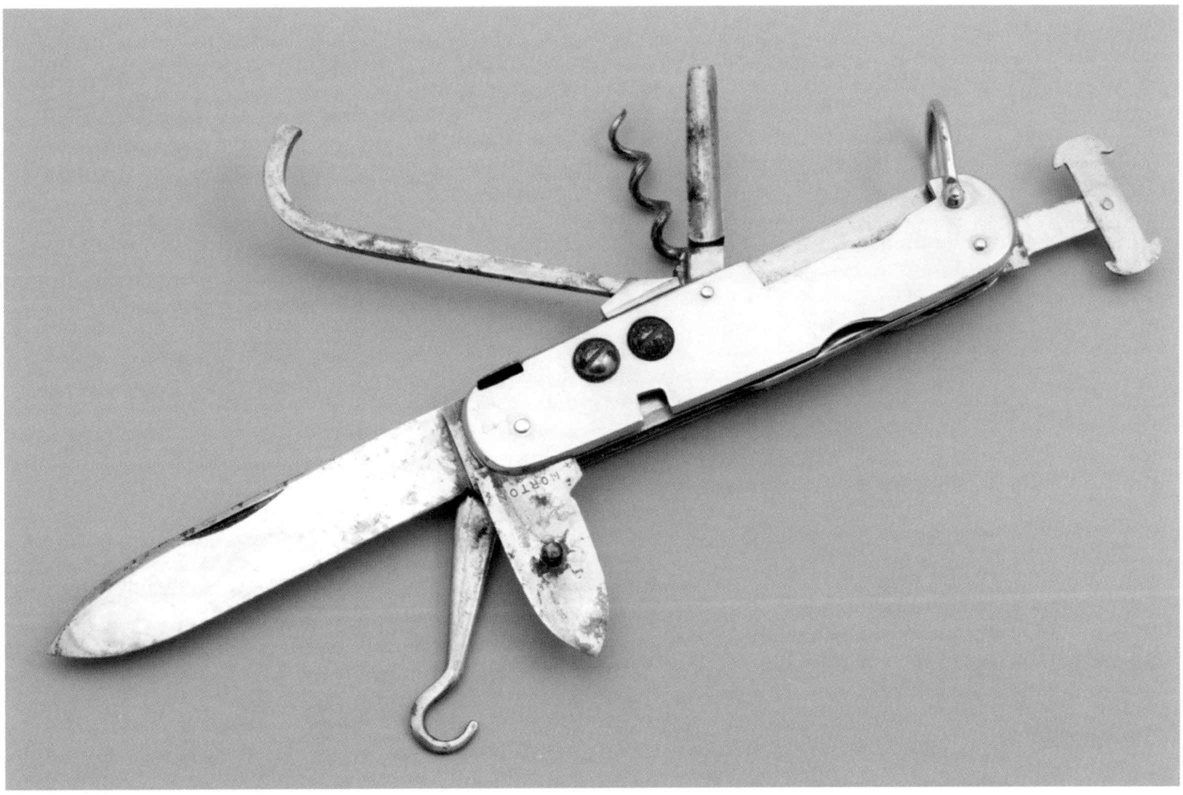

Plate 120.
All metal sportsman's knife which carries Morton's 39 CHEAPSIDE address

MORTON, JOSEPH & GEORGE.

It is not clear if there is link to Charles Morton, though he was possibly the father of Joseph but a Joseph Morton is listed in *1829* at 9 Clement's Lane. The firm is then listed throughout much of its history as Joseph and George Morton. Formed around *1834* Joseph and George Morton are recorded as working cutlers having premises at 2 Craven Building Drury Lane. In *1846* they are recorded as also having premises at 8 Great Turnstile and by *1850* have also added 39 Cheapside. The indications in the *1850* directory are that they are retailers. By *1855* the firm seems to split with George occupying 39 Cheapside whilst Joseph is at 8 Great Turnstile and 343 Oxford St. The directory entries change again in *1860* to George and Joseph Morton 39 Cheapside, and Joseph Morton 343 Oxford St. At this time the directory also list them as manufacturing cutlers. Things remain like this until *1883* when Joseph's address changes to 223 Oxford St. In *1895* only Joseph is recorded, occupying both the Cheapside and Oxford St. premises. Sometime between *1900* and *1910* Joseph must have passed away as by *1910* the firm is recorded as Mrs Matilda Morton, 39 Cheapside. It is still listed as such in *1912* but in *1915* the firm has become Morton and Co. and listed in *1925* as manufacturing cutlers.

MOSELEY & SON.

A somewhat complex history and one which the directories do not necessarily help in unscrambling there being entries for a John Moseley and Son, and a Moseley and Son.

In the *1870* directory there is an advertisement for a John Moseley and Son of 54 and 55 Broad St., Bloomsbury stating that they were established in *1730* in New Street, Covent Garden. They were certainly at 17 and 18 New St. in

Plate 121.
A most intriguing knife which is only sharpened for part of its length. The grip is of ebony and the cross-guard is a sandwich of two nickel silver plates with a highly worked insert between them. The blade is marked:

MOSELEY & SON
NEW STREET
COVENT GARDEN

1852. From the nature of the advert and entries in the trade directories John Moseley and Son were manufacturers of planes, lathes, saws etc. and also cutlers, manufacturers of razors, scissors, pen knives and table knives. They were at 54 and 55 Broad St., Bloomsbury and Leman St. Whitechapel in *1884*. Also in *1870* the entry " Moseley and Simpson (late John Moseley and Son) 17 and 18 King St. and 27 Bedford St., Covent garden WC (established in New St. *1730*) wholesale, retail and for exportation" appears. They are also recorded as manufacturing cutlers, needle and razor makers. There is no record in *1883* but in *1885* the name has reverted to Moseley and Son 63 New Oxford St. There is then no apparent trace after *1887* until *1915* when they reappear as Moseley and Son at the Oxford St. address. It is of course always possible that they were in some other section of the directory, but given their previous listing as manufacturing cutlers this seems unlikely. They remained at this address up until *1925*, but are not recorded in *1930*. It is however of note that British Plane Makers from *1700* states that the firm was taken over by William Marples and

Plate 122.
A highly unusual sticking/stabbing knife by Moseley. The knife has a turned lignum vitae hilt with brass ferrule and nickel silver top plate, the blade is inches long and only inches wide. A small flat in the ricasso area is marked:

MOSELEY & SON
LONDON

The knife came with a strange tubular steel sheath with large bulbous brass piece mounted towards the tip. The whole piece may have some form of veterinary significance.

Son in *1894* and transferred to Sheffield in *1910*.

MOSELEY, ROLAND CHARLES.
1 Henstridge Place *1915*

MOSELEY, ROLAND CHARLES & Sons.
1 Henstridge Place and 7 Netherwood St. *1920-1940*. *1945* only at 7 Netherwood St.

Plate: 123.
This small "Bowie" style knife is stamped:

MOSELEY & SON
COVENT GARDEN
LONDON

Along with a stamping which reads TARANAKI STEEL. This form of steel was made developed in New Zealand during the late 1800's and was based on the smelting of Iron Sands.

MOSELEY, WILLIAM.
1846 at 2 St. James Walk, previous entry in 1836 has him listed as Mosley. This spelling returns in *1850*.

MOSLEY, R.F. & CO.
Manufacturing Cutler. 3 Charterhouse St. *1905-1920*. 59 Holborn Viaduct *1925-1935*. 18 to 20 Holborn Viaduct. *1940-1945*.

MOSLEY, THOMAS.
9 Clerkenwell Close *1855-1860*

MOSLEY, THOMAS.
16 Wynyatt St., Goswell Rd. *1870-1885*

MOSLEY, THOMAS.
57 and 58 St. John's Square *1895*. 162 Clerkenwell Rd, *1900*, 148 Clerkenwell Rd. *1905-1915*

MOSLEY, WILLIAM.
Working Cutler. 80 Great Saffron Hill *1823-1829*

MOSLEY, WILLIAM.
Working Cutler. 21 Little Saffron Hill *1832*

MOUAT, GEORGE.
Percy Passage, Rathbone Place *1836*

MOXWORTHY, RICHARD.
56 High St. *1829*

MUELLER, PAUL.
29 Furnival St. *1905*

MULCUTE MANUFACTURING Co.
Manufacturing Cutler. 31 to 33 High Holborn *1910-1915*

MULLER BROTHERS (J&E).
90 Newgate St. *1870*. 32 Queen St. *1875*

MULLER BROTHERS & Co.
12 Newgate St. *1880*

MUNDY & Co.
162 Fenchurch St. *1935-1945*. *1945* also at 87 London Road, Southwark.

MUNDY, ARTHUR.
Working Cutler. 247 Walworth Rd. *1890*. 3 Carter St. Walworth *1895-1935*

MUNDY, EDWARD.
15 St. John's St. Clerkenwell *1850*

MUNDY, WALTER.
87 London Rd. Southwark *1920-1935*

MUNDY, WILLIAM.
5 Little Cross St. Islington *1860-1870*, at 2 Little Cross St. and 16 Artillery St., Bishopsgate *1875*. 87 London Rd. and 16 Artillery St. *1880-1885*

MUNDY, Mrs. WILLIAM.
Working Cutler. 87 London Rd. and 16 Artillery St. *1890*. Only at London Rd. *1895-1915*

MUNDY, WILLIAM SAMUEL.
58 London Rd. Greenwich *1935*. 241 Greenwich High St. *1940*

MURPHY, JAMES G.
3 Middle Row Holborn *1860-1866*. 328 High Holborn *1870 -1885*

MURRAY, JOHN RIDER.
215 Upper St. Islington *1875*

MUSGRAVE & Co.
Manufacturing Cutler. 37 and 38 Hatton Gardens *1935*

Plate 124.
Lock back folder with two secondary pen blades.
Marked:
G. NAZER
31 ROYAL EXCHANGE

NATHAN, ALFRED JERROLD & Co.
Agents 24 New Bridge St. *1915*

NATHANSON, ABRAHAM.
Frostic Place *1920*

NAZER, GEORGE.
A company that did not survive the Second World War being listed in *1940* but not in *1945*. George Nazer was established *c.1870* being listed as a razor maker of 31 Royal Exchange. They remained at this address throughout their history. During the course of their existence they were also listed as manufacturing cutlers and pen and pocket knife makers.

NEAL, JOHN & Co.
23 to 25 Hampden Gurney St. *1875-1885* in *1890* also at 44, 46 and 48 Edgware Rd.

NEIDHARDT & SCHULZ.
27 East Rd. City Rd. *1905* in *1910* as NEIDHARDT & SON *1915*

NICHOLS, MARY.
47 London Wall *1822-1840*

NORMAN, WILLIAM.
10 Maidenhead Court *1850*

NORTZELL & SON.
21 Bouverie St., Fleet St. *1836*

NURSE, CHARLES & Co.
182, 184, 173 Walworth Road, 48 Finsbury Pavement, 144 Bishopsgate Street without, 100 Fleet Street. *1895-1920*. Listed as Plane makers and tool dealers. British Plane Makers from *1700* places their dates of operation from *1887* to *1949*.

NYE, GEORGE.
38 Crammer Place, Waterloo Road *1855*

NYE, Mrs. ELIZA.
136 Westminster Bridge Rd. *1885-1890*

Bank of England & Royal Exchange, London.

Plate 125.
A fine Bowie knife with reported Boer war usage circa 1900. The knife has chequered horn scales, nickel silver guard and fullered blade. Note the lanyard ring fitted to the hilt. The blade is marked:

GEORGE NAZER
31 ROYAL
EXCHANGE

Size: blade 9 inches, 14 inches overall.

OAKES, F. J.
17 Albert Terrace, Notting Hill *1875-1885*

OFFELL, Mrs. ELIZABETH.
280 Goswell Rd. *1915*

OLDHAM, HENRY.
10 High St., St Giles and 11 Lambs Conduit St. *1850.* 66 Kings Road, Chelsea *1860-1875.* As OLDHAM BROTHERS. 64 and 66 Kings Road, Chelsea *1880.* Listed as Frank and Ernest Oldham in *1885*

OLDING, ALBERT HENRY.
Working Cutler. 23 Church St. Soho *1905.* 17 West St. Golden Square. *1910-1935.* 17 Newburgh St. Golden Square. *1940-1945*

OPENEASY KNIFE Co.
(see Minter and Sons Ltd.) *1900-1905*

OPPERMANN, WILLIAM J. F.
19 Southampton Row *1866*

ORME, J.
Cutler and Goldsmith. 4 Coade's Row, Bridge Row, Lambeth. *1820.*

OSBORN, JOHN.
100 Fleet St. EC4 *1925*

OSBORNE, GARRETT & Co.
Manufacturing Cutler. 51 to 54 Frith St. and 11 Bateman St. *1908-1920* Proprietors of the Kropp, Klein, Elmo, Carrara, Birr, Ogee and Oagar brand of razors

OSBORNE, GEORGE.
9 Wells St. *1822-1823*

OSBORNE, GEORGE.
Working Cutler. 9 Hanover Place, Regents Park *1829*

OSTERMANN, FREDRICK WILLIAM.
27 Leadenhall St. *1885-1900*

OVENS, WILLIAM & THOMAS.
Butchers Cutler. 5 and 54 St John St. *1905.* In *1910* 5 St John St. dropped but at 1 Cowcross St. *1915-1935* also at 54 St. John St.

OWEN, EDWARD & Co.
1 and 2 Dashwood House, New Bond St. *1900.* 9 New Bond St. *1905-1910*

OWEN, FREDRICK.
Manufacturing Cutler. 18 Endell St., Long Acre *1866-1900*, also at 29 Wellington St. Strand *1895-1900.* 57 Endell St. *1905-1930*

OWEN, WILLIAM.
18 Endell St., Long Acre *1855-1860*

OXLEY, FRANK.
Cutlers and tool grinders to the trade. 82 Caledonian Rd. *1910-1930*

P

Plate 126.
This large knife by PAGET is typical of his products, similar large knives being shown by Adams et al. in The Bowie Knife book and by Bruce Voyles in his Auction Catalogue No 3. Paget knives are also known to have been used by Samuel Baker, the Victorian Hunter who was known for hunting with hounds and knife. Baker wrote in 1890, 3 years before his death that his old hunting knife is at this moment hanging on the wall. He further wrote that:
"It was difficult to arrange a knife that would comprise all desiderata, but Mr Paget of Piccadilly (long since dead) was first rate cutler and he produced the perfection of a blade. The knife weighed exactly 3 pounds including sheath. The blade was 1 foot in length, 2 inches wide at the base and double edged for 3 inches from the point."
Size: blade 10.5 inches, 15.75 inches overall.

PACKER, MISS ETHEL ALICE.
85 Newington Butts *1925*

PACKER, JOHN CHARLES.
247 Victoria Dock Road. *1925-1935*

PAGET.
This firm started with a Richard Paget who is first recorded as a cutler in *1823* at 163 Piccadilly. In *1832* he is listed under cutlers but with a notation stating that he is a surgical instrument maker, however there is no entry under surgical instrument maker's for him during this year. His address at this time was 184 Piccadilly. Richard Paget is recorded at 195 Piccadilly in *1839* but not in *1840*. In *1844* a William Paget of 195 Piccadilly appears, being listed in both the cutlers and surgical instrument maker sections of the directory. In *1850* the name Richard Paget reappears at the 195 Piccadilly address. In *1860* the name changes again to a John Paget this time at 196 Piccadilly.

A further name change occurs around *1866* when a Philip Paget of 31 Duke St. is recorded. In *1870* his address was 37 Myddelton St. and by *1885* he was at 13 Baron St. No trace after *1888*.

It is also likely that another famous Victorian hunter i.e. Henry Astbury Leveson "The Old Shekarry" may have had a knife made by Paget. The image of him in his hunting attire shows a knife very similar to those shown by both Adams and Voyles in wear. Although he was also a great fan of knives by Thornhill.

PALMER, GEORGE.
Cutler to the Royal Family. 1 St James St., Pall Mall *1820-1836*. No Royal Warrant listed for *1836*.

PALMER J.
40 Castle St., Leicester Square *1820-1836*

PALMER JOHN.
Inventor of the Absolutorism razor rectifier. 11 and 12 Royal Arcade Pall Mall *1832*

PALMER, WILLIAM THOMAS.
Working Cutler. 68 Lots Road, Chelsea *1895-1915*

Plate 127.
Large Bowie by Paget.
Size: Blade 12.5 inches,
15.5 inches overall.
(Photo courtesy of Bill Adams)

Henry Astbury Leveson
"The Old Shekarry"
wearing what may be a
Paget knife.

Plate 128.
Paterson & Co. Bowie.
(Photo courtesy of Bill Adams et al.)
Size: blade 14 inches, 20.75 inches overall.

PAPE, WILLIAM.
84 Vauxhall Walk, Lambeth *1846-1860*

PAPE, HENRY JAMES.
8 Westmoreland Rd. *1885*

PARKER, HENRY.
25 Richmond St. St. Luke's *1910*

PARKER, WILLIAM.
50 and 382 Strand *1823*

PARKINS & Co.
16 Vere St. Oxford St. W (London agents for Joseph Rodgers and Sons, Sheffield) *1880*

PARKIN, WILLIAM.
382 Strand 1820. 50 & 382 Strand *1822*. 50 and 406 Strand. *1829*. 440 Strand *1836*

PARSONS, HENRY.
5 Lamb's Conduit Street *1836*

PARTON, SON & Co.
105 Regent St. *1910* agents for Sprock's razors

PARTRIDGE, E.J.
7 Hatton Gardens *1905*

PASHA COMPANY (The).
40 Bishopsgate St. within *1905*

PATERSON & Co.
46 Moorgate St. The magnificent Bowie shown in plate 128 was retailed by the firm of Paterson and Co. who where recorded in 1860 as electroplated goods manufacturers.

PATON, BRADY & Co.
41 Queen St., Cheapside *1875*

PATRICK, Mrs. LOUISE.
46 Union Rd, Rotherhithe *1900*

PATRICK, L & SONS.
46 Union Rd. Rotherhithe *1905-1925*

PAYNE, GEORGE.
12 Rochester Row, Westminster *1866-1910*

PEACOCK, CHARLES GILBERT.
1 Bishopsgate St. without and 38 Camomile St. *1880-1890*. 47 Houndsditch and 11 Goring St. *1895-1905*

PEARCE, A.R.
56 Queen Victoria St. *1880-1885*

PEARCE, JOHN & Co.
Manufacturing Cutler. 112 and 113 Fore St. *1910-1920*

PEARCE, JOSEPH ROBERT.
77 Cornhill *1860-1875*

PELLETT, THOMAS.
Manufacturing Cutler. 62 High Holborn *1890 1895*. As Walter William in *1900*. *1905-1910* as PELLETT Ltd. *1915-1920* as PELLETT (*1912*) Ltd. *1920*

PENNY, VALENTINE.
277A High Rd. Kilburn *1905*. 25 Ball's Pond Rd. *1910-1940*

PEPYS.
A family of Cutlers and Surgical Instrument Maker who operated from 22 Poultry throughout their history.
JOHN. *1760-1863*
ROBERT EDWARD *1860-1870.* Also listed as razor maker
WILLIAM H *1822-1839.* Took freedom and livery from the Cutlers Company. Master in *1822* and *1828.*
PEPYS & WILLIAMS, *1846-1855*

PERKINS, T.
Working Cutler. 15 Portland St., Soho *1823*

PERRY, HENRY & SON.
Deptford Bridge *1855*

PETTIGREW, CHARLES.
181 Whitechapel Road *1860*

PFEIFFER, ALBERT.
2 Walbrook Buildings, City *1860*

PHILIP & WHICKER.
see SAVIGNY

PHILIP, WHICKER & BLAISE
see SAVIGNY

PHILLIPS, JAMES JOHN.
41a North St., Chelsea *1855-1875.*
14 North St. *1880-1885*

PHILLIPS, THOMAS.
Manufacturing Cutler 22 Judd St. *1870*

PHIPPS & SON.
68 Newgate St. *1823*

PHIPPS, JAMES.
Razor maker. 68 Newgate St. *1823-1829*

PIERCE, THOMAS H.
Church St., Hackney *1846*

PIGALL, FRANZ.
Razor maker.
5 Noel St., Soho *1855.*
22 Tichborne St. *1860-1880.*
4 Rupert St. *1885-1910*

Plate 129.
A notable feature of this knife is its split guard. The blade is marked:
PIGALL
LONDON
Size: blade 6.25 inches long, 1.25 inches wide, 10.5 inches overall.

Plate 130.
A small Bowie marked on the blade:
POOLE
144 FLEET ST

PIGALL, FRANCIS.
49 Whitcomb St. *1915*
The relationship between Franz and Francis is unknown but it may only reflect the Anglicisation of the name and a continuation of the firm under the Francis name after Franz had died. Franz Pigall was born in Austria circa *1821/22* and died in London in *1884*. In the *1861* census he is recorded as a Master Cutler employing 2 men and an apprentice. The firm was awarded a medal at the *1873* Vienna Universal Exhibition for knives and razors. In addition they also held Royal warrants between *1904* and *1913* for King Edward VII and King George V for cutlery.

PINDER, WILLIAM.
69 Stanhope St., Hampstead Road 1850

PINKUS, SAMUEL & SONS.
80 Commercial St. *1900-1945*

PLADOFF, GEORGE.
8 Jerusalem Passage *1823*

PLATINOR INDUSTRIES.
Manufacturing Cutler. 66 and 67 Shoe Lane *1940*

PLUMB, GEORGE.
13 Russell St., Drury Lane *1823* and *1829* It is possible that this name is a misprint in the trade directory given that Plum, R.G. and J were operating

Plate 131.
Marked on the blade
POOLE
& SON
along with the mark of a cross which is has LONDON MADE in a circle around it. This mark has been noted on other London knives (see Hinde and Herbert). The knife is either a hunting knife or possibly part of a carving set.

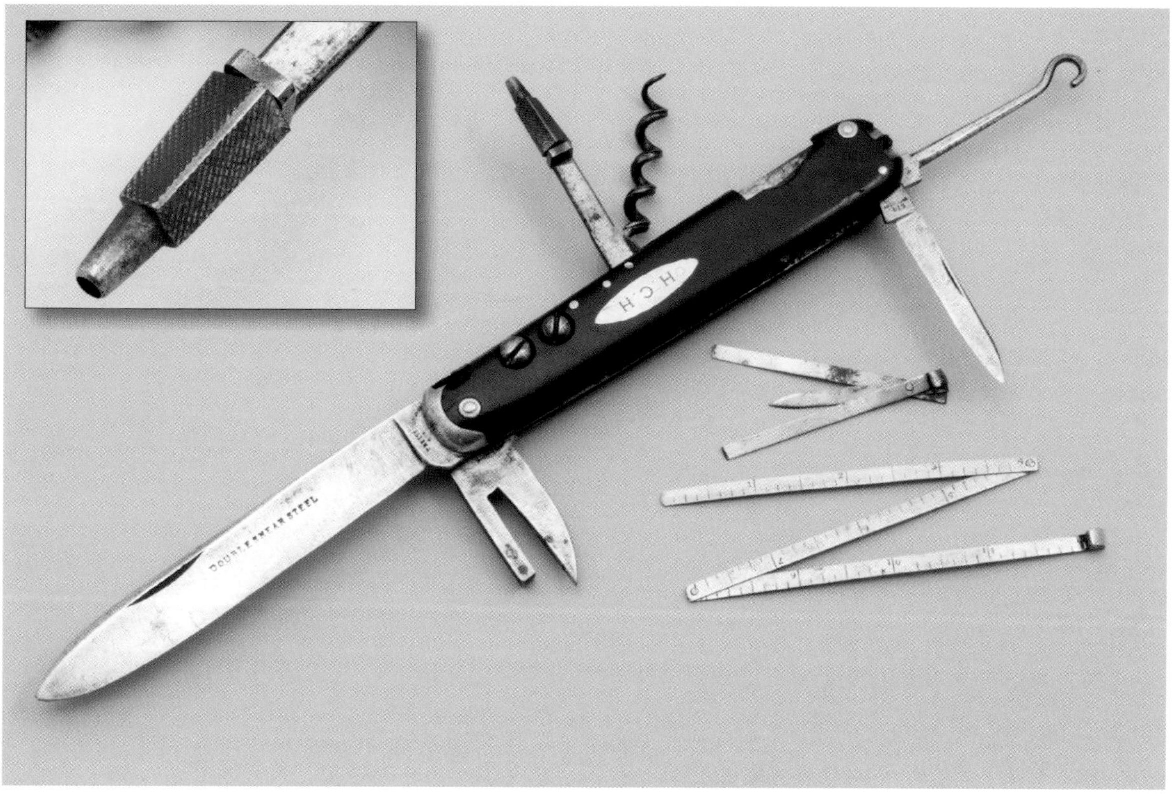

from this same address during this *1820's* period.

PLUM, CHARLES TUCKER.
Shear maker and Manufacturing Cutler. 448 Oxford St., 3 Dolphin St. *1855*. In *1860-1880* at 448 Oxford St. and 9 Lawrence St. *1885-1895* at 97 New Oxford St. and 9 Lawrence St.

PLUM, GEORGE.
Working Cutler and Surgical Instrument Maker. Occupied the following London premises-17 Picket St., Strand *1832-1846*. 262 Strand *1840-1850*
(The above PLUM's were a well known Bristol company, the Bristol business continued long after the London branch closed.)

PLUM, R.G. & J
13 Russell St., Drury Lane *1820-1825*

POLLEN, MICHAEL.
Working Cutler. 16 King St., Golden Square *1832*

POLLITZER, DIXON & Co.
(Agents) 11 Bartlett's Buildings *1895*

POND, ROBERT.
29 Bell St. Edgware Road *1846-1850*. 44 Weber Row, Blackfriars Road *1860-1866*

PONTIFEX, J.H.
89A and 89B Buckingham Palace Rd. and 205 and 207 Victoria St. *1900-1910*

POOLE. H.
8 Yate's Rentals, Pear Tree Court, Clerkenwell *1855*, as Herbert and Son *1860-1880*

POOLE, R.
8 Yate's Rentals, Pear Tree Court, Clerkenwell *1850*

POOLE, R.
23 Clerkenwell Close *1822-1823*

POOLE, ROBERT.
57 and 58 St. John's Square *1895*

Plate 132.
A fine and unusual gentleman's/horseman's knife. This knife has rosewood scales and besides the usual accoutrements found on such a knife has an unusual punch tool. The main blade is stamped on the flat DOUBLE SHEAR STEEL and is marked on the ricasso:

PRIEST
& CO

Plate 133.
The wonderful little knife is marked:

W PRIEST
53 OXFORD ST

Which William this refers to is not known. The knife has a bolster integral with the blade fancy ferrule and pommel and a grip of mother of pearl.

Plate 134.
Folding knife which is unusual in that it has two identically-sized locking blades. Both blades are marked:

DOUBLE SHEAR STEEL

and on the ricasso:

PRIEST & CO

with the address:

514 OXFORD ST.

on the reverse. The scales are of ivory

POOLE, SAMUEL.
144 Fleet St. 1875-1890.

POOLE, S & Co.
51 Burlington Arcade *1910-1925*

POPE, WILLIAM & SON.
80 and 81 Edgeware Row *1866*. 190 and 192 Edgeware Rd. *1870-1875*

POPPLEWELL & Co.
9 Bury Court St. Mary Axe *1910-1915*

POSTON, A.E. & Co. Ltd.
6 Dowgate Hill *1930-1935*. Lonsdale House, Dowgate Hill *1940*

POTTS, WALTER HENRY.
Working Cutler. 10 Colvill Place, Tottenham Court Rd. *1910*

POUND, JOHN & Co.
Manufacturing Cutler. Founded by a Henry Pound in *1823*. Not listed under cutlers until late in the 19th century when in *1885* recorded at 81, 82, 83 Leadenhall Street, works

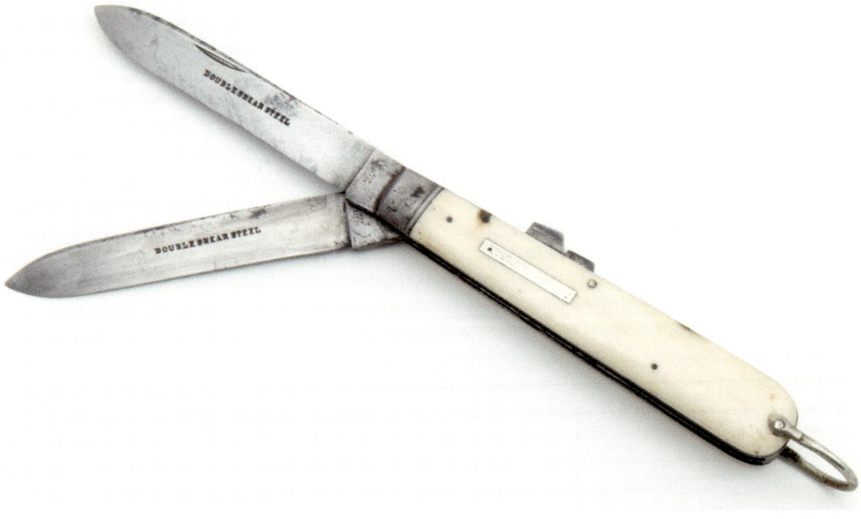

135

Plate 135.
This spear point bowie has ebony scales, which are quite large, a brass cross-guard and spear point blade. The blade is marked:

PRIEST
253 OXFORD ST

along with **LONDON** in a half circle. The Brass mounted sheath whilst contemporary with the knife is probably not original to it.
Size: blade 10 inches, 15 inches overall.

Plate 136.
Two examples of the same knife, similar examples of which have been noted by other makers/suppliers. These are interesting in that whilst they are of the same pattern they bear different addresses. The left specimen is stamped:

PRIEST
253 OXFORD ST

The right specimen is stamped:

PRIEST
514 OXFORD ST

Plate 137.
This piece is marked: PUTLEY with no street address however given the style of the knife it more than likely that of Isaac Putley.

at Great Alie St. In *1900-1905* at 81, 82, 83 and 84 Leadenhall Street, 67 Piccadilly, 211 Regent St., Works at Halfmoon Passage. *1910* also listed at 243 Brompton Rd. and recorded as "with works London and Sheffield". Maintained premises in Leadenhall Street, Oxford Street and Piccadilly up to *1940*. John Pound was a Lord Mayor of London *1904/05* and was created a Baronet in *1905*. A knife has been noted with their Leadenhall Street address.

POWELL, J.T. & Co.
Manufacturing Cutler. 83 Clerkenwell Road *1915*. 55 Hatton Gardens *1920-1935*

POWELL, MARY.
3 Great Turnstile, Holborn *1823-1836*

PRASSE, EMIL.
295 Bethnal Green Rd. *1900*

PRATT, J.
48 Newington Causeway *1823-1832*

PRATT, J. F.
Cutler and Surgical Instrument Maker. 10 Chase St. and 420 Oxford St. *1852-1855*

PRIEST.
The firm had a history which spanned from *1779* to *1915*. James Priest was an apprentice to cutler Thomas Squire he was also a master of the Cutlers Company. He became free of his apprenticeship in *1779* and is recorded by the Cutlers Company has having died in *1839*. His working address was the Strand and he had as apprentices both John Tiercelin and Edward Stammers.

No James Priest is recorded in the *1822* directory record but in *1823* a William Priest, working cutler of 1 Melina Place is noted. In *1832* a Preist at 32 Norfolk St. is listed, note the spelling of the name and this mis-spelt entry is repeated in *1834*. In *1836* the spelling is corrected with William having two entries as Priest William 253 Oxford St. and Priest Wm 32 Norfolk St. In *1840* only the Oxford St. premises in listed.

William is no longer listed in *1844* his place at the Oxford St. premises being occupied by John Priest who remains at this address until *1860* when a William reappears. During this period i.e. in both *1855* and

1860 they are listed as razor makers. In *1870* the firm's name was changed to Priest and Co. which remained unchanged until its demise. Although remaining in Oxford St. in *1885* they had moved to 514. Their directory entries in the last 10 years or so of their existence read "cutlery manufacturers, razor makers: silver medal 1885, gold medal 1888".

PRIESTLEY & MOORE.
Manufacturing Cutler. 7 Ely Place *1940*

PRIME, THOMAS & SON.
19 Ely Place *1880-1885*. 3 and 5 Charterhouse St. *1890*

PRITCHARD, SARAH.
28 Seward St. *1832*

PROCTOR, ELIZA.
Duke St. West, Smithfield *1822-1823*

PROCTOR, HENRY.
Working Cutler and Surgical Instrument Maker.
182 Union St. *1832 -1836*

PRYOR, NATHANIEL.
20 Gracechurch St. *1829-1832*

PRYOR, ELIZABETH.
20 Gracechurch St. *1836-1839*

PRYOR, THOMAS.
Cutler and Surgical Instrument Maker. 67 Minories *1826 -1836*

PULLEN, MICHAEL.
16 King St. *1829*

PULVERMANN, MARTIN & Co.
26 Minories *1900*

PUTLEY, ABRAHAM.
Working Cutler. 114 High St. *1820-1829*. As & Son in *1832-1840*

PUTLEY, ISAAC.
Manufacturing Cutler.
114 Borough High St. *1846 1850* also at 44 in *1855*. Only at 44 in *1860-1866*. 127 Borough High St. in *1870-1875*. 175 Borough High St. *1880-1890*. 45 Pembridge Road *1900*. More than likely the son of Abraham Putley. Isaac Putley had two sons, Isaac and Alfred, both of whom are listed in the *1861* census returns as Cutlers. In *1881* there is only a record of Alfred who is listed as a Cutler and Opticians.

QUINCY HARCOURT.
(Export) 150 Fenchurch St. *1866.* 5 Bond Court in *1870-1875*

RAMSPOTT & WILLIAMS.
96 Great Tower St. *1895*

RANDALL & FREEMAN.
60 Burlington Arcade (Cutler and travelling bag makers) *1832*

RASMUS & GORDON.
78 Seven Sisters Road *1930*

RAWCLIFFE & WALDRON.
19 St. Dunstan's Hill *1905*

READ & ELVIDGE.
13 Warwick Court High Holborn *1900-1945*

READER, GEORGE HENRY.
14 St. John's St. *1895*

REDBARD, GEORGE.
120 Wardour St., Soho *1823*

REDBURN, GEORGE.
126 Wardour St., Soho *1829*

REED, JOSEPH.
167 Long Lane Bermondsey *1846-1850*

REES, RICHARD.
9 Red Lion Passage, Red Lion Square, Holborn *1820-1829*

REES, RICHARD. & SON.
45 George St., Portman Square *1832-1836.* As RICHARD. J REES *1839-1855*

REILLEY, E.M. & Co.
Reilly was a wholesale gun maker and rifle manufacturer from *1861* to *1917.* Operated primarily out of Oxford St. occupying at various stages numbers 502, 315, 295 and also 16 New Oxford St. (1883-1898) and 13 High St., Marylebone.

REMOLINE Co.
Razor Makers. 4 Denman St. *1920*

REVELL, FRANCES.
Cutlers and Surgical Instrument Maker. 67 Marylebone Lane *1832*

RICHARD, GEORGE.
19 Whitehart Yard, Drury Lane *1839*

RICHARDS, ROBERT.
57 and 58 St. John's square *1895*

RICHARDS, WILLIAM.
483 Strand. *1839*

RICHARDSON, GEORGE.
14 High St., Kensington *1832*

RICHARDSON, G.
Mayfield Place, Kensington High St. *1846*

RICHARDSON, HENRY.
77 Finsbury Pavement *1885-1890*

RICHARDSON, JOHN.
43 New Bond St. 1836-1840

RICHARDSON, & Co.
26 King St. St James's. Richardson's actual business is listed as East India Agent but this also included being a sword retailer who not only sold swords made by Wilkinson, they also sold swords etched with their name which had been made by Wilkinsons. Richardson operated between *1915* and *1942.*

RICHARDSON, WILLIAM & SON.
273 Whitechapel Rd. *1880-1895.* 18 Whitechapel Rd. *1900.* 96 and 183 Whitechapel Rd, *1905-1945* by *1945* only at latter.

Plate 138.
A Superb spear point Bowie marked:

REILLY, NEW OXFORD ST.

Chequered ebony grip. Oval guard and unusual shaped pommel. The sheath is unusual in that it still has its frog, a feature that is rarely seen.
Size: blade 10 inches, 16 inches overall.

Plate 139.
This knife may have associations with Wilkinson. The piece also has some features similar to the knife shown in Plate 1 of my book on British and Commonwealth Military Knives. However the etching on the blade whilst partially erased presents something of a mystery in that whilst the remains of the address reads JAMES St. the start of the name seems to read RITCH--- which does not fit the name of RICHARDSON. Unless of course it was incorrectly etched.

The knife itself is almost a shortened version of the 1890 Pattern Cavalry Sword.
Size: blade 10 inches, 15 inches overall.

RICHFORD & Co.

52A High Holborn *1905*. 153 Fleet St. *1910-1915*. In *1915* also at Milner Works, Barnsbury St.

RIGGE, JOHN and THOMAS.

Cutler and razor tablet maker. 65 Cheapside *1832-1836*. As RIGGE, T.H. and Co *1840-1846*

Plate 140.
Skinner marked:
G. RUSHBROOKE (SMITHFIELD) LTD.
along with:
SPECIAL HAND FORGED.

ROBERTS, A.J. & Co.
15 to 18 Bishopsgate St. *1880*

ROBERTS & BELK Ltd.
Manufacturing Cutler. 24 Holborn Viaduct *1910-1920*

ROBERTS, EDWIN.
356 Caledonian Rd. *1880-1890*

ROBERTS, Mrs. SOPHIA.
356 Caledonian Rd. *1895-1900*

ROBINSON, E. H. & Co.
Pen and Pocket Knife Makers.
52 Bishopgate *1846-1935*

ROBINSON, J.
19 Kingsland Road *1822*

ROBINSON, JONATHAN.
Working Cutler 101 Wardour St. *1823*

ROBINSON, J.
2 Catherine St., Strand *1832*

ROBINSON, MARIA.
Working Cutler 12 Hart St. Grosvenor Sq., *1836*

ROBINSON, SAMUEL.
15 Chapel St., Liverpool St. *1855*

ROBINSON, THOMAS.
Working Cutler. 15 Russell Court, Drury Lane *1820-1832*

RODRIGUES, HENRY.
42 Piccadilly *1890-1905*

ROMAN, FRANCIS.
2 Oxford Row, Old Kent Road *1855*

ROMAIN, N.A.
26 Shoreditch High St. *1910*

ROSIN, A & I.
Manufacturing Cutler.
18 Australian Ave. *1935*

ROTTON, JOSEPH.
86 Great Saffron Hill *1839*

ROTTON & SON.
25 Sackville Road Piccadilly *1820-1832*, as & Co. in *1832*

RUFF, GUSTAV WILLIAM.
95 and 97 Charlotte St., Fitzroy Square. *1910-1915*

RUFF, R.I.
Manufacturing Cutler, makers of the RA MI keen edge stainless steel table cutlery. 36 Penton St. *1925*

RUSHBROOKE, G.
Butchers Cutler. 67 and 69 Charterhouse St. EC. *1890-1900*, stayed at 67 until *1924*. Also at 71 in 1900. *1908-1920* also at Greenhill's Rents, Cowcross St., EC In *1925* at 73 Charterhouse St. *1925* at 146 Aldersgate St., and in *1926* at 73 Charterhouse St. and listed as G. Rushbrooke (Smithfield) Ltd. Continued in operation into the *1960's*

RYAN, GEORGE.
312 Euston Rd. *1895*

RYLEY, JOHN.
20 Webb St. *1829*

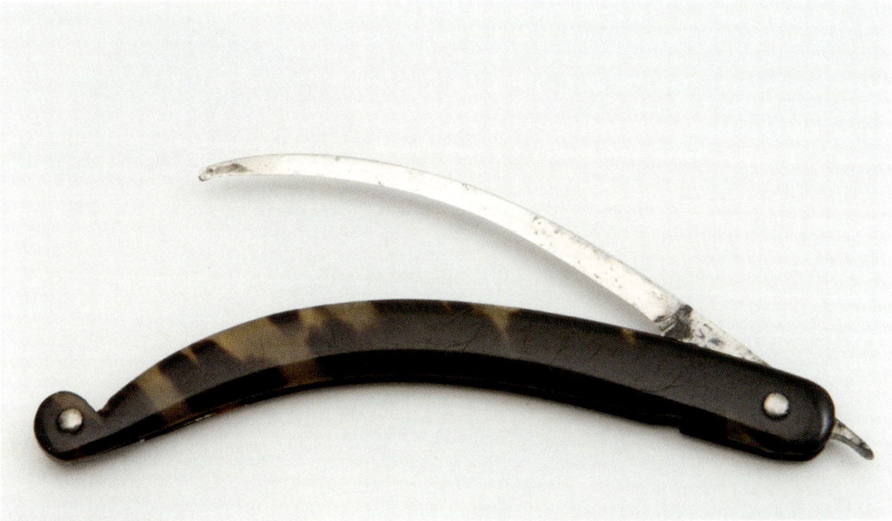

Plate 141.
A Bistoury with tortoiseshell scales. The ricasso is simply marked:
SAVIGNY.

S

SALT, ISSAC.
45 Edgware Road *1846*

SALT, WILLIAM.
118 Piccadilly *1846*

SAMUEL, CHARLES.
58 Rosebery Avenue *1900*

SAMUEL, CHARLES & Co.
Butchers Cutler. 56 Long Lane, West Smithfield. *1905-1930*

SANSOM & SONS.
16 Thavies Inn, Holborn *1840*

SAVIGNY & Co.
Probably established in about *1720* the history of Savigny is a classic example of how the published information can be misleading when trying to establish the history of London cutlers. Southwick in his write up on Savigny indicates that the firm started with John Fessier Savigny, cutler and razor maker, who was probably the son of Oliver Fessier, with John not adopting the surname Savigny until the early *1720's*. He was succeeded by a John Horatio Savigny cutler and surgical instrument maker whose premises where at Pall Mall and 29 King St., Covent Garden from *1795* to *1808* though for *1807* and *1808* a partnership of Savigny, Everill and Mason are recorded at the site.

Plate 142.
A quill knife by Savigny with superb nickel silver scales. The tang is marked:
SAVIGNY
& Co

From *1809* to *1822* the three-man partnership is recorded at 67 St James St. being described as Wholesale and retail cutlers and surgeons instrument makers and manufacturers of patent razors. The records for *1822* do however show Savigny's name crossed through and Everill and Maison listed as having succeeded though they are still listed under the Savigny, Everill and Mason name in *1823*.

Plate 143.
A superb example of the London cutlers skill is this knife in the style of a Khanjar with carved hilt in the style of a camel's head. The blade bears the name and address of:

SAVIGNY & Co
67 St. JAMES'S
STREET
LONDON

This would appear to date the piece in the period 1840-1875.
Size: blade 9 inches, 13.25 inches overall.

Plate 143.
A fine example of an early folding knife with stag scales a large oblong back to the spring. Stamped on the ricasso:

SAVIGNY
& CO

However according to Bennion in her book on Antique Dental Instruments this firm founded circa *1720* by a Paul Savigny who succeeded the business of the late Widow How. In *1726* she lists the firm as a John Tessier (note the different spelling) Savigny and notes that in *1784* the firm was known as John Henry Savigny 129 Pall Mall.

The London trade directories do

Plate 145.
A further early folder with tortoiseshell scales and surgical instrument lock. Blade marked:

SAVIGNY & CO

however make the history of the company from the *1820's* a little clearer. So even though there are discrepancies in the records the history of Savigny seems to run along the following lines noting some of the records are far from clear as differently named firms occupied the same premises during similar dates.

Established c.*1720* when a Paul Savigny succeeded to the business of a Widow How.
1726 John (Tessier or Fessier) Savigny cutler and razor maker.
1784 John (Henry or Haratio) Savigny 129 Pall Mall, and 29 King St
1794 John (Henry or Haratio) Savigny 67 St James St.
1810 to c.*1834* Savigny, Everill and Mason surgical instrument makers 67 St James St.
1836 Everill, Philip and Wickes (Bennion records this name as Whicker) 67 St James St.
1840-c.1847 Everill, P and W 67 St James St.
1855 Philip, Whicker and Blaise 67 St James St.
1856 Whicker and Blaise 67 St James St.
1860 Savigny and Co. (wholesaler) 67 St James St.
1860 Whicker and Blaise 67 St James St. manufactory, Young's Place, Wood St., Westminster.
1870-c.1877 Louis Blaise 67 St James St.
1840-1875 Savigny and Co. 67 St James St.
1880-1886 C Wright and Co. from Louis Blaise and Co. (late Savigny and Co.) 108 New Bond St.
1896-1960 Alfred Cox (late partner of C Wright and Co. from Louis Blaise and Co. late Savigny and Co. 108 New Bond St. Moved to 120 New Bond St. c.*1902*, to 54 Duke St. c.*1930* and to 108 Whitechapel Road c.*1940*. Dropped the association with Blaise and Savigny from his name c.*1901* and became known as Alfred Cox (Surgical) Ltd. in *1945*.

SAVORY, JOSEPH.
Cutler and Silversmith.
48 Cheapside. *1820*

SCHAFER, P & F.
48 Cornhill. General Merchants, Agent for Shannon Ltd. *1900-1915.*

SCHERF, F.A.
57 Cheapside *1875*

SCHMIDT, ALFRED.
6 Eldon St. Finsbury *1900-1905*

SCHULTZ, CARL.
27 Sloane Square *1890*

SCHWARTE (JOHN & DANIEL).
18 Finsbury Circus *1880*

SEARLE, JAS EDWARD.
52 Kent St. *1855*

SELINGER & SONS.
51 Milton St. *1900-1905.* No trace for a number of years but in *1920* as Edward Selinger.

SELWYN, A.H. Ltd.
8 Lawrence Lane *1920*

SETTLE, D.
4 Hudson's Court, Strand *1829*

SETTLE, DENIS.
9 High St., Marylebone *1840*

SEWELL JOHN.
195, 197 and 199 Victoria St. *1895*

SEWELL JOHN & SON.
49 Fore St., Cripplegate *1832* (wholesale)

SEWELL, JOSEPH & CHARLES JOHN.
49 Fore St., and 128 London Wall *1880-1885*

SHARPE, RICHARD. & SON.
Wholesale Table Knife and Fork Manufacturers. 9 Great New St., Fetter Lane *1820-1829*. As Jonathan and Richard in *1836*. *1840* as Sharpe, Richard, 4 Gough Square. In 1846, as John and Richard at 5 Gough Square *1850*

SHEARER, MAUNDY & MILES.
5 Lillypot Lane *1860*

SHELDRAKE, & BIGG.
29 Leicester Square *1832-34*

SHELL, RICHARD.
88 St. Stephen's Row, Bow *1875*

SHEPEARD, HENRY A.
51 Marshall St., Golden Square *1860*

SHEDRICK, S.
2 Youl Place, Old Kent Road *1829*

SHINWELL, THOMAS.
25 Union St., Bishopsgate *1866*

SHOLL, RICHARD.
Manufacturing Cutler. 3 Cleveland St., Mile End Road *1860-1866*. *1870* at 3 Colt St., Old Ford. *1870*. 88 St. Stephen's Row *1880-1885*

SHORT, JOHN.
Wholesaler. 15 Lime St. *1950-1880*

SHREWSBURY, ABRAHAM.
87 Queen St. *1890*

SHUBRICK, JOHN.
32 Clifton St., Finsbury *1860-1870*. At 49 in *1875*

SIDDALL, CHARLES.
Working Cutler and Hardware man. 4 Myddleton St., *1829*. 7 Charles St. *1832-1836*

SIDDALL, CHARLES.
8 Kent Place, Old Kent Road *1846-1855*

SIDDALL, JAMES.
8 Kent Place, Old Kent Road *1860-1866*. 101 Kent Place *1870-1900*

SILBER & FLEMMING.
Dealers. 56 to 62 and 71 Wood St., and 2 London Wall *1890-1895*

SILVER, S. W. & Co.
A retailer who seemed to like very large Bowies with evidence which appears to indicate that the bowie knives he sold under his name were made by Joseph Rodgers.

As a retailer Silver had extensive interests. Their interest in the India rubber and gutta percha

Silver advertisement from 1914

Plate 146.
A massive bowie, which could have been made by Joseph Rodgers. With chequered horn scales and with a sheath that has the usual clip the blade is some 15 inches in length. Overall length 20 inches. Ricasso marked:

S.W.SILVER & Co
CORNHILL

Size: blade 14.75 inches, 20 inches overall.

business resulted in one of the biggest factories in the Royal Victoria Dock area of London; the factory was so large that it gave the name Silvertown to the area. An advertisement in *1859* shows the marketing of vulcanised rubber, engineering equipment and machinery, furniture, clothing and for Outfitting Naval and Military Officers. The company's interest also extended to outfitting those destined for immigration to the Colonies as this piece from the *Illustrated London News* of *1848* shows:

> *Immigration being much required in AUSTRALIA, NEW ZEALAND, &c., and as the supposed expense of an Outfit often prevents Individuals Emigrating, S. W. SILVER and Co., CLOTHIERS, OUTFITTERS, and CONTRACTORS (having a large interest to maintain in those Colonies), have been advised to make known that they can supply a comfortable OUTFIT, including Bedding, for Male or Female Emigrants from Four Pounds (net) upwards, or less (Two Pounds, if needful); and for Children in proportion, at No. 4, Bishopsgate-street Within, opposite the London Tavern, where lists will be given on application.*
>
> *S. W. S. & Co., being the makers of nearly every article in all the Outfits they supply, and as one of their objects is to promote Emmigration, they neither receive from agents, or pay the too usual commission to any person introducing passengers to be fitted out, so that the passage and outfit may be procured at the least possible expense; but they will, on application, advise passengers how to obtain the most economic passage to the Colonies. They leave a representative in every Australian*

Plate 147.
Stylistically similar to a Shakespear Knife this piece is marked SILVER & Co LONDON a mark which is just visible under the down turned guard. (On the reverse side there is a mark as shown - a mark which is found on some other London Knives). The grips are of wood chequered on the top in the manner of a Shakespear Knife. The sheath is wood covered in leather and carries positions for a knife and fork.
Size: blade 10.5 inches, 16.25 inches overall.

Plate 148.
Spear point bowie almost certainly made by Joseph Rodgers and retailed by Silver.
Stag scales and oval nickel silver guard. The sheath is fitted with the knife retention clip.
The ricasso is marked:

S.W.SILVER & CO
66 & 67 CORNHILL

Plate 149.
Green River Knife marked:

SILVER & CO
2 EASTCHEAP

Colony, to whom they ship Clothing monthly; thus they would forward small parcels free of expense. Naval and Military Officers, Midshipmen, Cadets, Civilians, Ladies, &c. are outfitted as heretofore at the Cabin-Passenger Outfitting Warehouse, Nos. 66 and 67, Cornhill (the Emmigration Outfitting being exclusively at No.4 Bishopsgate-street Within) London, and each branch at St. George's-crescent, Liverpool.

Their main premises were at 66 and 67 Cornhill, the Cornhill address being found on all of the bowies bearing their name which have so far been noted. They did however also occupy other

premises, 10 Cornhill, 3, 4 and 5 Bishopsgate, 11 Leadenhall St., 29 Old Bond St., 15 Bury St. and warehouses at Bishopsgate, Woolwich and Silvertown Amalgamated with B. Edgington Ltd. *1899* and traded after that as Silver and Edgington Ltd. In *1914* located at King William House 2 East Cheapside. An advertisement in the *1914* Telephone directory mentions their long association with Cornhill. Are listed in "The London Gun Trade" as sword cutler and rifle manufacturers up until *1913*

They survived the 2nd World War and finally went out of business in *1967/68.*

SIMMONDS BROTHERS.

"The trade supplied with knives, forks and cutlery on hire in any quantity." 6 to 15 Newton St., Holborn 1875. 4, 6, 8 Newton St. *1880-1890.*

SIMONS, EMANUEL.

100 and 101 Houndsditch
1915-1920

SIMPSON & SMITH.

Cutler and Surgical Instrument Maker. 55 Strand *1820-1823.*

SIMPSON, JAMES.

James Simpson is recorded in *1832* as a surgical instrument maker of 55 Strand. There is no trace in the cutlery section of *1840* directory but a Mrs Susan Simpson 55 Strand is listed under surgical instrument makers. At the same time a T Simpson and Co. with an address at 156 Leadenhall St. appears. However to further confuse the lineage by *1846* three Simpson's are listed:

Fred Simpson and Co. 57 Borough High St
S Simpson 55 Strand (Simpson and Smith *1823, 1829*)
T Simpson, jnr. and Co. 156 Leadenhall St

Plate 150.
What appears to be a fixed blade pruning knife with a blade marked with a crown over:

SIMPSON
55 STRAND
LONDON

By *1850* the entries are Frederick and Thomas Simpson and Co. 57 Borough High St., and Henry Simpson 55 Strand (listed both as cutler and surgical instrument maker), but by *1855* Thomas's name no longer appears. Neither branch of the name appears in *1870*. It does however appear likely that at this stage they amalgamated with Moseley

Given the address on the piece illustrated the lineage of the Simpson's who occupied 55 Strand must have been along the following lines:

James Simpson *1832*
Mrs Susan Simpson *1840*
Henry Simpson *1850 1860*

SIPPEL, B & J. Ltd.
Manufacturing Cutler. 5 and 6 Macintosh Lane, Homerton. *1935*

SKEGGS, GEORGE.
Wholesaler. 1A Liverpool St. *1866*. 12 Shoreditch High St. in *1870*

SKINNER, ALFRED & SON.
33 Martin St. Stratford. *1925-1940*

SKINNER, J.C.
36 Basinghall St. 1880

SMEE, JAMES
1 Minories *1832*

SMITH, ABRAHAM.
Working Cutler. Curaitor St. *1832*. 66 Fetter Lane 1836.

SMITH, Mrs. ANN.
72 King William St., City *1846-1850*

SMITH, MISSES A & E.
72 King William St., City *1855-1875*

SMITH, BENJAMIN.
Working Cutler. 8 Kensington Cross *1832-1839*

SMITH & BLASTER.
22 Bridge Rd, Lambeth *1840*

SMITH & CARTER.
25 Finsbury Pavement *1855*

SMITH, CHARLES D.
11 Southville, Wandsworth Rd. *1855*

SMITH, FREDERICK.
Noted in Hinde and Herbert. A Frederick Smith took the freedom of the Cutlers Company in *1835* and was Master in *1869*. The knife shown by Hinde and Herbert has the address obliterated but is clearly marked: LONDON MADE. However no record in the cutlers section of the directories could be found for a Fredrick Smith

SMITH, GEORGE.
30 Lamb's Conduit Street *1820*

SMITH, GEORGE.
4 Feather Court, Drury Lane *1829*

SMITH, GEORGE.
Surgical Instrument Maker. 1 Turk's Row *1832*

SMITH, GEORGE.
5 Turk's Row *1836*

SMITH, GEORGE.
Gunsmith. George Smith operated between *1859* and *1897*. He was based at 82 New Bond Street during *1870*.

SMITH, Mrs. HARRIET A.
20 Barnsbury Place *1850*

SMITH, ISAAC.
85 Great Saffron Hill *1836*

Plate 151.
Kukri marketed by Smith but probably not made by them. The scales are of horn which the rivets covered by black horn disc. The scabbard is interesting with its brass mounts . The piece is marked:

SMITH
NEW BOND ST
LONDON

Size: blade 10.5 inches, 15 inches overall.

JAMES SMITH & SONS (UMBRELLAS) Ltd.
James Smith and Sons Ltd. are a umbrella and cane maker and one of the few firms mentioned in this book that are still in existence.

Founded in *1830* by James Smith with premises at Foubert St. the firm was moved to New Oxford St. in *1857* by his son, also called James. Their New Oxford St. premises still exist and is a classic example of a Victorian shop. The frontage of the shop shows the association with knives etc. by the advertisement for swordsticks.

SMITH, JOHN.
Working Cutler and Surgical Instrument Maker. 19 Cock Lane, Giltspur St. *1832 –1836*.

SMITH, J.
Working Cutler and dressing case maker. 38 Cheapside *1823-1837.*

SMITH, J.
Working Cutler. 70 St. John St., Clerkenwell 1829-1832.
59 St. John's St. 1836-1840

SMITH, JOSEPH.
Working Cutler. 86 Whitechapel Road *1829*

SMITH, WILLIAM TENNISON.
Working Cutler and razor maker. 86 Lombard St. *1820-1836.*
72 King William St. in *1840*

Plate 152.
This Officer swagger stick with concealed blade was frequently sold by such firms to officers going overseas. During WW1 many hundreds of thousands of military swagger sticks were sold to soldiers. The blade was in all likelihood made in Sheffield and etched with Smith's name. The blade is etched with foliate panels and marked:

JAMES SMITH & SONS LTD.
NEW OXFORD ST.
LONDON

SMITH, SIDNEY & Co.
52 Long Lane, Smithfield *1866*

SMITH, WILLIAM.
Working Cutler and Surgical Instrument Maker. 4 St. Saviour's Churchyard *1803 -1831*

SMITH, WILLIAM.
Working Cutler. 4 Peartree Court, Clerkenwell *1832*

SMITHERS, H.W.
Studio Yard, Bromley Rd., Catford *1935*

SNOOK, GEORGE.
Cutler and grinder. 47 James St., Manchester Square *1823*

SNOWDON, ROBERT Jnr.
7 Netherwood St. Kilburn *1915*

SOILLEUX, ALBERT.
Cutler and weavers instrument maker. 146 Brick Lane, Spitalfields *1823-1829*. 46 Sclater St. in *1836-1855*

SOUTHCOMBE, JOHN.
c.1865-1875. John Southcombe

Plate 153.
The knife shown was undoubtedly purchased by someone of means. It has ivory scales; silver mounts and comes complete with a silver mounted belt. The size of the belt indicates it was either made for a Lady or child but one from a titled family as the locket is engraved with a coronet over the letters EE back to back. When originally made this must have been superb example of the WINGFIELD KNIFE. The silver marks reflect a date of 1868.

Plate 154.
Dirk with sheath made from deer skin with silver mounts and locket engraved with a monogram which appears to read WD. The pommel is also engraved with what appears to read from RB to C B Bruce. The hilt is of stag and the blade is pierced with small holes both along the flat and on the back edge. The blade is marked:

SOUTHCOMBE
130 & 131 JERMYN ST

The locket and chape bear London silver hallmarks for 1866
Size: blade 8.5 inches, 15.5 inches overall.

of 130 and 131 Jermyn Street, St. James was a hairdresser, dressing case maker, and fancy repository. The concept of a hairdresser selling knives may seem odd but during the Victorian period people such as this would have catered for the needs of the rich by offering a wide range of fancy goods.

SPEAR, Mrs. MARY.
2 Well St., Wellclose Square *1846*

SPILLER, FRANCIS EDWARD.
39 Newington Causeway *1860-1875*. 71 Newington Causeway *1880-1890*

SPILLER, ROBERT.
166 Upper St., Islington *1875-1890*. 204 Upper St. in *1895-1905*

SPINK, HARRY.
Working Cutler. 105 Great Russell St. *1915*

SPURRIER & Co.

Manufacturing Cutler. 42 Wool Exchange, Coleman St. *1890*, also at 41a in *1895-1900*, 15 Wool Exchange, Basinghall St. *1905*

SPURRIER, JOHN WALTER.

15 Wool Exchange, Basinghall St. *1915-1920*.

STACEY, WILLIAM KING. (late GREER)

London made table cutlery, pen/pocket and sportsmen's knives, scissors, shear, razors, corkscrews and skates. Established *1780*. 23 Newgate Street. *1875 -1880*. The 1875 directory records the name as STACEY, thereafter it is STACY. In *1885* Railway Approach, London Bridge and 4 Newgate St. In *1890* as STACY, WILLIAM KING & FREDRICK. FREDRICK dropped in *1895*. *1900-1905* at 19 Newgate St. *1908-1912* at 98 Newgate St. Listed as "Safety" carving forks, table and pocket knives, "Facile" American shears; patent aluminium wallets; chatelaines and surgical instruments for nurses. *1915-1935* as STACY, LONDON Ltd. *1920*. A knife with the 4 Newgate Street address has been noted but with the name spelt as Stacey.

STAMMERS, EDWARD.

Edward Stammers was a knife, fork, razor maker, cutler and silversmith established circa *1807* at 32 Wych St. In *1811* he was at 21 Strand and

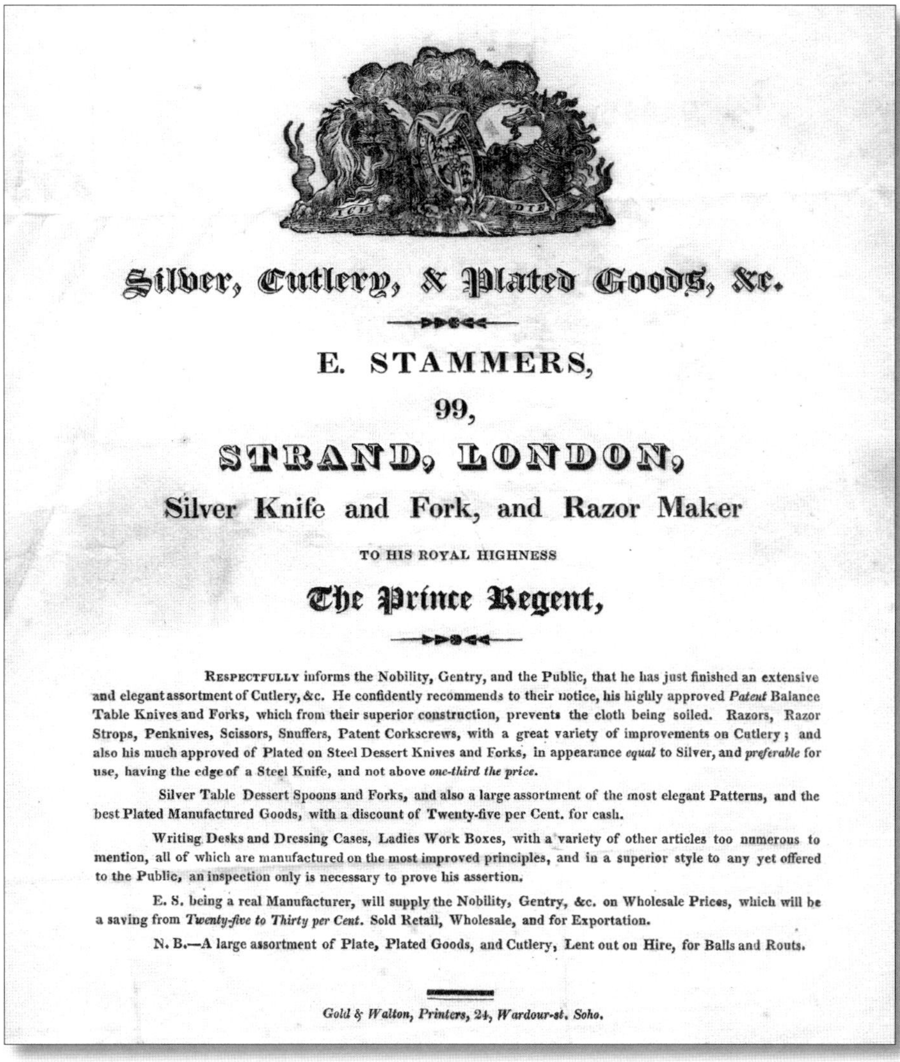

Silver, Cutlery, & Plated Goods, &c.

E. STAMMERS,

99,

STRAND, LONDON,

Silver Knife and Fork, and Razor Maker

TO HIS ROYAL HIGHNESS

The Prince Regent,

RESPECTFULLY informs the Nobility, Gentry, and the Public, that he has just finished an extensive and elegant assortment of Cutlery, &c. He confidently recommends to their notice, his highly approved *Patent* Balance Table Knives and Forks, which from their superior construction, prevents the cloth being soiled. Razors, Razor Strops, Penknives, Scissors, Snuffers, Patent Corkscrews, with a great variety of improvements on Cutlery; and also his much approved of Plated on Steel Dessert Knives and Forks, in appearance *equal* to Silver, and *preferable* for use, having the edge of a Steel Knife, and not above *one-third the price*.

Silver Table Dessert Spoons and Forks, and also a large assortment of the most elegant Patterns, and the best Plated Manufactured Goods, with a discount of Twenty-five per Cent. for cash.

Writing Desks and Dressing Cases, Ladies Work Boxes, with a variety of other articles too numerous to mention, all of which are manufactured on the most improved principles, and in a superior style to any yet offered to the Public, an inspection only is necessary to prove his assertion.

E. S. being a real Manufacturer, will supply the Nobility, Gentry, &c. on Wholesale Prices, which will be a saving from *Twenty-five to Thirty per Cent*. Sold Retail, Wholesale, and for Exportation.

N. B.—A large assortment of Plate, Plated Goods, and Cutlery, Lent out on Hire, for Balls and Routs.

Gold & Walton, Printers, 24, Wardour-st. Soho.

An interesting piece of cutlery ephemera dating from the 1811-1820 period, when the future King George IV was Prince Regent.

Plate 155.
Skean Dhu. The blade bears the names and address

HENRY STARCK
31 DRUMMOND
TERRACE
NW

whereas the reverse of the locket on the sheath is marked:

H STARCK
MAKER
LONDON

The front of the locket is engraved

W.C.H.
1.1.08
J.M.S

from *1812* at 99 Strand, and later at 100 Strand. In *1836* he is noted at 90 and 100 Strand. According to Southwick he remained at 100 Strand until *1866*.

STARCK, HENRY.
1897-1921. Henry Starck was a musical instrument maker located at 31 Drummond Crescent, St. Pancras, and subsequently at 6 Kentish Town Road.

STATTER, GILES.
Working Cutler. 75 Shoreditch *1823*

STATTER, GEORGE WILLIAM.
90 Leonard St., Shoreditch *1832*

STEER, THOMAS.
69 Oxford St. *1846-1850*

STEER, Mrs. MARY & Co.
69 Oxford St. *1855-1860*

STEIN, GEORGE & Co.
Working Cutler. 8 Crutched Friars *1836*

STEWART CHARLES & Co.
22 Charing Cross *1850*, at 9 in *1855*

STEWART, LEWIS.
13 Birchin Lane *1855*

STILL, ALEXANDER.
4 Leicester Place *1836*

STODART, DAVID.
Cutler and Surgical Instrument Maker. 401 Strand *1787-1839*

STOKER, ALFRED W.
88 Bishopsgate St. within *1880*

STONE, FREDRICK.
6 Greycoat St., Westminster *1855*. 4 Marchment St. in *1866*

STONE, FREDRICK.
80 Tonbridge St. *1890-1895*

STONE, WILLIAM BUTLER.
Phoenix Place, Ratcliffe Crescent *1866*

STONE, WILLIAM.
8 Queen St., Ratcliffe Crescent *1870-1875*

STOREY, JOHN FREDRICK.
246 Regent St. *1895*

Plate 156.
A working knife of some sort marked:

**J.W.STUTTER
MANUFACTURER
173 SHOREDITCH**

along with a large 6. It also bears the mark of a shield around which are the words:

LONDON MADE

STOUT BROTHERS.
10 West India Dock Road *1875-1905*

STOUT, WILLIAM.
2 & 3 Victoria Place, Commercial Road, Limehouse *1855*. 1 to 3 Victoria Place in *1860*.

STRATFORD, WILLIAM.
Working Cutler. 212 Tottenham Court Road *1829-1832*

STRONG, JAMES.
26 Moorgate St. 1905

STRUDWICK, THOMAS.
14 New Bond St. *1846-1850*

STRUDWICK, ARTHUR.
194 Morning Lane, Hackney *1915*

STUTTER, GILES.
Cutler. 75 Shoreditch *1822*

STUTTER, JOEL W.
Manufacturing Cutler. 184 High St., Shoreditch *1829-1875*. In *1880-1885* also at 133 Bishopsgate St. without and 138 Goswell Rd. *1890-1930*. 268 Bishopsgate and 173 Shoreditch High St. *1935-1940*. Only at 268 Bishopsgate *1945*

SUTTON, SAMUEL.
68 Old Bailey *1846-1850*. 144 Fleet St. in *1855*

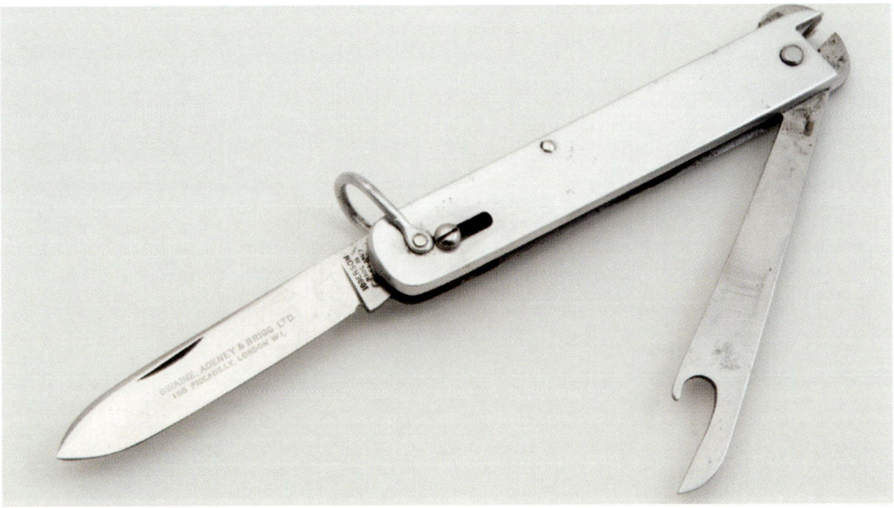

Plate 157.
Made for Swaine, Adney and Brigg by George Ibberson. This wire cutter knife is of a style known to date back to the 1st World War when officers were required to carry a pair of wire cutters. The ricasso of the blade is marked:

IBBERSON, MADE IN ENGLAND

along with their violin trademark and SHEFFIELD MADE. On the flat of the blade it is etched:

**SWAINE, ADNEY AND BRIGG LTD.
185 PICCADILLY
LONDON W1**

Plate 158.
Commando Knife made by George Ibberson and Co, and retailed by Swaine and Adeney. Stag grip, brass guard and commando blade which is beside the George Ibberson trade mark marked:

SWAINE & ADENEY LTD.
185 PICCADILLY
LONDON W1

A number of similar examples have been noted and the sturdy leather sheath is of a style noted on some other knives retailed by Swaine and Adeney.

SUTTON, WILLIAM.

144 Fleet St. and 68 Old Bailey *1836*, only at Fleet St. *1840-1850*

SWAINE ADENEY Ltd.-SWAINE ADENEY BRIGG & SON'S LIMITED

A firm whose lineage was through leather goods, umbrella, gentlemen's outfitters but who retailed a number of knives and other edged weapons such as swagger sticks with concealed blades. A number of their edged products were made by George Ibberson of Sheffield.

Founded in *1750* by a John Ross whose Whip making business was located at 238 Piccadilly, London W.1. The business was purchased by James Swaine business in *1798*, who had been foreman of a successful whip-making business in Holborn. The firm gained royal appointment to His Majesty King George III and to his sons, The Prince of Wales and the Dukes of York, Clarence, Kent, Cumberland and Cambridge.
The Royal appointments were renewed in the reigns of His Majesty George IV and His Majesty William IV. In the year *1835* James Swaine moved his business to larger premises at 185 Piccadilly. The business continued to flourish and in *1845* Edward Swaine took his nephew into partnership and Swaine Adeney was born.

Swaine Adeney products were exhibited at the 1851 Great London Exhibition and they won several prize medals for their leather goods.

The Briggs link starts with a Thomas Brigg and Son's which was established in *1836* at 23 St. James's Street. The company specialised in the manufacture of umbrellas, walking sticks and hunting crops.

The two firms amalgamated in 1943 During to become Swaine Adeney Brigg & Son's Limited and is still in business.

TACKLEY, E.
9 Charlton St. *1829-1860*

TANNER, RICHARD.
Working Cutler. 17 Brunswick St., Hackney Road *1832*

TAYLOR & MORRELL.
161 Oxford St. *1844-1846*

TAYLOR, J.
Heathcock Road, Strand *1822-1823*

TAYLOR, J & SON.
12 St. Martin's Church yard *1829*

TAYLOR, JOHN.
45 Edward St. Star Corner *1870*

TAYLOR, JOHN JAMES,
161 and 161A Oxford St. *1850*

TAYLOR, WILLIAM & SON.
22 Pavement, Finsbury *1832*

TAYLOR, WILLIAM BOWERS.
4 Pitt Place, Drury Lane *1855*

TEMPLE (K) & CROOK (F).
Cooks Knives. 20 Motcombe St., Belgrave Square *1875-1880*

THOMAS, ALBERT.
68 Aldersgate St. *1900*. 317 Upper St., Islington *1905*

THOMAS, JOHN.
Working Cutler. 425 Oxford St. *1822-1832*

THOMPSON, CHARLES, HENRY.
49 Carnaby St. *1860*. 79 Dean St., Soho *1866*

THOMPSON, GEORGE.
Working Cutler. 5 Duke's Row, Pimlico *1823*

THOMPSON, JAMES.
Great Windmill St. *1817-1843*. Taken over by MAW

THORNHILL.
With a history stretching back to *1734* Thornhill was a prolific maker of knives including some very high quality Bowies and folding knives. Originally founded by a Joseph Gibbs the firm by the early 19th century was known as Morley and Thornhill. This partnership was dissolved around *1820* with the firm of Morley and Co., manufacturing

An extract from "Camp Life and its Requirements" Part I *"Soldiers and their Equipment" by H.A.L. "The Old Shakarry". HAL is H.A. Levenson, soldier and explorer.*

Levenson was a great fan of Thornhill Knives. In his book: Hints to Sportsmen and Travellers published in 1874 he describes a belt and equipment and states: "Belt and Appurtenances I usually wore when in pursuit of large game, manufactured by Thornhill of 144 New Bond Street, the most practical man in the trade." When further describing his Hunting Knife, this being of the type described as the Old Shekarry's Hunting Knife in the catalogue shown he states "With one of the Thornhill's knives I can cut through a dollar."

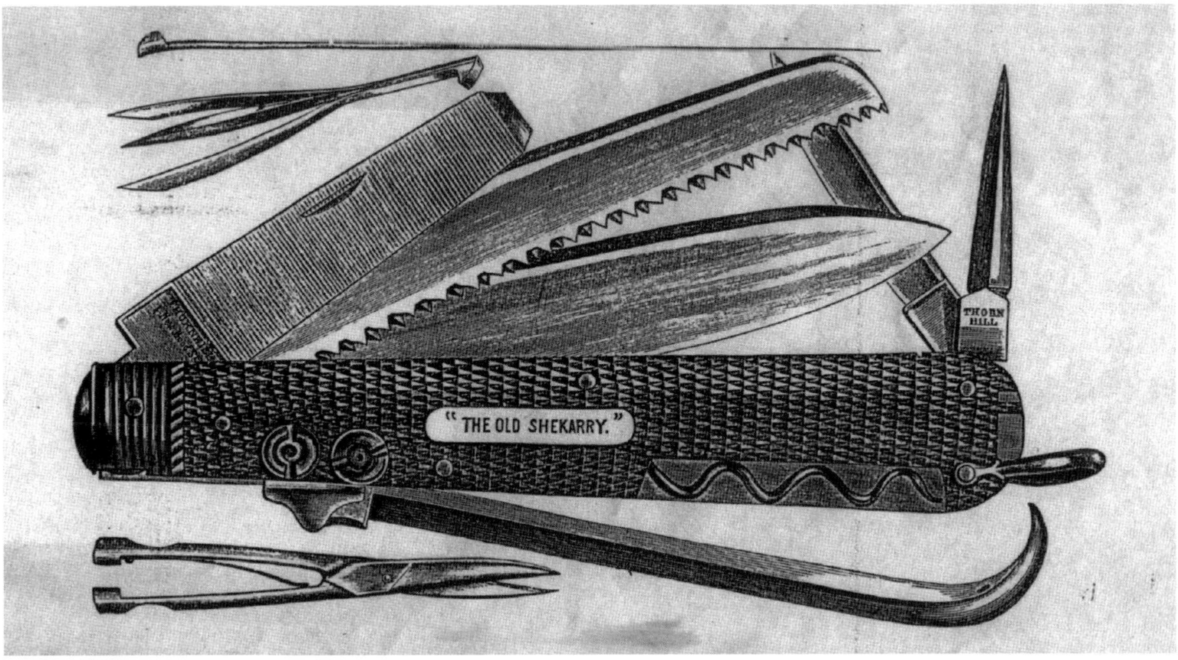

Plate 159.
This knife is the image of that shown on page 273 of *The Bowie Knife Book*. Size: blade 7 inches, 11.75 inches overall.

Plate 160.
A folding bowie marked with a VR crown and THORNHILL, LONDON. The grip conceals four tools, tweezers, pricker, scissors, and a small folding knife. The locket of the sheath carries a family crest. The chape has London silver hall marks for 1875.
Size: blade 11 inches, 15.75 inches overall.

Plate 161.
An example of a knife known as the ELLIS KNIFE the name of which is etched in a panel on the blade. The grip has ebony scales and contains probe and a small folding knife. The steel guard is pierced to accommodate the scabbard clip. The ricasso is marked:

V (CROWN) R
THORNHILL
LONDON

Size: blade 7.75 inches, 12.5 inches overall.

Plate 162.
Thornhill-made hunting axe. Rosewood scales fitted to a steel shaft. The hammer head of the axe is unusual in that it is cut to form an I I stamp.

Plate 163.
This interesting hunting style knife was carried by a member of the Coldstream Guards during the 1870/80s. The pommel cap is engraved with the guards badge and the name of the owner.

cutlers operating from 42 Leadenhall St. and the firm of Thornhill and Co. operating from 144 New Bond St. By *1822* two Thornhill's appear in the directory, Thornhill and Co. at 144 New Bond St., and W.J.S and F Thornhill 23 Fish St. Hill and 34 Castle St. Thornhill and Co. are listed in this same directory as working cutlers. The relationship between the two is not known.

In *1832* the entries are a little more specific being given as John James Thornhill 144 New Bond St. and William and Frederick Thornhill 23 Fish St. Hill. By *1836* only John James remained listed. In *1850* the name is recorded as Walter Thornhill but they are not at this stage listed as working cutlers carrying the notation that they are desk and dressing case makers. The entry continues in the form for a number of years but in 1885 the entry reads as follows

> *THORNHILL, WALTER & Co. 144 and 145 New Bond St., and 6 Little Bruton St. W. Cutlers to the Queen and their Royal Highnesses the Prince and Princess of Wales; 2 prize medals, Paris 1878, 2 medals Calcutta 1884. The entry notations also list them as Needle makers, desk and dressing case makers, razor makers, shears makers, and manufacturing cutlers.*

The *1886* entry provides an interesting insight into the origins of the Company as it states;

> *"by special appointment cutlers to the Queen, established 1734"*

Went out of business circa *1912* with the original premises being demolished.

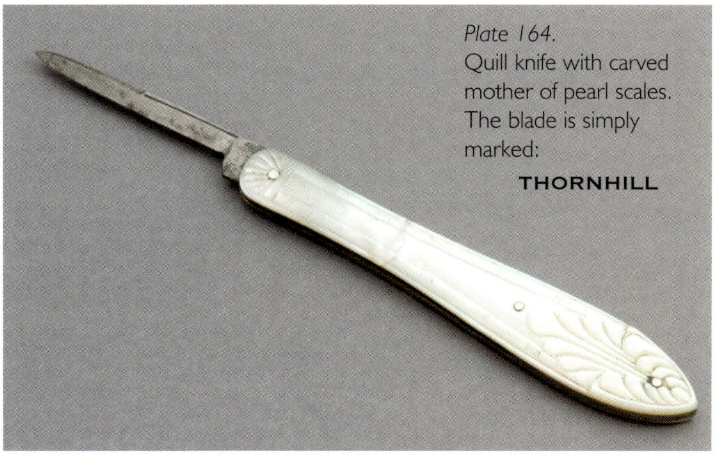

Plate 164.
Quill knife with carved mother of pearl scales. The blade is simply marked:

THORNHILL

Plate 165.
Push Dagger which has appeared in Flayderman's book: *The Bowie Knife*. This highly unusual knife is etched on one side

THE IRISH "THUG" KNIFE

and on the other a dedication etching which reads:

DR LAWDER, HYDHERBAD AVEC LES COMPLIMENTS DE M GEO SHEPARD PAGE

The knife is also marked with the rarely seen Thornhill trade mark of the Thornbush along with:

V (CROWN) R
W THORNHILL & CO
LONDON

Plate 166.
A knife style typically known as the Wingfield knife by THORNHILL. Which on the sheath locket bears the crest and initials of a member of the Courtenay family-the Earls of Devon.

Plate 167.
A rather plain but superb hunting knife by Thornhill. The blade is marked with:

V (CROWN) R
THORNHILL
LONDON

The barrel shaped grip has chequered horn scales and the hilt contains the usual probe and scissors. The sheath locket is dated 1859

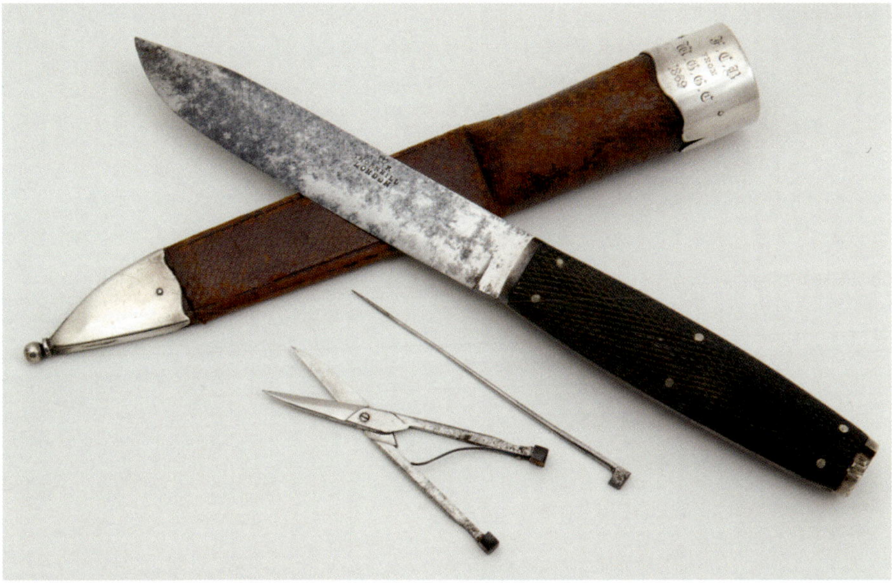

THURKLE.

Numerous addresses in the Soho, High Holborn area of London. *1766-1920* A Francis Thurkle was listed has Master of the Cutlers Company in *1766* when his prime business was as a hilt maker with an address in New Street Square He was later joined by his son Francis II and the firm became Thurkle and Co. A number of further changes took place in the Company name with the old Francis dying and Francis II's son George joining the Company. There was also a short-lived partnership with Skynner. By *1827* the Company was run by Abraham Thurkle with an address in Dean Street, Soho, London. The company had evolved into one making both small arms and swords.

In *1834/35* another Thurkle joined the firm-a Benjamin and he moved the business to 104 High Holborn in *1864*. About this time an Edward Thurkle appears with an address at 200 High Street, Holborn, however by *1865* he his back at 104 High Holborn. His relationship with Abraham is not known. Edward either liked or was forced to move as between *1876* and *1899* his address was 5 Denmark Street, Soho.

Plate 168.
Plain spear point Bowie with stag grip steel guard and pommel cap. This piece is not of the same quality as other Thornhill knives. Ricasso marked:

V (CROWN) R
THORNHILL
LONDON

Plate 169.
A very unusual knife whose exact purpose is unknown. The leaf-shaped blade is flat on one side but ground with a central ridge on the other. Rosewood scales with pouch style sheath. Ricasso marked:

V (CROWN) R
THORNHILL
LONDON

Size: blade 8.25 inches, 14.25 inches overall.

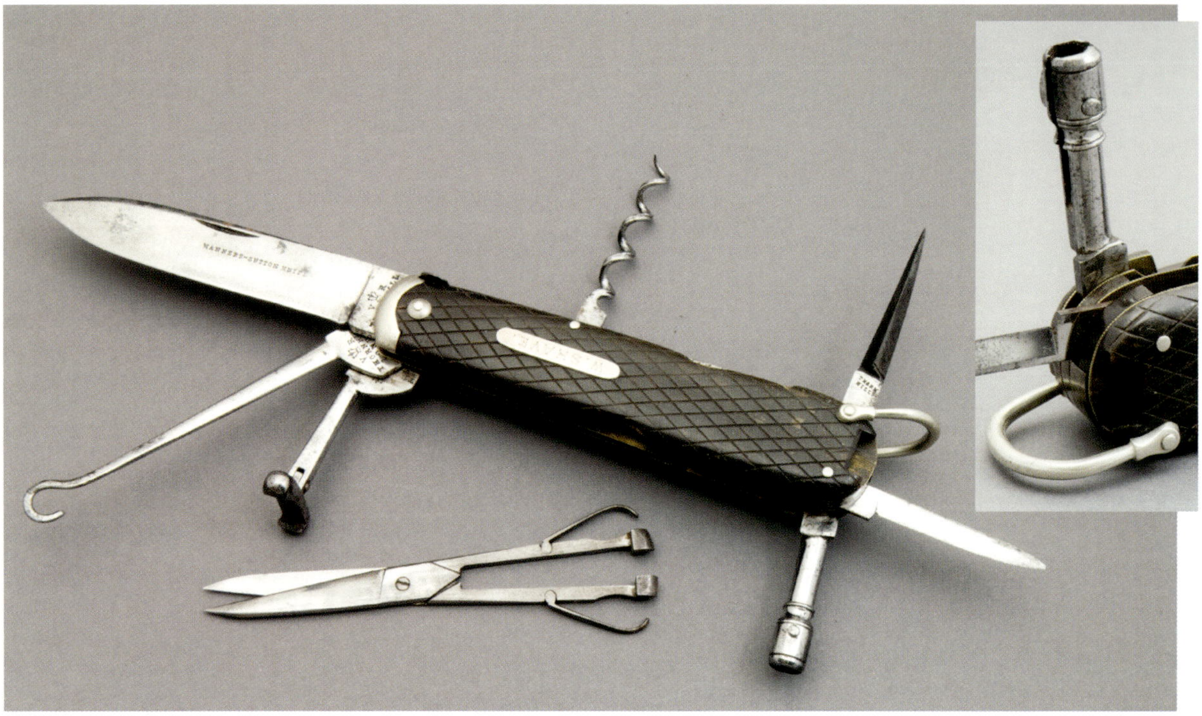

Plate 170.
A magnificent gentleman's shooting knife marked on the main blade:

THE
MANNERS SUTTON KNIFE

along with the previous owners name of the shield. The knife besides the main blade has a cartridge extractor, nipple key, small pen blade, corkscrew, punch, and within the grip probe, tweezers and scissors. The main blade is stamped on the ricasso:

V (CROWN) R
THORNHILL
LONDON

Plate 171.
Hunting knife with the blade marked:

V (CROWN) R
W. THORNHILL & CO
LONDON

Plate 172.
A Khyber-style knife with horn scales and blade which is formed to provide an integral bolster. Blade marked:

V (CROWN) R
THORNHILL
LONDON

Plate 173.
This Thornhill knife is marked on the blade flat:

DARROCH KNIFE

Plate 174.
A 5 blade folder with surgical instrument style lock. The hilt contains a small screwdriver, pencil, scissors and tweezers. The circular shield bears a monogram consisting of the letters PF surmounted by a ducal crown indicating ownership by a titled family. The blade is simply marked:

THORNHILL

172

WALTER THORNHILL,

POPULAR SPORTING KNIVES.

THORNHILL'S PAGET KNIFE, 42/-,

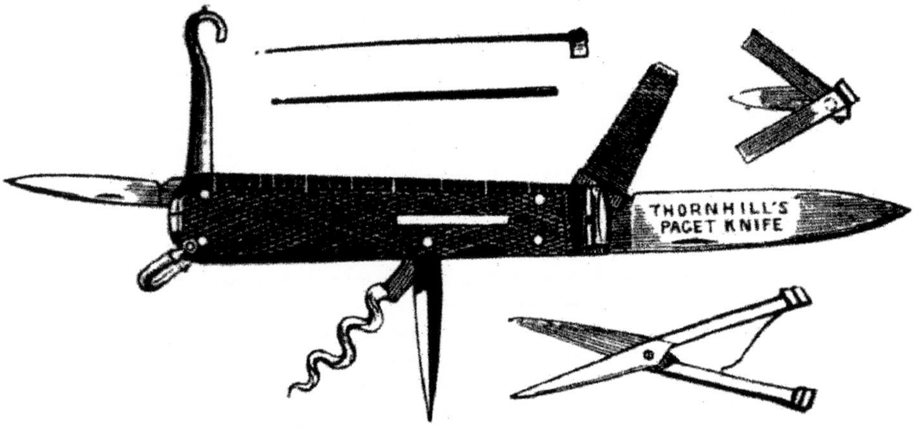

Is a most useful pattern knife for general purposes, and is a true friend to the sportsman and traveller. It contains a large and small blade, a file and turnscrew in one, a button hook, corkscrew, borer for making holes in straps, good useful pair of scissors, lancet, tweezers, gun pick, bodkin, and inch rule.

It is made in four sizes, 5-in., 4½-in., 4-in., 42/- each, and a small size for the waistcoat pocket, 3 inches long, 35/-

STALKING KNIVES.

The Corbett, 45/- Dalkeith, 45/- Darrock, 55/- Graham (in sheath), 21/- Ossulston, 28/- Percy, 32/- Prince of Wales, 63/- Richmond, 18/6.

HUNTING KNIVES.

The Bedale Hunt, 35/- Berkeley Hunt, 35/- Coke Hunting Knife, 21/- North Warwickshire Hunt, 18/6 Manchester, 42/-

FISHING KNIVES.

The Adair, 42/- Coke Fishing Knife, 32/ Falmouth, 55/- Guest, 38/- Pennell, 25/- Walton, 35/- Wingfield (in sheath), £5 5s. 6d., see page 4.

THORNHILL'S HAREWOOD KNIFE.

A very thin knife containing one large spring blade, one small blade, corkscrew, borer, lancet, tweezers, gunpick, and turnscrew. Made in four sizes, same as Paget Knife, 18/6, 21/-, 26/., and 28/-.

THORNHILL'S CLAYTON LANCER KNIFE.

Designed by Capt. Clayton, of the 9th Lancers.

It is extremely thin in order to be able to be worn attached to a belt under the tunic.

Contains one large spring blade, borer, corkscrew, and gun-pick. Price, 25/-

THORNHILL'S RANDOLPH KNIFE.

Designed by Col. Randolph, for service in the Crimea.

Contains a large spring blade, small blade, a turnscrew, the sides of which form a file and the edge a cutting file for wire, button hook, gouge, borer, corkscrew, pair of scissors, lancet, tweezers, gun-pick, pair of compasses, two steel screws and nuts for repairing traces, hoof picker, gimlet, inch scale marked on outside of knife; it has a D loop for attaching it to the belt, or it can be carried in a leather case. Price 75/-

COUNTRY KNIVES.

The Eglington, 35/- Escric, 32/- Jolliffe, 35/- Kitchener, 34/- Potts, 38/- Blandford, 42/- Milton, 12/6 Botanical, 25/-, &c.

144, NEW BOND STREET.

CUTLER TO THE QUEEN.

LADIES' INSTRUMENT KNIVES.

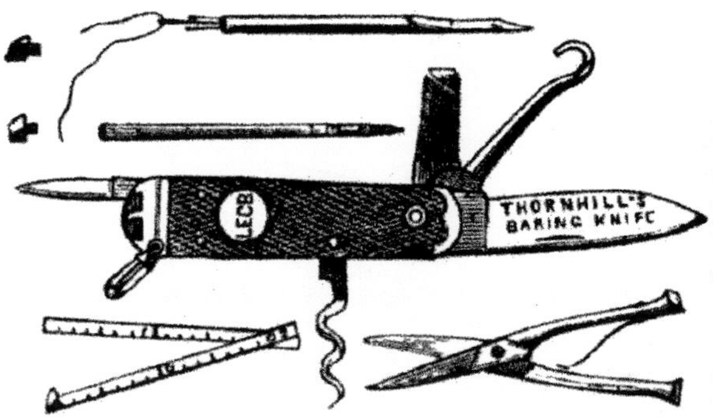

THORNHILL'S BARING KNIFE,

2¾ inches long.

Contains one large spring blade, one small blade, button hook, turnscrew and file for cutting wire used in fancy work, a corkscrew, a needle case and pencil combined, elongating penholder, with gold pen and reserved leads for pencil, pair of scissors, and a folding 4 in measure. Price 4½ guineas.

THORNHILL'S Improved Baring Knife.

Contains a pair of compasses, lancet, and tweezers in addition to the above. Price 5 gs.

The Miniature Paget Knife. 35/-

The Miniature Harewood Knife. 18/6.

THORNHILL'S MINIATURE KNIFE.

1¾ inches long.

Contains large and small blade, button hook, pair of scissors, nail instrument, and silver picker; made with Pearl, Ivory, Gold, Silver, or Russia Leather sides. Prices 21/- to 63/-

THORNHILL'S LADY'S KNIFE.

2¼ inches long.

Contains one large blade, small blade, button hook, stiletto, corkscrew, and nail files; also made with the addition of a pair of scissors. Price 12/6.

The Ladies' Wingfield Knife in Silver Mounted Sheath, £5 5/-

THE CHILD'S FIRST KNIFE, 1/-, 1/6, and 2/-

With round end blade and not too sharp.

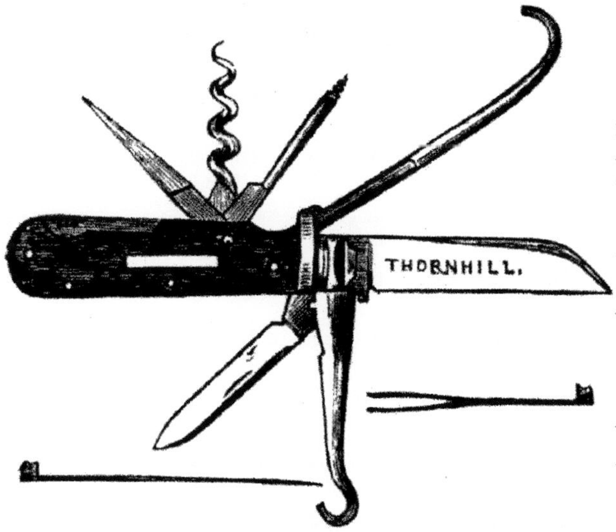

BOY'S INSTRUMENT KNIFE.

Contains one large blade, one small blade, button hook, corkscrew, borer, gimblet, horse pick, nutcrackers, tweezers, gun-pick, and name plate.

Price 8/6.

The same knife may be had with a saw instead of a button hook.

Also of a larger size.

Price 10/6.

Also a similar knife not quite so complete,

Price 5/6.

SMOKING KNIVES.

The Gleichen, 32/-   The Skeleton (all steel), 12/6.

The Smokers' "WAISTCOAT POCKET KNIFE," 2 inches long and very thin, containing one large and one small blade, glove button hook, nail file, and cigar piercer, 8/6.

ESTABLISHED 1734.

THORNHILL'S SHEATH KNIVES.

THE OLD SHEKARRY'S HUNTING KNIFE.

For large Game. Price, in Pigskin Sheath, 42/-

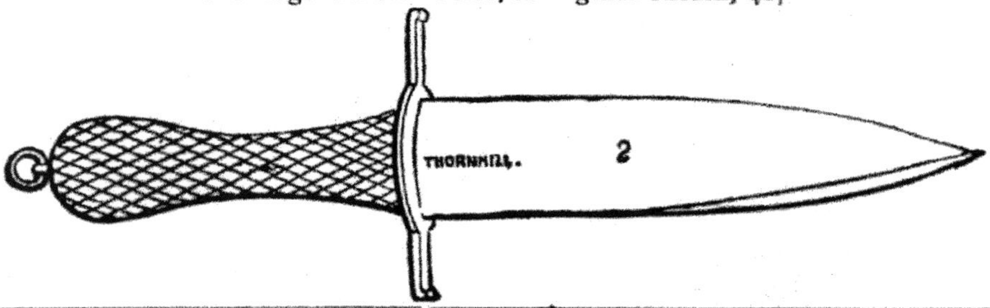

THORNHILL'S GRAHAM SKINNING KNIFE.

Price, in Pigskin Sheath, 21/-
The Graham Knife may also be had with instruments similar to the Wingfield Knife.
Price, in Pigskin Sheath, 38/-

THORNHILL'S WINGFIELD KNIFE.

Price, with Silver Mounts and in Silver Mounted Sheath, 5 guineas.

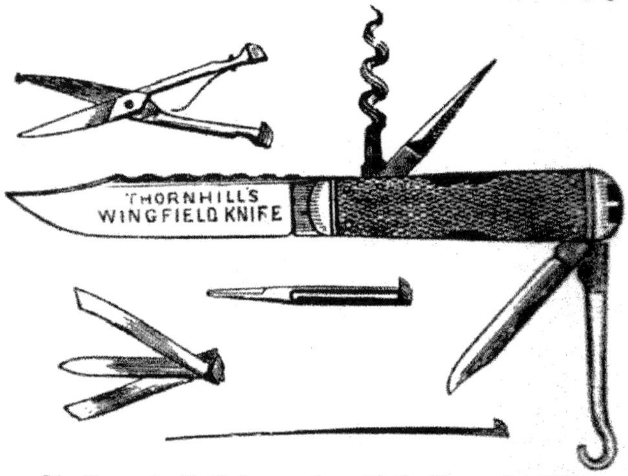

The Favourite Knife for wearing with the Norwegian Belt.

THORNHILL'S SHAKESPEARE KNIFE.

In Sheath, 31/6.

THORNHILL'S NORWEGIAN SHEATH KNIVES.

Of a variety of patterns, with and without instruments.

WALTER THORNHILL having a Factory in London, and employing several particularly clever and ingenious workmen, is enabled to undertake the manufacture of any peculiar or out-of-the way pattern knife that may be required.

WALTER THORNHILL,

CUTLER TO THE QUEEN, SILVERSMITH, &c.,

144, NEW BOND STREET, LONDON.

Established 1734.

Printed by Walter Thornhill, 5000 | 5 | 75.

In *1899* a split took place in the firm with the part owned by Edward being taken over by J. R. Gaunt and Son. George Thurkle who owned the remaining portion continued alone working at 3 different addresses between *1900* and *1912*.

In *1913* George Thurkle was now at 149 High Holborn, and was the sole bearer of the name to continue working. In *1920* and in the aftermath of the World War I when business proved difficult the firm was it was sold to Wilkinson Sword.

The Thurkle has primarily been associated with the manufacture of swords and no Bowie or other similar knife has been located which bears their name. Also the name does not appear in any of the standard references on Bowies. The only reference found to them making any sort of knife is in relation to a Scottish Dirk of the Liverpool Scottish, a volunteer regiment raised during the Boer War (see The Scottish Dirk by James D Foreman) The Boer War took place between *1899* and *1902* during the period when George was part of the Company. This piece is however stated as being made by a C Thurkle, Soho, London. The reference must therefore partially be in error because no family member with the initial C was operating during this period, it is more likely to be G for George.

THURLING, GEORGE.
Butchers Cutler. 64 Long Lane *1890-1910*. *1915-1935* also at 15 Newbury St. 76 Long Lane, West Smithfield *1940*.

THURLOW, GEORGE.
58 Mortimer St. 1866 -1875.

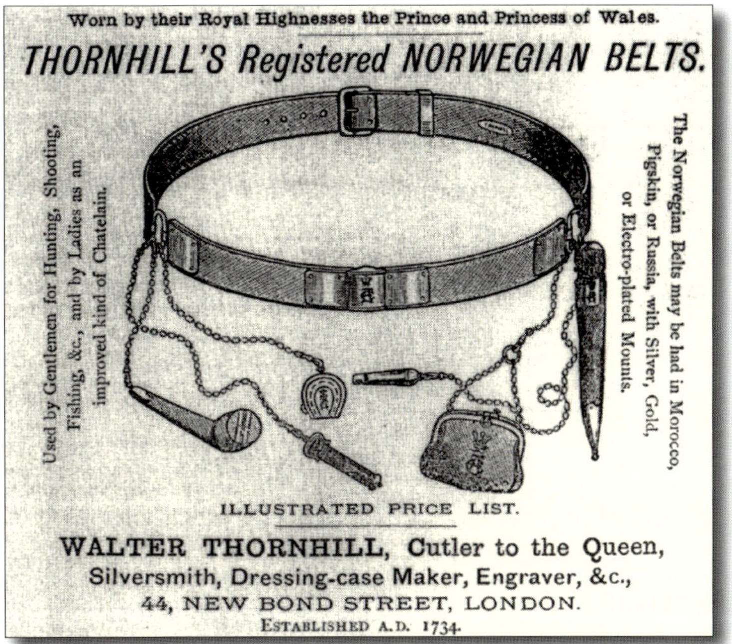

Advertisement from 1881 for THORNHILL'S Registered NORWEGIAN BELTS

TIDBURY, CHARLES.
Cutler and razor maker. 20 St. Martin's Court *1820 -1829*

TIDBURY, ELIZABETH.
20 St. Martin's Court *1832*

TIERCELIN JOHN JOSEPH.
1789-1838. Founded by Joseph a Huguenot who is listed as a razor maker and cutler at 7 Piccadilly. By the early *1800's* they were at 3 Piccadilly as Tiercelin and Son. In *1820* his son John took over the business, at which time he is also recorded as Cutler to the Prince Regent. John had been an apprentice to Priest. Went out of business in *1839*.

TIMM, J.
75 Leather Lane, Holborn *1823-1829*

TISSINGTON, GEORGE.
6 Sutherland Terrace *1860-1870*. 20 Caledonian Rd. in *1875-1885*

TOMLIN, JOSEPH.
36 Leather Lane *1840*. 9 Market St. in *1846*

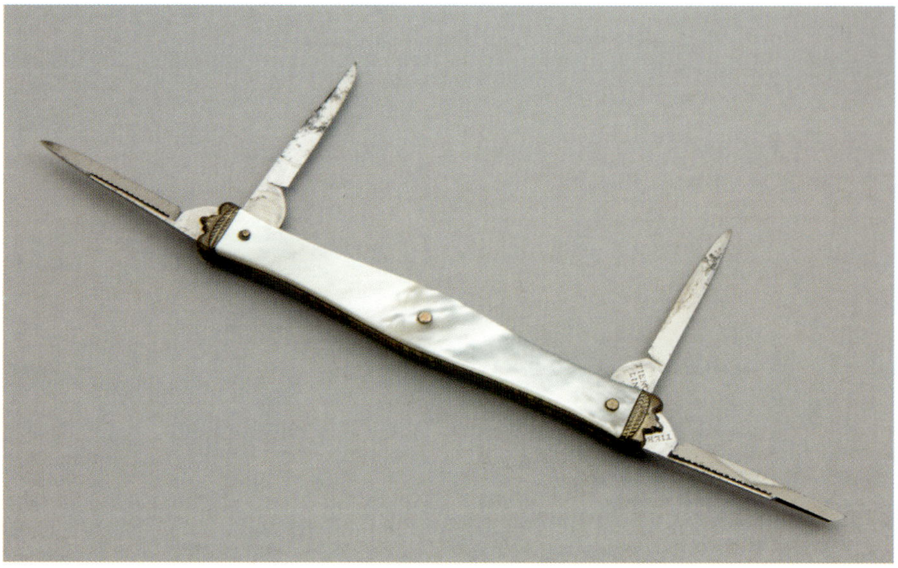

Plate 175.
Of the highest quality and a very early knife this piece has 4 quill knife blades, mother of pearl scales. The mounts are of gold and the back springs have gold wash along with superb file-work. The blades are marked:
TIERCELIN

TONKS, WILLIAM HENRY.
Working Cutler and razor maker.
50 Burlington Arcade *1832-1840*

TRIMBY, GEORGE & Co.
41 Queen St. Cheapside *1866-1870*

TUDOR, HENRY.
14 Bridle Lane, Golden Square
1885-1895

TURNER, EDWARD. CHARLES.
44 St. John St., Smithfield *1846-1850.*
75 St. John St. *1855-1866.*
113 St. John's St. *1870 -1875*

TURNER, EDWARD CHARLES & Co.
153 St. John's St. *1890*

TURNER, JOHN.
50 Tothill St. *1832-1846*

TURNER, JOHN L. B.
10 Old Compton Road *1866-1870*

TURNER, JOSEPH.
29 Charlotte St., Whitechapel *1832*

TURNER & KNOTT.
153 St. John's St. *1880-1885*

TURNER, MILLER & Co Ltd.
155 Edgware Rd., and 7, 8, 9 and 10 Burwood Mews, Edgeware Rd.
1915-1925

TURNER, ROBERT.
50 Tothill St. *1822-1829*

TURNER, Mrs. SARAH
23 Frith St., Soho *1855*

TURPIN, RICHARD.
25 Eyre St. Hill *1846-1850.*
29 High St., Kensington *1855-1875*

TURTON, JOHN & Co. Ltd.
Manufacturing Cutler. 3 Amen Corner *1925* 23 Thavies Inn.
1935-1940

TYLER, WILLIAM WICKHAM.
9 Ebury St., Pimlico *1855-1875.*

UNDERWOOD.
Along with Thornhill, Hill and Son one of the more frequently found London makers. The history of the cutler bearing this name has two separate threads: commences circa *1791* with a Yeeling Underwood who was sworn free of the Cutlers Company in *1791* after an apprenticeship with Yeeling Charlwood. The other branch of the name was Henry Thomas Underwood who was also indentured to Yeeling Charlwood in *1791*. It is not actually clear if there was any blood relationship between Yeeling Underwood and Henry Thomas but given their backgrounds as recorded by Southwick it appears they where not related.

Yeeling Underwood held a number of positions with the Cutlers Company including that of master in *1819*. He did however die in *1834*. He is listed in the *1820*, *1832* and *1834* directories as being located at 8 Great Turnstile. A George Underwood, presumably his son, is then listed at 8 Great Turnstile but is not recorded for a number of years but then makes a re-appearance in *1860* as George Underwood and Co. This however was a short-lived reappearance as although they are listed in *1866* there is no trace in *1870* or thereafter.

The other branch of the name i.e. Henry Thomas succeeded the business of Charlwood when Sarah Charlwood willed the business to him and he established premises at Russell Court in *1803*.
Listed in *1820* at the Corner of Russell Court, Drury Lane and in *1822* occupying premises at 74 Drury Lane and 56 Haymarket. Drury Lane is dropped from the list by *1832*. The firm remained under the same name and Haymarket address until the early *1860's*, which coincides with Henry's death in *1860*, when it became known as Underwood and Farrant. Although it does not appear that they stamped this name on their products as knives of much later than this *1860's* date are found just with the Underwood stamp. Remained in business under that name until circa *1925*.

Although there is no clear family link it is possible that Henry Thomas was related to a John Underwood who died in *1803*. He provides a link back to James Bernardeau (see frontispiece) as they all operated from Russell Court.

Plate 176.
Ink Eraser with rose wood handle. Blade is marked:
UNDERWOOD
56 HAYMARKET

Plate 177.
Folding pruning saw with surgical lock rose wood scales nickel bolster and scales. Blade is marked:

UNDERWOOD
LONDON

Plate 178.
Tea plantation knife, rosewood scales. Ricasso marked simply:

UNDERWOOD

Another Underwood does however appear for a short period. A Miss M Underwood is recorded in *1839-1840* at 8 Burlington Arcade, there is no trace of the name in *1844* and whether there was any family link with the Yeeling or Henry is unknown.

Plate 179.
This magnificent Bowie is similar to that shown in *The Bowie Knife Book*, page 247, except that this knife has a spear point blade. The ricasso is stamped:

UNDERWOOD
56 HAYMARKET
LONDON

The similarities of the guard and grip to that in *the Bowie Knife Book* leads one to assume they are by the same maker.
Size: blade 11 inches, 16.5 inches overall.

Plate 180.
Large bowie with the owners monogram of ERNR etched on the blade. Chequered ebony grip, blade is stamped on the ricasso:

UNDERWOOD
56 HAYMARKET
LONDON

Plate 181.
Small hunting style knife in the Woodsman's form. Blade is marked:

UNDERWOOD.

Plate 182.
A fine Edwardian period hunting knife with its very well made tubular-style sheath. Rosewood scales. Blade stamped:

E (CROWN) R
UNDERWOOD
56 HAYMARKET
LONDON

A smaller version of this knife has been noted.

Plate 183.
Having one of the typical London features of a scabbard/cross-guard clip a fine bowie by Underwood which besides their name and address which includes the name LONDON bears the V (crown) R stamp.

Plate 184.
Of the general same pattern as the previous knife except is this example the grip is if horn. The pommel cap is engraved G.H.EVANS. The blade is marked:

V (CROWN) R
UNDERWOOD
56 HAYMARKET
LONDON

Plate 185.
Of generally the same design as the previous two knives this piece has a spear point blade which is marked in the same manner as above. The pommel cap is engraved with the name:

CECIL RUSSELL.

Plate 186.
This fine skinning knife has a bolster integral with the blade and tang, and chequered ebony scales. The blade, similar in style to some San Francisco knives, is marked:

V (CROWN) R
UNDERWOOD
56 HAYMARKET
LONDON

Plate 187.
Bearing the crown VR stamp this hunting axe is similar to others seen with other makers names. The piece has rosewood scales on the shaft and a fold-out saw which is stamped:

UNDERWOOD
LONDON

Such axes were generally sold with a belt pouch but these are rarely seen today.

Plate 188.
A highly unusual push dagger with rosewood grip. Blade is stamped:

UNDERWOOD
LONDON

Plate 189.
This very unusual knife of yataghan form was either made for export, presentation or for someone who was going to the Balkans area. The horn scales are decorated with silver pins, and the bolster and back of the tang is chased with various designs. The blade is marked:

V (CROWN) R
UNDERWOOD
LONDON

Size: blade 14 inches, 19.75 inches overall.

UNITED CUTLERY & HARDWARE WORKS (LONDON) Ltd.

Manufacturing Cutler. 8 and 9 Chiswell St. *1930*

Plate 190.
An early 20th century hunting knife with ebony grip with blade marked:
VERINDER
ST. PAULS
It is highly likely this is a Sheffield product.

Plate 191.
A very early folding dirk with surgical instrument style lock marked H.V. St Paul's. Stag scales.

VAUGHAN, D.

Working Cutler. 1 King's Head Court *1823-1829*

VERINDER.

John Verinder started his apprenticeship in *1765* with a Joseph Bayzand. Bayzand died during the period of the apprenticeship and Verinder continued under a James Lyon. Lyon worked from St Paul's Churchyard and once he became free so did Verinder.

John Verinder' son Henry was a Master of the Cutlers Company on two occasions. He operated from 79 St Paul's Churchyard and is variously listed as Henry Verinder and Co. working cutler and as Henry Verinder working cutler and wholesale. According to Southwick

Plate 192.
An early hunting knife by VERINDER which bears the name and address:

VERINDER
ST. PAULS
LONDON

Stag grip and a cross-guard which appear to have been fitted incorrectly i.e. the finials are up- pointing. The sheath is unusual in that it retains its frog.

he died in *1846* however the directory for *1850* still list a Henry Verinder. However it would seem that either his brother or his son retained the name after his death.

John Richard was also the son of John but served his apprenticeship under his older brother Henry. John Henry Verinder was the son of Henry and served his apprenticeship under his father. He sworn free in *1828* being recorded as Cutler of St. Paul's Churchyard.

The firm continued under the name Henry until at least *1855* but in *1860* it is recorded as Mrs E Verinder 79 St Paul's Churchyard. In *1870* it is listed as John Verinder and remained as such until at least *1887*. In *1890* it appears as Henry Verinder still at the St. Paul's address. However the link with St Paul's was broken circa *1895* when he is recorded at 17 A Ludgate Hill. His name still appears in *1925* but not in *1930* or thereafter.

VICKERS, HARRY.

78 Red Lion St. Clerkenwell *1875*

VICKERY, J. C.

183 Regent Street *1890-1930*
A retail business that was established circa *1890* by a John Vickery and a Thomas Hobbs at 183 Regent Street. Listed as dressing case and bag makers, jewellers, silversmiths, stationers and dealers in fancy goods. The partnership was dissolved in *1891* with Vickery continuing the business at 181 and 183 Regent Street. In the period *1900* to *1925* it variously occupied premises at New Burlington Arcade, and at 145 and 147 Regent Street along with the first floors of 143. 145 and 148 Regent Street and a part of 149. The firm failed in *1930*. The company was however continued under the Vickery name for a numbers of years by James Walker Ltd.

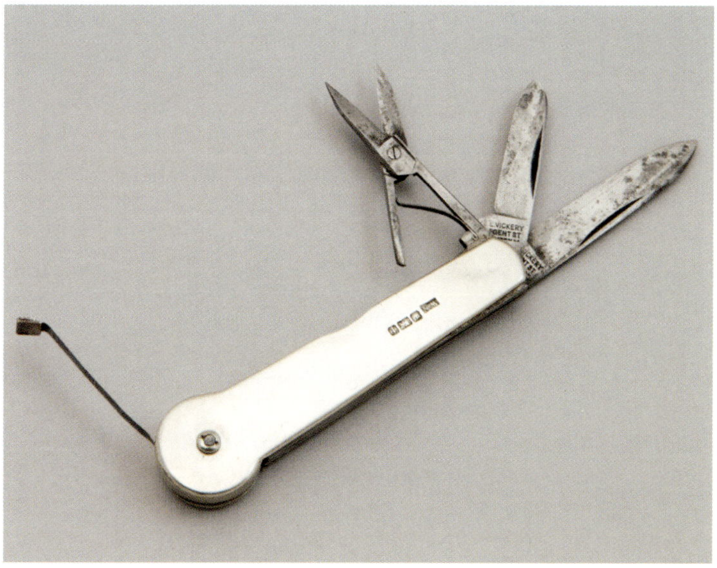

Plate 193.
All metal knife with nickel silver scales which has a small retractable ruler, scissors, main and pen blades which are both marked:

J.E.VICKERY
REGENT ST

VICTORIA & WESTMINSTER SAW, TOOL & CUTLERY WORKS (F.E. OXLEY)

Working razors and scissors a speciality. 9 Tachbrook St. Pimlico *1935-1945*

VINCE, GEORGE.

Manufacturing Cutler. 1 Yates Rental's, Clerkenwell *1855-1870*

VINCENT, JOHN.

201 Hoxton Old Town *1855-1866*

VINING, RICHARD.

Working Cutler, razor maker and Surgical Instrument Maker.
125 Regent St. *1832-1850*
(Sometimes listed as Vinning). As VINING, Mrs. HANNAH. 125 Regent St. in *1855* (Business taken over by Mechi)

VORSTER, R& H.

Manufacturing Cutler. Billiter Square Buildings *1900-1910*

WADDINGTON, HENRY.
4 Amen Corner, Mitcham Road, Tooting *1935-1945*

WADDINGTON, JOHN THOMAS.
154 Borough High St. *1900-1940*

WADE, ALFRED & Co.
Manufacturing Cutler. 98 Great Tower St. *1925*

WALKER & HOLTZAPFFEL
(Retail) Ltd. 61 Baker St. *1935*. See also HOLTZAPFFEL

WALLACE BROTHERS.
Manufacturing Cutler. 63 Basinghall St. *1900-1920*, also at 62 *1915-1920*. 87 Queen Victoria St. *1925*

WALLACE BROTHERS, and HENRY & SONS.
8 and 9 Clerkenwell Green *1900*

WALLIS, THOMAS & Co.
Holborn Circus *1905-1910*

WALSH, JOHNATHAN.
12 St. Bartholomew's St. *1839*

WARD, FREDERICK WILLIAM.
Cutler and Surgical Instrument Maker. 67 Hackney Rd. *1839*

WARD, GEORGE.
23 Clerkenwell Close *1836*

WARD, GEORGE.
6 Providence Place, Kentish Town *1855-1866*

WARD, GEORGE.
109 Kentish Town Road *1870*

WARD, GEORGE.
8 and 9 Clerkenwell Green *1920-1925*

WARD, GEORGE & SONS.
16 Clerkenwell Green *1935-1940*

WARD, HENRY.
10 Yates Rents, Clerkenwell *1850-1866*

WARD, HENRY.
24 Clerkenwell Green *1875*

WARD, HENRY & SON.
8 and 9 Clerkenwell Green *1885-1915*

WARD, Mrs. JANE.
18 Lowther Arcade *1870*, also at 19 in *1875*, a Miss Alice Ward also listed at the same addresses in *1875*

WARD, JESSE.
Old Chapel Row, Kentish Town *1832*

WARD, JOHN.
Working Cutler. 16 Artillery St. *1822-1832*. As John and Son in 1836. In *1840-1850* as WARD, Mrs E and Son.

WARD, JOHN.
3 Artillery St. *1855*, at 16 in *1860-1866*

WARD, MATTHEW HENRY.
Working Cutler. 442 Mile End Rd. *1910-1935*. 494 Mile End Rd. *1940-1945*

WARD, THOMAS & SONS Ltd.
Manufacturing Cutler. Morley House, Holborn Viaduct *1930*. 26 to 30 Holborn Viaduct *1935-1940*

WARDER, PERVIVAL.
149 Westbourne Grove *1900-1915*

WARING & GILLOW Ltd.
164 to 180 Oxford St. *1920-1930*

Plate 194.
Dating from the WW2 period a fighting knife, and next to it a slightly smaller version.
Both knives are etched on the blade:

W J WATERER
55 YEARS
SWORDMAKER &
CUTLER
9 PUGHS PLACE
CARNABY ST
LONDON W1
ENGLAND

Plate 195.
This exceptionally fine piece of London cutlery bears the Watson name. This knife has a hilt with of a waisted shape with chequered ebony scales secured by 5 pins. Steel cross-guard and spear point blade:

WATSON
29 OLD BOND ST
LONDON

along with the stamp:

LONDON MADE

on the blade.
Size: 8.5 inches, 13.5 inches overall.

WARNER THOMAS.
25 Sackville St. *1829-1855*

WARNER THOMAS.
67 Park St. Grosvner Square *1860*

WARNER THOMAS.
12 Upper Seymour St. *1866.*
43 Queen St., Edgeware Road *1870*

WARREN & RUDGLEY.
20-21 Chenies Mews *1826-1887*

WASS, R.
Patent razor maker to HRH the Prince Regent and manufacturer of cutlery. 76 Cornhill *1820.*

WATERER.
W. J. W. J. Waterer is something of an enigma because despite the etching on a knife stating that he was a Sword maker and Cutler for 55 years virtually nothing is known about him. He was not recorded in the *1935* or earlier directories but in the *1940* directory is listed under Sword Cutlers and Manufacturers as William John Waterer 9 Pugh's Place, Carnaby St. and he remained at this address until *1958.* Some very basic biographical details are however available from the census returns and death records. Born in *1874* he is listed with an age of 27 and occupation of sword cutler in the *1901* census. Ten years earlier in the *1891* census he is also listed as sword cutler. This seems a little strange because with an age of 17 he is more than likely to have been an apprentice rather that a fully qualified sword cutler. He died in *1964.*

WATERMAN & ADWAS.
Eden St. Hampsted Row *1885*

WATERMAN, CHARLES.
31 Meridith St., Clerkenwell *1846.*
13 Duck Lane, Wardour St. in *1855*

WATERMAN, CHARLES.
182 Seymour St., Euston and 24 Clerkenwell Green. *1870* latter address dropped in *1875* but note HENRY WARD at this address *1875*

WATSON.
A number of Watson's appear in the trade directories and other references but it is not totally clear if they were all related though the commonality of some addresses would appears to indicate that some were indeed related. In the LONDON ARMS TRADE there are references to 5 Watson's i.e.

WATSON & HANCOCK.
Gun and rifle makers. 308 HIGH HOLBORN 1886-1890

WATSON, THOMAS WILLIAM.
Rifle Manufacturers. 4 Pall Mall 1878-1884

WATSON BROTHERS.
Gun and Rifle makers, and sword cutlers. 4 Pall Mall 1885-1895 and 29 Old Bond St. *1896-1920*

WATSON JAMES.
35 Queen Victoria St. *1892*

WATSON, WILLIAM & SON.
Gun and Rifle makers. 313 High Holborn *1868-1881,* 308 High Holborn *1882-1885*

In the cutlers section of the *1832* trade directories a Mrs Ann Watson of 26 St. John's Square appears as a working cutler, there is however no trace in *1836* or subsequent years. The next appearance of a Watson is c.*1855* when there are two entries for a Henry Watson, one at 9 King St., Lower Road,

Plate 196.
Large folding locking jack knife bearing the name. Stag scales.

WATSON & SON
308 HIGH HOLBORN

the other at 16 Norton Folgate. In *1860* only one Henry is listed being at 9 King St. There are no further entries for Watson until *1885* when W Watson and Son of 308 High Holborn makes an appearance. In *1886* the name has become Watson and Hancock. No mention is found in *1895*. However the next appearance of the name is in *1908* with a Watson. J.J of 25 Richmond St. This was however a very short-lived appearance as there is no trace in *1910* or after.

WATSON, SON & Co.
70A Basinghall St. *1920.*

WEATHERLEY, WILLIAM ELLIOT.
186 Fleet St. *1829-1832*

Plate 197.
Stag handle bowie marked:

WATSON & SON
308
HIGH HOLBORN

WEBB, JOHN.
Butchers Cutler. 14 Newbury St.
1925-1935

WEBB & REEVES.
Butchers Cutler. 9 Newbury St.
1920

WEBSTER, JAMES.
8 Long Lane, Smithfield *1855.*

WEBSTER, JAMES.
49 Rochester Row *1866*,
at 25 Bishopsgate *1870*

WEBSTER, JOHN.
70 Bunhill Row *1866-1870*

WEDELL, S.
Working Cutler. 57 Chiswell St.
1915-1920

WEDGEWOOD, RALPH & SON.
9 Cornhill *1866-1875*

WEEDON, THOMAS.
Cutler and Surgical Instrument Maker. 18 Little Eastcheap, 42 Heart St. *1789-1856*

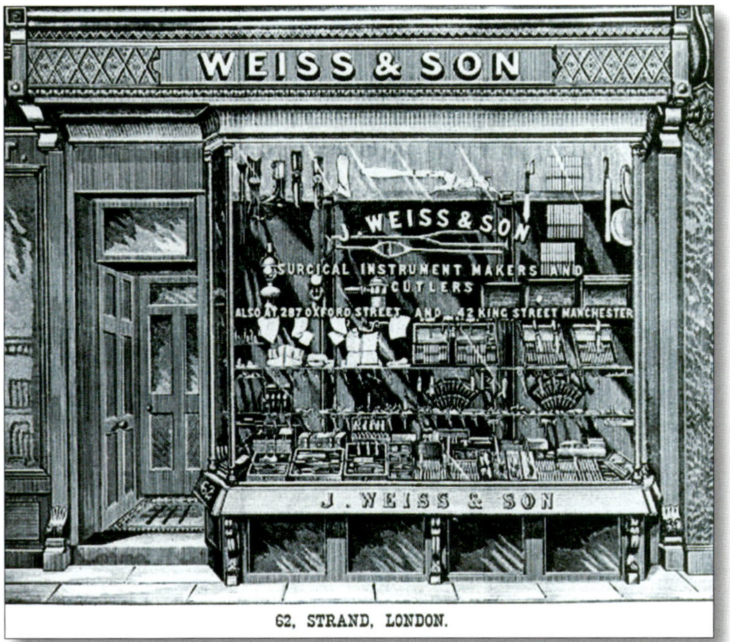

The shop frontage of Weiss premises in the Strand

WEBSTER, JAMES.
49 Rochester Row 1866

WEBSTER, JAMES WILLIAM.
25 Union St., Bishopsgate *1870*

WEISS, JOHN.
John Weiss was a Swiss national who established the firm in *1787* at 42 Strand. Between *1811* and *1822* the firm is listed at 33 Strand as surgeon's instrument maker and razor maker, however by *1823* they

Plate 198.
A interesting lock back knife with an unusual shaped blade. Stag scales. The blade is marked:

WEISS & SON
287
OXFORD ST

and hand forged. The absence of 'London' in the address may indicate that this was not made by Weiss but only retailed by them.

Plate 199.
All metal early motorist knife with tool for adjusting magnetos. The main and pen blades are marked:

WEISS & SON
287
OXFORD ST.

Plate 200.
A skinning knife with rosewood grips and spear point blade marked:

V (CROWN) R
WEISS
LONDON

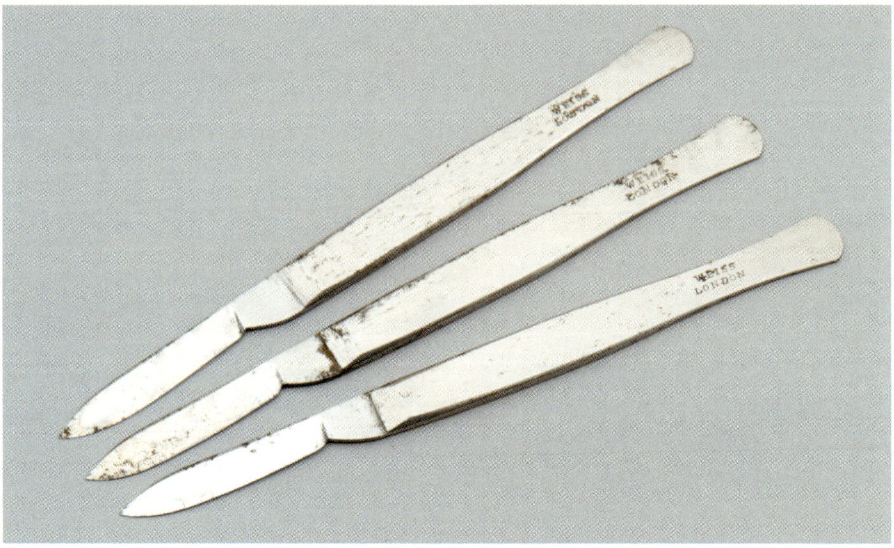

Plate 201.
All metal scalpels by WEISS.

Plate 202.
A magnificent Bowie with the locket engraved as follows:

A H SMITH
FROM
HAMILTON GEARY
ROYAL ARTILLERY
1863

Size: 9.75 inches, 14.75 inches overall.

Plate 203.
WEISS dagger which has well-formed ebony scales, nickel silver guard and a blade which is fluted on both sides. The grip is a smaller but almost identical form to that found on the knife shown in Plate 202. Blade marked:

WEISS
LONDON

Size: blade 7.25 inches, 11.5 inches overall.

Plate 204.
Dating from prior to 1830 this hunting knife has an ebony hilt carved with a lions mask pommel. The ricasso is marked:

G (CROWN) R
WEISS
LONDON

Size: blade 10 inches, 15.25 inches overall.

Plate 205.
Shown in *The Antique Bowie Knife Book* this is again a knife which dates from prior to 1830. Ebony grip, recurving guard with file work to the edge and spear point blade.
Size: blade 8 inches, 13 inches overall.

Plate 206.
This early WEISS dagger is unusual in that it not only bears a stag grip, ebony been that most commonly found on WEISS knives but it also carries the street address of 33 STRAND. This is uncommon in WEISS knives, which in general only bear the name of LONDON. The grip is silver mounted as is the sheath. The pommel cap engraved with a thistle emblem, possibly indicating a Scottish connection and the locket engraved with the name:

W P DOBREE.

Size: blade 7 inches, 11.75 inches overall.

(opposite page and following):
Pages from the Weiss 1925 catalogue showing a range of surgical knives.

are listed at 62 Strand as surgeon's instrument makers and cutlers. At this time the firm consisted of a partnership of a Fredrick Foveaux Weiss, Alfred Markes, Henry Joseph, Francis Foveaux and Richard Williams. The partnership was dissolved in late *1868*/early *1869* with Fredrick Foveaux Weiss trading under the John Weiss and Son name moving to 287 Oxford Street. They were still at this address in *1955* but by *1960* had moved to 17 Wigmore St.

John Weiss and Son exhibited at the 1851 Great Exhibition and the 1862 International Exhibition.

Weiss output of knives must have been relatively high as he is one of the more common London makers which the collector can encounter. Generally his work was of very high quality reflecting the surgical instrument background.

The Company now part of the HAAG STREIT Co. and located in Milton Keynes Union St.

Plate 207.
Another unusual WEISS dagger with its ebony grip carved in the form of a pot-bellied imp. Fancy recurving guard with acorn finials, ricasso scalloped in the same way as Plate 203. Blade marked:

WEISS
LONDON

Knives.

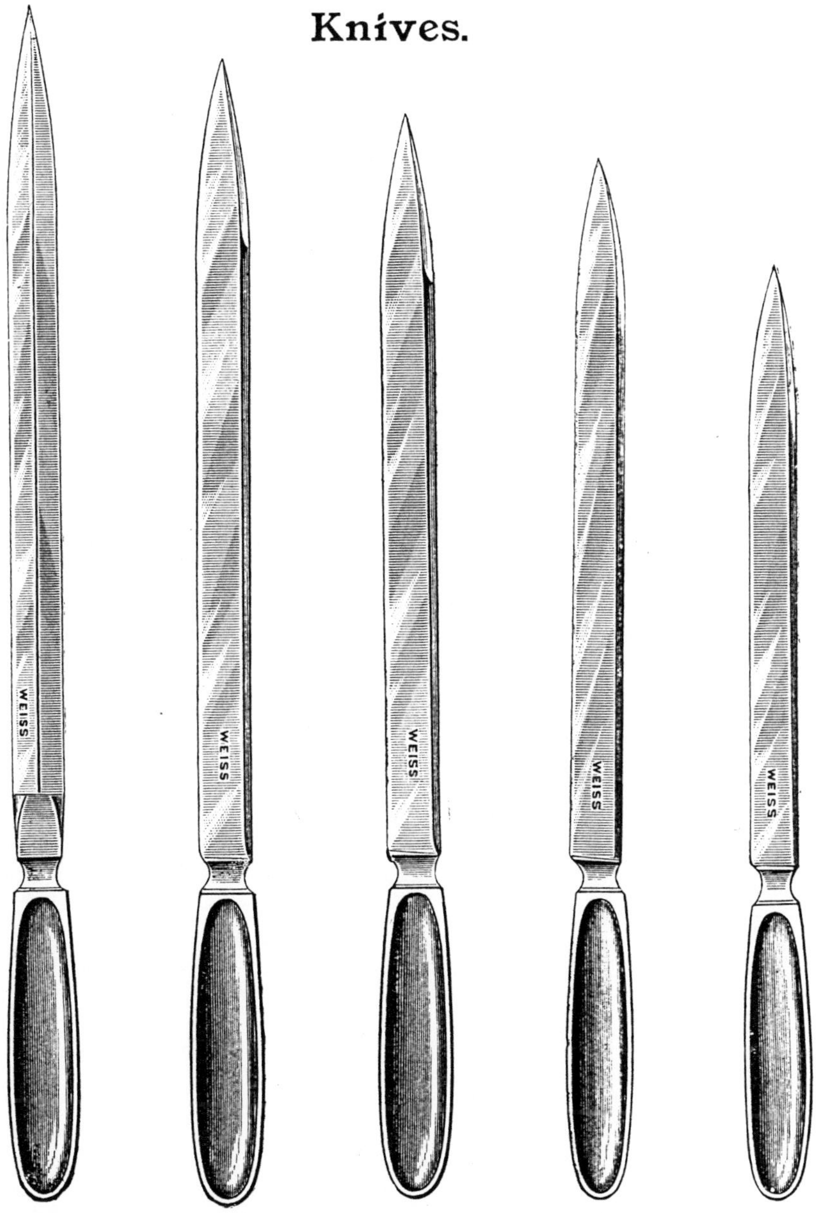

791 792 793 794 795

Amputation Knives, Aseptic, the blades and handles forged out of solid steel ; the handles grooved and nickel-plated.

791.	**Amputation Knife,** double-edged, Lisfranc's 7-in. blade, **22/-** ; 8-in., **24/6** ; 9-in.	**£1**	**8**	**0**
792.	Ditto single-edged, Liston's 11 in. ...	**1**	**8**	**6**
793.	Ditto do. do. 10 in. ...	**1**	**6**	**6**
794.	Ditto do. do. 9 in. ...	**1**	**4**	**6**
795.	Ditto do. do. 8 in. ...	**1**	**3**	**0**
***796.**	Ditto do. do. 7 in. ...	**1**	**1**	**0**
***797.**	Ditto do. do. 6 in. ...	**0**	**19**	**6**

* Not illustrated.

Knives.

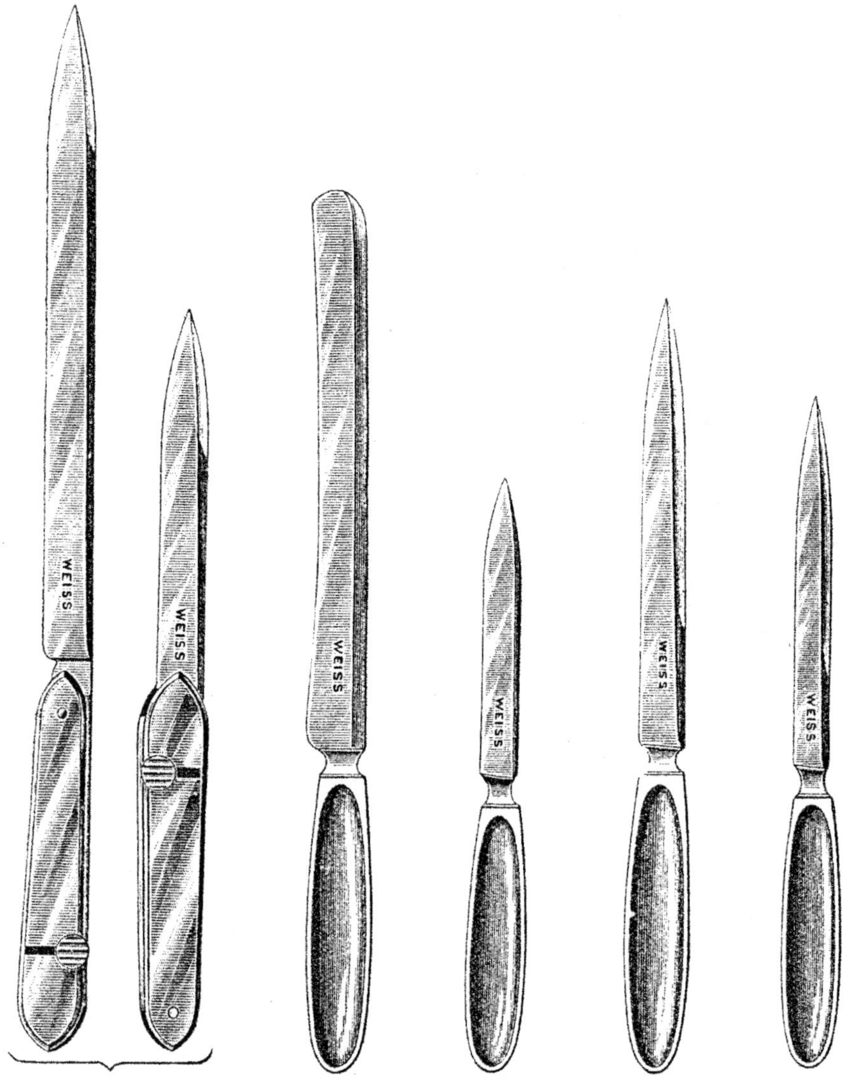

798 799 801 802 803

Amputation Knives, Aseptic, the blades and knives forged out of solid steel; the handles grooved and nickel-plated.

798.	**Amputation Knife,** folding, in spring handle ...	£2	2	0
799.	Ditto for circular operation, $7\frac{1}{2}$ in. ...	1	3	0
***800.**	Ditto do. $8\frac{1}{2}$ in. ...	1	4	6
801.	Ankle-joint Knife, Syme's	0	16	0
802.	Catlin, double-edged, 6 in.	0	18	6
803.	Ditto do. 5 in.	0	16	0

If with fluted backs, extra, each

* Not illustrated.

Knives.

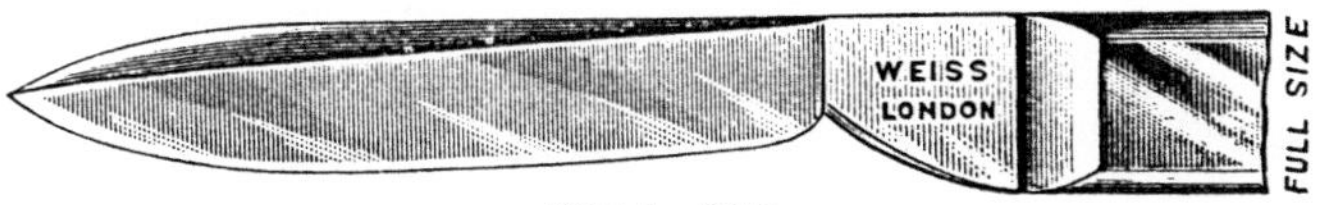

827 to 830

Scalpels, double-edged, five sizes, as Fig. 804 :—

827.	In hollow metal handles, nickel-plated ...	each	**£0 5 0**
828.	Solid forged, dull-plated handles	do.	**0 4 6**
829.	Ditto polished handles	do.	**0 5 0**
830.	Ditto fluted and hollowed handles ...	do.	**0 7 0**

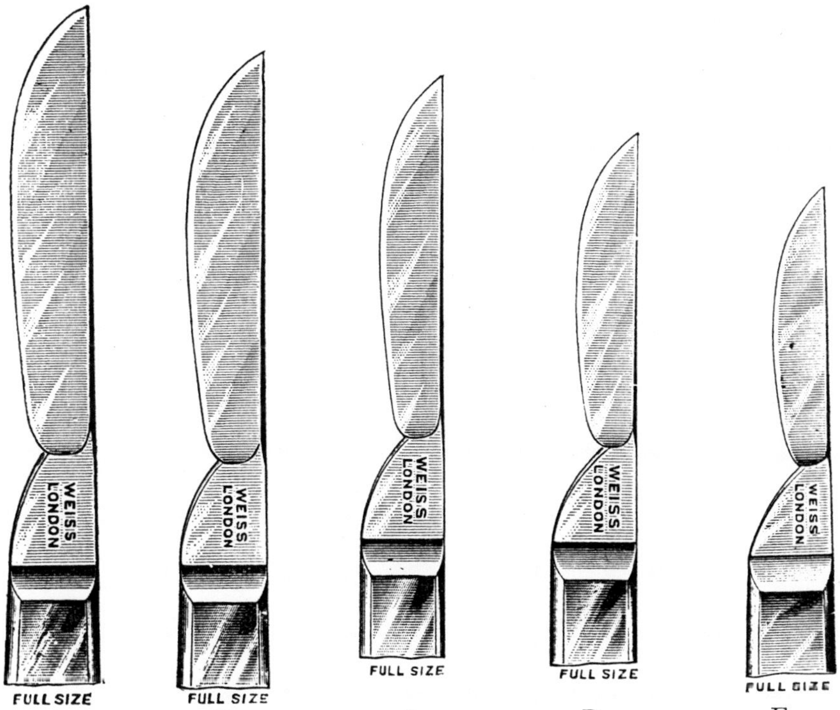

A B C D E

831 to 834

Scalpels, with back-pointed blades, five sizes, A, B, C, D, E :—

831.	In hollow metal handles, nickel-plated	**0 4 6**
832.	Solid forged, dull-plated handles	**0 4 0**
833.	Ditto polished handles	**0 4 6**
834.	Ditto fluted and hollowed handles	**0 6 6**

835

835. Tang Scalpel, with Raspatory in metal handle ... **0 7 6**

JOHN WEISS & SON, LTD. 283

Pocket Dressing Instruments.

Folding Knives, in metal handles, nickel-plated, with French or spring locks.

2024

2024. **Bistoury,** straight, sharp (finger knife), French lock £0 6 9

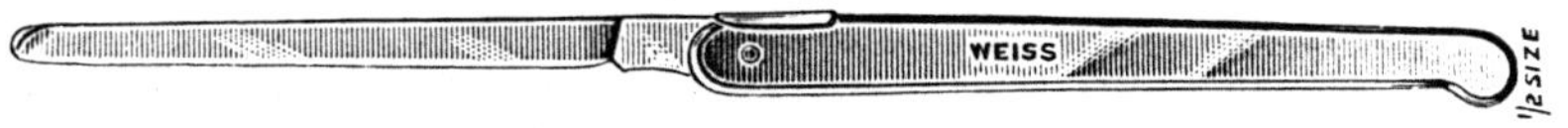

2025

2025. **Bistoury,** straight, probe, French lock 0 6 9

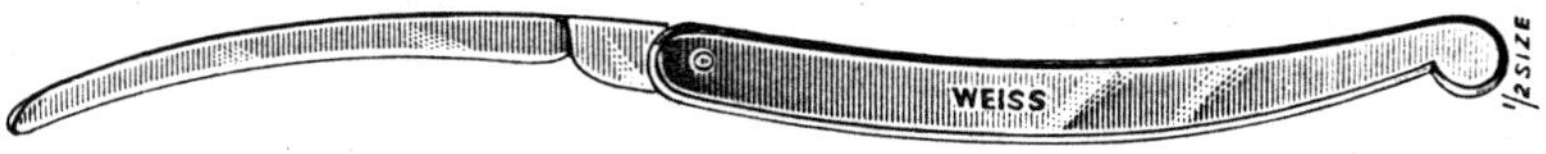

2026

2026. **Bistoury,** curved, probe, spring lock 0 6 9

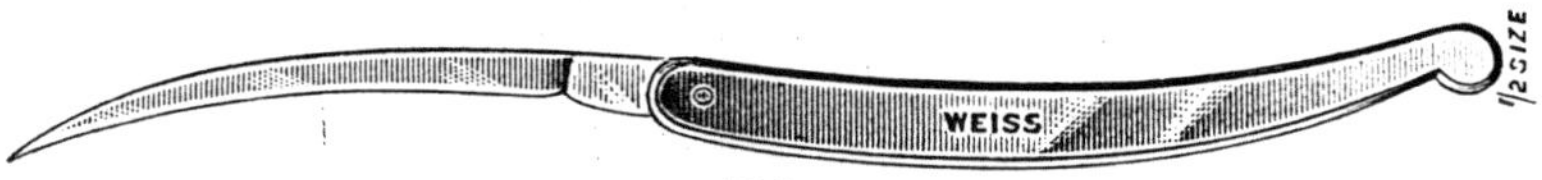

2027

2027. **Bistoury,** curved, sharp, spring lock 0 6 9

2028

2028. **Bistoury,** double, sharp and probe, spring locks... 0 11 6

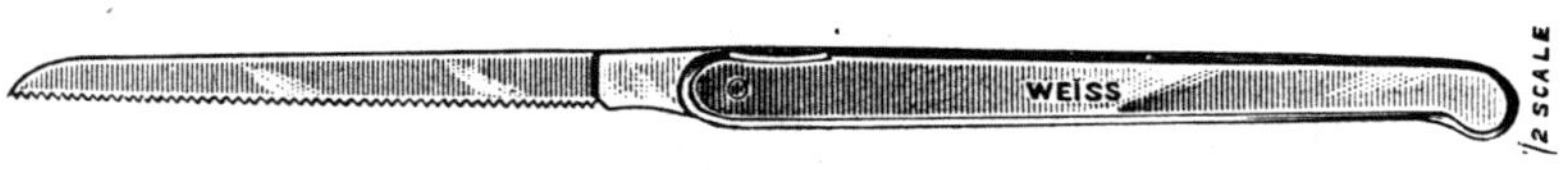

2029

2029. **Finger Saw,** French lock 0 10 0

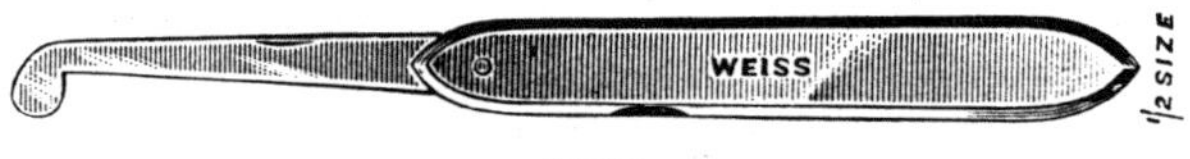

2030

2030. **Gum Lancet,** spring lock 0 6 0

2031

2031. **Gum Lancet** and **Syme's Abscess Knife,** spring locks 0 10 6

287, OXFORD STREET, LONDON, W.

Pocket Dressing Instruments.

Folding Knives, in metal handles, nickel-plated, with French or spring locks.

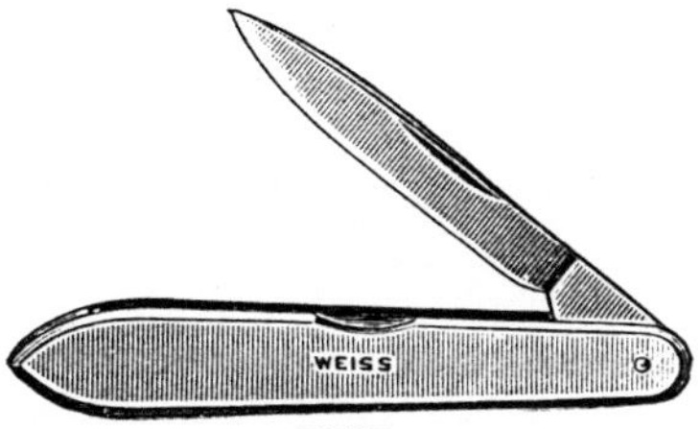

2037

2037. Scalpel, spring lock £0 6 0

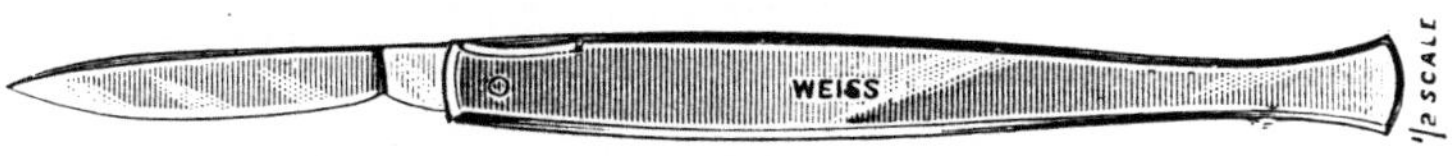

2038

2038. Scalpel, long handle, French lock 0 8 3

2039

2039. Scalpel, double, spring locks... ... ... 0 10 6

2040

2040. Scalpel and Finger Knife, spring locks 0 10 6

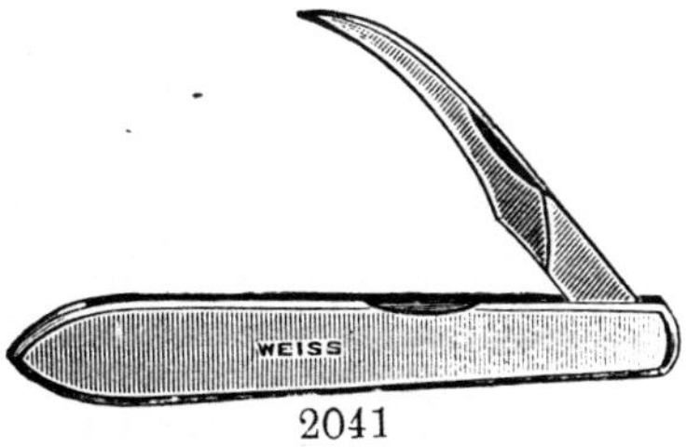

2041

2041. Syme's Abscess Knife, spring lock 0 6 0

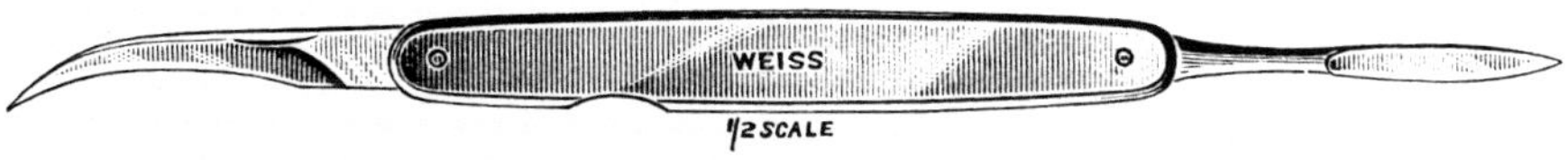

2042

2042. Syme's Abscess and Paget's Tenotomy Knives, spring locks 0 10 6

Pocket Dressing Instruments.

Folding Knives, in metal handles, nickel-plated, with French or spring locks.

2043

2043. Suture Needle, double, spring locks £0 13 6

2044

2044. Tenotomy Knife, double, spring locks 0 10 6

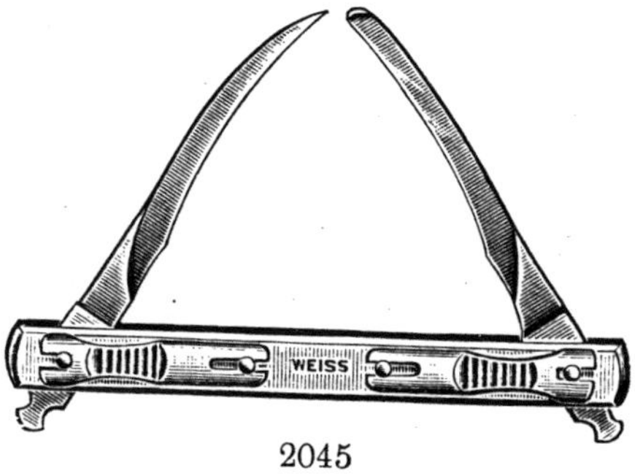

2045

2045. Double Knives, with nickel-plated metal handles, detachable sides and slide bolts ... each 0 12 9

(Any combination of blades can be made in this pattern.)

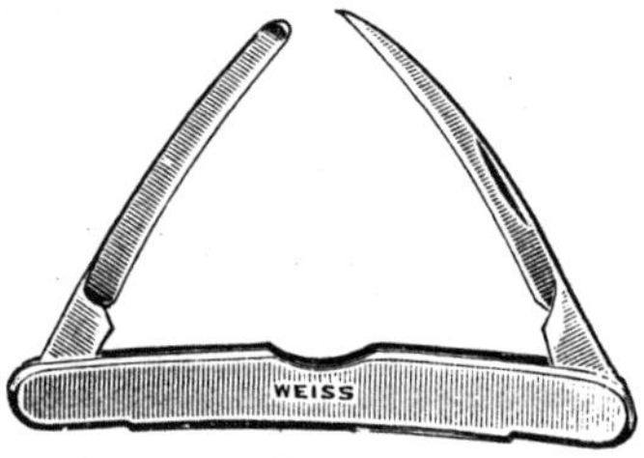

2046

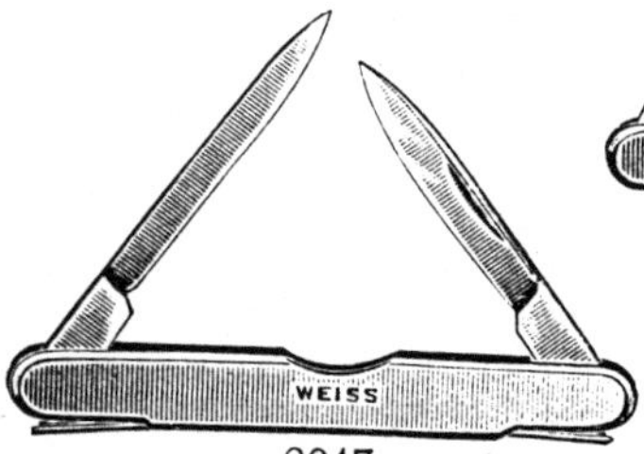

2047

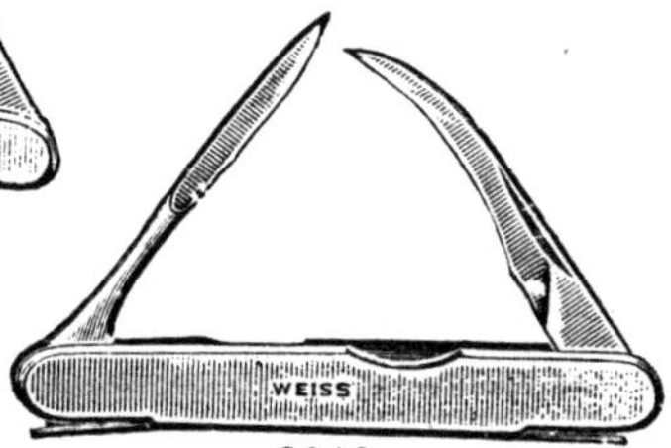

2048

Double Knives, Miniature, with French locks :—

2046.	**'Double Bistoury**	0	10	6
2047.	**Scalpel and Finger Knife**	0	9	9
2048.	**Syme's Abscess and Paget's Tenotomy Knives**	0	9	9

Pocket Dressing Instruments.

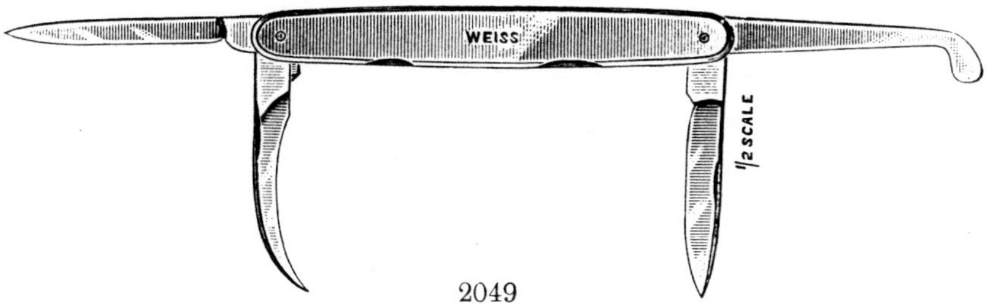

2049

2049. Four-bladed Pocket Instrument containing :—
Gum Lancet, Scalpel, Syme's Abscess and Pen
Knives £0 16 0

2050

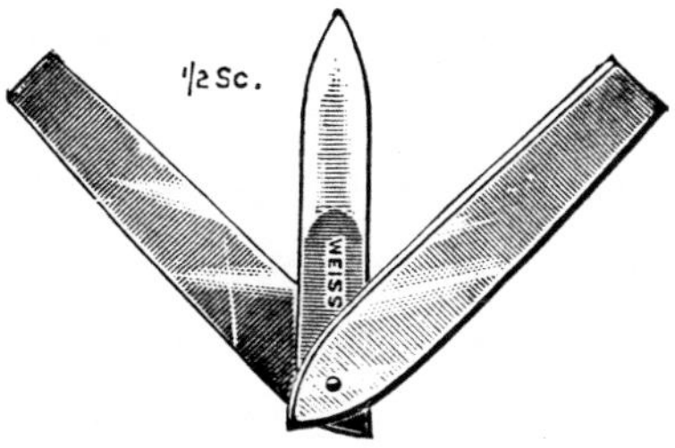

2051

2050.	**Abscess Lancet,** in metal scales	0 3 0
2051.	**Bleeding Lancet** do.	0 2 3
***2052.**	**Cases,** leather, for Lancets ... ... each, from	0 0 10
***2053.**	Ditto, silver do. ... each, from **21/-** to	1 18 6

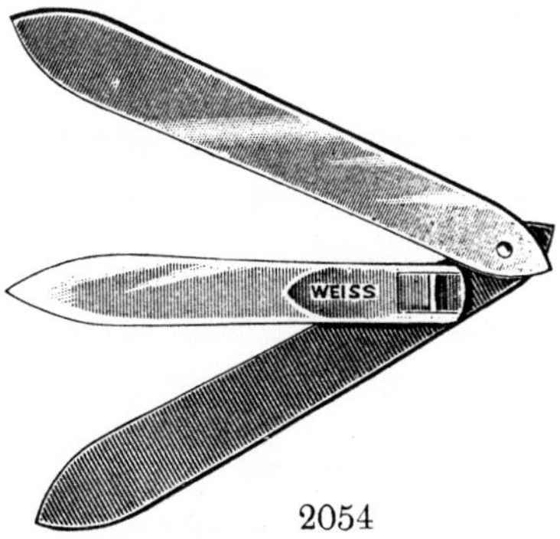

2054

2054.	**Seton Needle,** in metal scales	0 5 3
***2055.**	Ditto **Tapes,** elastic gum ... ... each	0 0 10

* Not illustrated.

Plate 208.
A superb folding knife with etched panels and marked:

SPANISH KNIFE

and:

LONDON MADE

along with

B.B. WELLS

on the ricasso.

WELCH, WILLIAM.

4 Jubilee St. 1890

WELLS, BENJAMIN BLAKE.

Benjamin Blake Wells is found in the *1850* directory but not in that for *1846* so his appearance occurs between *1847* and *1850*. His address at the time was recorded as a Cutler and Desk and Dressing Case Maker of 431 Strand and 143 Leadenhall St. In *1870* these latter premises are no longer occupied instead he is at 138 and 431 Strand, by *1880* however only the 431 Strand premises are listed. In 1890 Wells entry in the directory indicates that he is a razor maker and manufacturing cutler. In *1895* he is additional listed as a pen and pocket knife maker. Is recorded in the *1912* directory but not in *1915*.

WENTLMAN, WILLIAM.

10 Mill Lane, Deptford *1880*

WEST, FITZMAURICE.

1 St James St. *1840*-c.*1863*. West is listed in the *1841* directory as (late G.Palmer) cutler, dressing case and needle manufacturer to her Majesty, HRH Prince Albert, the Queen dowager, and to HRH the Duchess of Kent, and King and Queen of the Belgians. In *1852* the reference to G Palmer does not appear and the "royal" connection is shortened to cutler and dressing case manufacturer to the Royal Family. Exhibited at the 1862 International Exhibition. Name does not appear under cutlers in the *1866* directory, thus appears to have gone out of business between *1862* and *1866*.

WEST, RICHARD.

Wholesale. 18 Lower Smith St. 1820. 73 Banner St. *1823-1836*

WEST, THOMAS.

8 Artillery Place, Westminster *1841-1846*

Plate 209.
Large spear point Bowie probably marketed by Wells as there is no indication of being London made in the markings. Size: blade 12 inches, 17.5 inches overall.

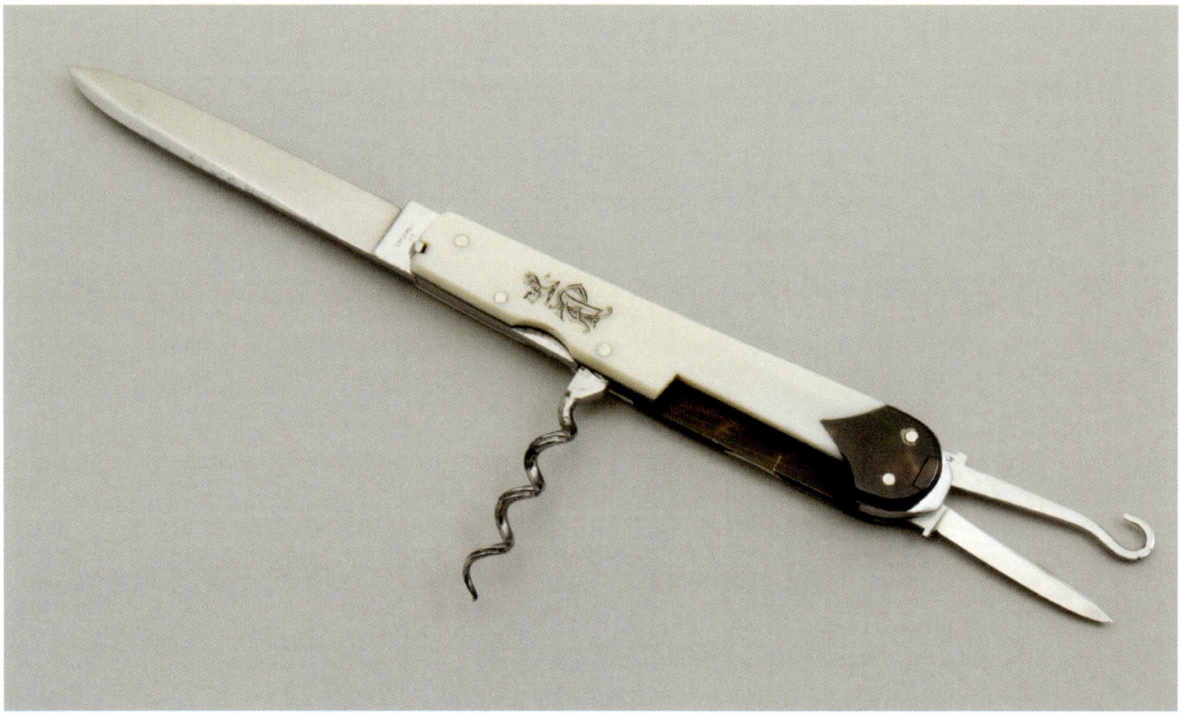

Plate 210.
Superb knife with ivory scales inset with tortoiseshell and marked with the crest of the Peel family along with the initials AP. The tang is marked WEST on one side, and on the other:

1 ST JAMES ST

WEST, W.
9 Boswell Court *1822 -1823*

WHEATON & BENNETT.
Working Cutler. 104, 106 and 108 Oxford St. *1895-1925*

WHICKER & PHILIP.
67 St James St. *1840-1850* (see Savigny)

WHICKER, PHILIP & BLAISE.
67 St James St., Pall Mall and Wilton St., Pimlico *1855* (see Savigny)

WHILTSHER, JONATHAN.
16 White Conduit St. *1855*

WHITE , L & J. B.
8 Great St. Andrew's St., Seven Dials 1846. As Mrs L in *1850*

WHITE, WILLIAM JAMES.
15 Union St. Whitechapel *1870*

WHITELY, WILLIAM.
51 to 58 Westbourne Grove and Queen's Rd. *1880*. 31, and 55 to 61 Westbourne Grove *1885*. 147 to 159 Queen's Road *1890-1895*

WHITELY, WILLIAM Ltd.
31 to 55 and 61 Westbourne Grove, 147 to 159 Queen's Rd. *1900*. 26, 31 to 55 and 61 Westbourne Grove, 147 to 159 Queen's Rd, and 49, 50, 51, 52 and 53 Kensington Gardens *1905*.

Plate 211.
Lock back folder with folding cross-guard, Stag scales. Blade marked:
WILD
ST. MICHAELS
ALLEY
CORNHILL

WHITTON, THOMAS MORGAN.
12 and 13 St. John's Lane, Clerkenwell *1866* also at 24 in *1870*. 14 St. John's Lane in *1875*

WHITTON BROS. & WHITTON.
12, 13 and 14 St. John's Lane *1920*.

WILCOX, THOMAS.
45 Edgeware Road *1850 1855 1860 1866*. 106 Edgware Rd. in *1870-1880*.

WILD, ALFRED RICHARD.
1 St. Michael's Alley *1885-1895*

WILD BROTHERS,
35 Kirby St., Hatton Gardens *1880-1900*

WILD, GEORGE.
58 Compton St. *1905*

WILD, WILLIAM.
21 Bowling Green Lane *1910-1915*

WILD, WILLIAM WALTER.
11 New Inn Yard, Tottenham Court Rd. *1930-1940*

WILKINS & SON.
Wholesale. 354 City Road *1880-1905*. In *1910* as WILKINS, JAS, RAWLINS & SON.

WILKINSON SWORD Co. Ltd.
1772-2005.
Besides being well known as sword makers Wilkinson produced some of the most historically important Knives i.e. the *Fairbairn Sykes Fighting Knife*, the *RBD Hunting Knife* commissioned by a R Beauchamp Drummond in *1869*, and the

Shakespear Knife. Tracing it history back to the gun maker Henry Nock, who founded his gun making business in *1772*. When Nock died in *1804* James Wilkinson inherited the business in *1804*. The exact relationship between Nock and Wilkinson is far from clear there being no evidence to support the frequently-told story that he was Nock's son-in-law. In *1825* James Wilkinson set up in his own name a business at 27 Pall Mall. James's son Henry took over the business in *1848* and continued to run it until his death in *1861*. The present name was adopted around *1889*.

Whilst Pall Mall (note that during their history they occupied a variety of premises in this location) remained the Company's main outlet the manufacturing premises they occupied at Chelsea became too small and they moved in *1903* to the Oakley Works, Southfield Road, Acton Green.
The Pall Mall premises closed in

Wilkinson's Pall Mall premises circa 1902, and (right), as they are today - and one of the few London Cutlers sites that still remain.

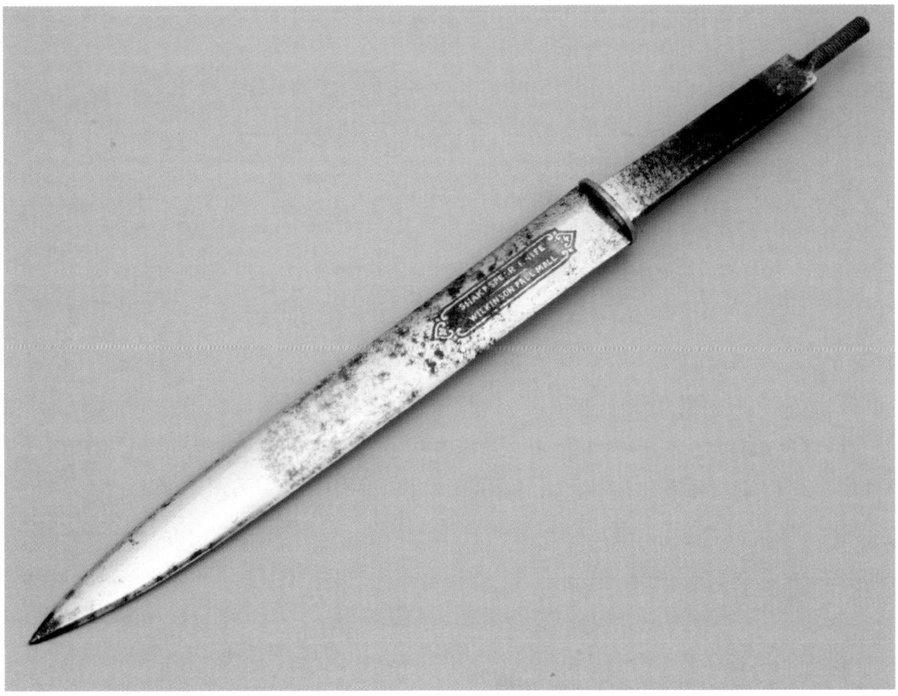

Plate 212.
Large version of the Shakespear Knife which unusually does not actually carry that name. The piece is just marked within a panel:

WILKINSON
PALL MALL
LONDON

Size: blade 9 inches, 14.25 inches overall.

Plate 213.
A very unusual, but uncompleted, version of the Shakespear Knife. The blade has the etched panel:

SHAKESPEAR KNIFE
WILKINSON PALL
MALL

1969 after some 140 years in this location. Oakley works remained until *1998* when they moved to the Sword Centre, Brunel Road Acton. Wilkinson Sword ceased all sword and knife manufacturing in *2005*.

WILKINSON, THOMAS & Co.

Tailors Cutler. 30 King's St., Cheapside *1855*. 115 Cheapside in *1870*

WILLATT, CHARLES.

31 Old St. *1832-1836*

Plate 214.
A classic example of the Shakespear Knife, in this case enhanced by the owners name and the words *Primo Assassino*. Size: blade 7.25 inches, 11.5 inches overall.

Plate 215.
One version of the well known but rare RBD knife. The RBD knife came in a number of sizes being etched No 1, 2 or 3 to reflect this.
This is a No. 1 example with a 6 inch blade.
The blade bears an etched panel containing the script: RBD HUNTING KNIFE Nº1
The ricasso in marked:

**WILKINSON
PALL MALL
LONDON**

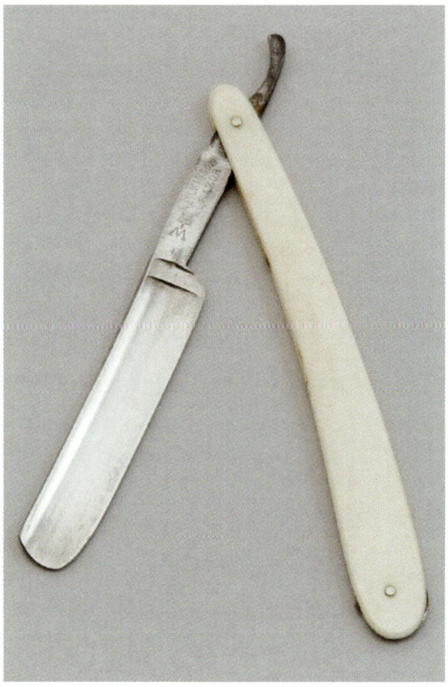

Wilkinson's Oakley works circa 1888

(above left):
Plate 216.
A Wilkinson razor known as the Figaro.

Plate 217.
Brass-mounted dirk by Henry Wilkinson.
Size: blade 12 inches, 17 inches overall.

Plate 218.
A very unusual knife which appears to be a variant of the RBD knife, though it is not marked as such. The knife has stag grip a RBD style cross-guard and sheath though this lacks the scabbard clip. The sheath is leather over wood with a nickel top mount. The blade has the Royal Coat of Arms with Kings Crown along with the Wilkinson trade mark of:

WILKINSON
SWORD CO LTD.
LONDON.

The back edge of the blade is etched with the name:

L.B.SANDERSON

Plate 219.
A group of one of Wilkinson's most famous knives, the Fairbairn Sykes (F-S) Fighting Knife.

Plate 220.
Although the blade of this piece is marked:
MANTON CALCUTTA
it was undoubtedly made for them by Wilkinson Sword a fact supported by the fact that the reverse of the scabbard locket is marked:
WILKINSON PALL MALL LONDON.
Made as a sidearm the blade is etched with symbols of the Royal Artillery along with a large etched panel bearing the words:

220 **FRONTIER KNIFE**
Size: blade 12.5 inches, 18 inches overall.

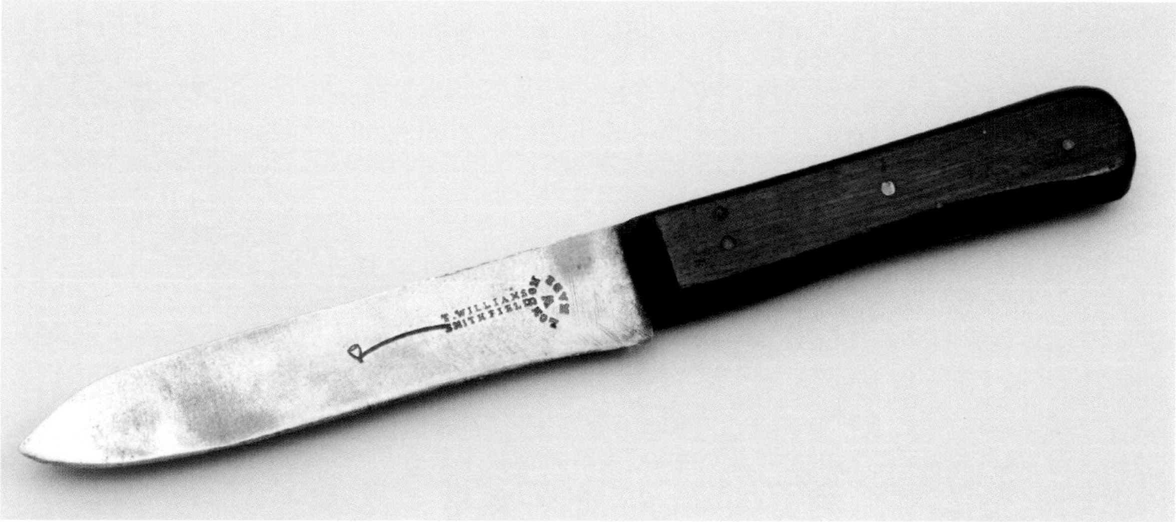

Plate 221.
A skinning knife with a strange set of stamps the blade bears the mark:

T WILLIAMS
SMITHFIELD

over a pipe trademark. The end of the WILLIAMS stamp partially over stamps the mark of:

LONDON
W
MADE

According to the Archivist of the Company of Cutlers in Hallamshire their records for 1900 when T Williams was at 8 and 14 West Smithfield indicate that the mark of a pipe with the words T WILLIAMS was a registered mark. They interestingly comment that the letter 'W' in the Sheffield trades usually indicated a 'waster' i.e. a reject.

WILLEY Mrs. ANN & MISS MARY.
21 Fish St. Hill *1855*

WILLEY, WILLIAM.
113 St. George St. *1846-1895*, also at 21 Fish St. Hill and 11 St. George St. in *1850*.

WILLIAMS.
At least two of the recorded Williams were at the less glamorous end of the cutlery trade being a makers and suppliers of butchers knives. Though there are some rather confusing references to at least two of them being surgical instrument makers.

Three Williams are noted in *1822*. Edward Williams 30 Lamb's Conduit St., Ebernezer Williams of 4 West Smithfield, and a Thomas Williams 106 Union St. and 14 West Smithfield. In 1832 both Ebernezer Williams and Thomas Williams are recorded as surgical instrument makers and butchers tool cutlers. It is of note however that their names do not appear under the surgical instrument maker section of the *1832* directory. There is no trace of Edward at this date.

In *1836* Ebernezer is at 82 West Smithfield and Thomas no longer occupied the 106 Union St. premises. At this time however a John Williams of 4 Long Acre is recorded. Ebernezer is no longer found in the 1840 record whilst John and Thomas continue to be listed up until *1860* but John's concern is now known as John Williams and Son 14 Little St. Andrew St. In *1866* there are further changes with the entries being:
Williams and Son 37 Castle St., Long Acre
Williams Alfred H, 135 Fenchurch St. (Desk and Dressing case maker)
Williams Thomas (butchers) 14 West Smithfield, and 7 Bank Building Metropolitan Cattle Market.

By *1880* only Thomas remains listed with an additional premises at Gee St., Goswell Road. There are further changes to his premises in *1885* when 8 West Smithfield is added but 7 Bank Building is dropped. More changes take place in 1890 with 79 Charterhouse and Great Arthur St. being additionally occupied. Various other changes to their premises took place in the early *1900*'s Williams appears in the *1930* directory but not in that for *1935*.

Plate 222.
Simple stag-gripped dirk stamped:

WILLIAMS
LONG ACRE

Possibly John Williams circa 1836-1860.

WILLIAMSON, ALBERT ARTHUR.
483 Harrow Rd. *1935-1940*

WILLIAMSON, EDWIN.
Working. 206 Mile End Rd. *1890*

WILLIAMSON, H. Ltd.
81 Farringdon Rd. *1905-1915.*
In *1920* at 77 to 81 Farringdon Rd, at 77 and 79 in *1925*

WILLIAMSON, WILLIAM.
21 Eyre St. Hill *1855*

WILLIAMSON, WILLIAM.
152 Praed St., Paddington *1860-1870*

WILLIAMSON, WILLIAM.
80 Harrow Hill *1875 -1885*

WILLIS, A & Co.
28 Hatton Gardens *1895-1910*

WILSON & DAVIS.
10 Hatton Gardens *1875-1880*

WILSON, FREDRICK & Co.
Manufacturing Cutler.
9 Hatton Gardens *1885-1895*

WILSON & SON.
Manufacturing Cutler, pen and pocket knives and razor makers. 7, 8 and 9 King William St. , Strand, works 7 Rose St. Soho *1890-1905*, works at Manette St. Soho. In *1910-1925* as WILSON & SMITH. 9 King William St. address dropped, not listed during this period.

WILSTSHIER, JONATHAN & GEORGE.
57 and 58 St. John's Square *1895* at 162 Clerkenwell Rd. in *1900*

WILTSHIRE, J.
8 Long Lane, Smithfield *1836-1846*

WILTSHIRE, J.
20 Crescent St., Euston Square *1855*

WINTER, JAMES
74 St. George St. and 2 and 3 Upper East Smithfield *1855-1866.* In *1870-1875* at 71 Upper East Smithfield and 221 Shadwell High St. Only at later in *1880*

WOLLOMS & Co.
299 Tottenham Court Road *1866-1870*

WOOD.
Bennion list four WOOD's - one based in York, one in Manchester and two in Liverpool she does not however record any for London. However a number of London-based Wood's are listed as surgical instrument makers i.e.

John Wood, 15 Aske St., *1855*, 16 Portpool Lane *1860*
James Wood and Co., 29 Paternoster Square, *1885*
Vincent Wood, 29 Paternoster Square, *1890*, 9 St. Andrew St., 1895

The absence of an address on the piece illustrated makes it of course impossible to establish whether or not it was made by either of the London based Wood's but it is typical of the period.

WOOD, ALFRED ROBERT.
65 High St. St. Giles *1890*

WOOD, HENRY.
Butchers Cutler. 6 and 7 West Smithfield 1866

Plate 223.
Small folding Abscess Lancet with horn scales and marked:
WOOD.

WOOD, J.
Working Cutler. 111 Bishopgate St. within *1820-1834*

WOOD, ROBERT.
7 West Smithfield *1823-1832* also at 5 West Smithfield in *1836*, 6 and 7 in *1846-1850*

WOOD, ROSETTA.
111 Bishopgate St. within *1836*. 39 Threadneedle St. *1840-1846*

WOODHOUSE, WILLIAM.
7 Portpool Lane, Gray's Inn Rd. 1895

WOODHOUSE, WALTER.
39 Leather Lane. *1900*

WOOLNOUGH, DRAPER & Co Ltd.
12 and 13 Chiswell St. *1925-1930*

WOOLLEY, SAMUEL
19 Piccadilly *1846*

WORMALL, ANTHONY
20 Union St. Lambeth *1832-1839*

WORMALL, ANTHONY Sen.
121 Lambeth Walk. *1846-1870* (spelling is WORMULL in *1850*)

WORMALL & PHILLIPS.
45 Union St. *1866*

Plate 224.
A knife of the style typically used from the Boer War up to and including World War 1. Horn scales, sheeps foot blade and marlin spike. The ricasso is marked:

J.A. WYLIE & CO
62 HOLBORN
VIADUCT

WORMALL, JOHN.
121 Lambeth Walk *1875-1880*, at 65 in *1885*

WORMULL, GEORGE.
45 Union St. *1870-1885*
(see also Evans & Co.)

WORTH, B & SONS.
Manufacturing Cutler.
1 Gresham St. *1905-1925*

WRIGHT, C & Co.
108 New Bond St. *1880-1895*

WRIGHT, CHARLES.
52 Baldwin's Gardens *1829*

WRIGHT, CHARLES.
Working Cutler. 57 Gray's Inn Lane *1822-1832*, as Charles David in *1836*.

WRIGHT, CHARLES DAVID.
87 Hoxton St. 1870 also at 21 Great St. Andrew's St. in *1875-1890*.

WRIGHT, EDWARD.
17 Homer St. Marylebone
1822-1825

WRIGHT, HENRY.
Cutler and Surgical Instrument Maker. 13 London Rd, 32 London Rd, 18 London Rd. *1794-1867*

WRIGHT, Mrs. CAROLINE.
Manufacturing Cutler 21 Drury Court, Strand 1870

WRIGHT, Mrs. ELIZABETH.
57 Grays Inn Lane *1839-1840*

WRIGHT, JOHN.
138 Ratcliffe Highway *1822-1825*

WRIGHT, STEPHEN.
59 Wych St., Strand *1850-1855*. 4 Drury Lane *1860*

WRIGHT, THOMAS.
4 Lowther Arcade, Strand. *1836*

WRIGHT, WILLIAM.
Working Cutler. 7 Ship Alley *1822-1834*. 12 Grenada Terrace. Commercial Road in *1836-1840*. 1 Rephidim St., Old Kent Road *1844*

WYLIE, J.A. & Co.
62 Holborn Viaduct *1915-1940*

YORKE, JOHN & ALEXANDER.
91 Watling St. 1860 -1866

YOUARD & Co.
24 Castle St. Houndsditch *1880.*

ZILLES, HENRY.
14 South St., Finsbury *1885.*

4 References & Sources

Sheffield Exhibition Knives. *Claussen, Watts, McMickle*. Old World Publishing Ltd, Salem, Oregon. 1999.

London Silver-hilted Swords, their makers, suppliers and allied traders with directory. *Leslie Southwick*, Royal Armouries 2001.

The Directory of Gold and Silversmiths and allied trades 1838-1915. *J Culme*. Antique Collectors Club 1987.

The Scottish Dirk, *James D Foreman*. Historical Museum Series No.26. Museum Restoration Service, Alexandria Bay N.Y., USA, and Bloomfield, Ontario, Canada.

Butterfield and Butterfield Auction Sale 4838A (March 1992) Catalogue. The Antique Bowie Knife Collections of Robert Berryman and Chas Schreiner III.

Butterfield and Butterfield Auction Sale 6552 (January 1997) Catalogue. The William R. Williamson Bowie Knife Collection.

The Knife Guide, *Bernard Levine*, Knife World Publications, Knoxville Tennessee, USA. 1981.

The Mark of the Sword. "A narrative history of the Cutlers' Company 1189-1975". *Tom Girtin*. Hutchinson Benham, London 1975.

The Worshipful Company of Cutlers of London - A BRIEF HISTORY, *Dudley Hayton*, 1956 (reprinted 1980).

Goin's Encyclopaedia of Cutlery Markings. *John and Charlotte Goins*. Idianapolis. 1998.

THE SWORDSMAN - Newsletters of the Wilkinson Sword Collectors Society.

Hitchmough of London, *Tony Tocci*, Fighting Knives, Winter 1992.

The London Hunting Knife, *Bernard Levine*, Knives 98.

Antique Medical Instruments. *Elisabeth Bennion*. Sotheby Parke Bennet Publications 1979.

Antique Dental Instruments, *Elisabeth Bennion*. Sotheby's Publications, London 1986.

John Weiss and Son Ltd, 1925 catalogue Section II.

Army and Navy Catalogue 1939.

The Antique Bowie Knife Book. *Bill Adams, J. Bruce Voyles, Terry Moss.* Museum Publishing Co. Inc Conyers, Georgia. 1990.

Bowie Knives - Origin and Development. La Commission des Avoyelles. 1979.

Sales and Auction catalogues - Wallis and Wallis, Jim and Cindy Crawford.

Pigot & Co. Directories of London and its Suburbs.

Kelly's Post Office Directories of London.

The Cutlery Industry, *Peter Smithhurst.* Shire Album 158, Shire Publications Ltd. 1987.

I*XL means I EXCEL. *William R Williamson.* Published by Robert. E. P. Cherry.

Swords and Sword Makers of England and Scotland. *Richard H Bezdek.* Paladin Press 2003.

THE BOWIE KNIFE Unsheathing an American Legend. *Norm Flayderman.* Andrew Mowbray Inc. Lincoln, Rhode Island 2004.

The Collections of the Worshipful Company of Cutlers of London. Part One London Made Knives and their Marks. *Keith Hinde and John Herbert.* Authors Online Ltd. 2005.

MY BOY JACK The search for Kipling's Only Son, *Tonie and Valmai Holt.* Leo Cooper, Yorkshire 1998.

Primer of Military Knives Part 1. *Gordon Hughes and Barry Jenkins.* Privately Published Brighton 1973.

The Sheffield Knife Book "A History and Collector's Guide". *Geoffrey Tweedale.* The Hallamshire Press, Sheffield 1996.

British Planemakers from 1700. 2nd Edition. *W.L. Goodman.* Arnold and Walker, Needham Market, Suffolk. 1978.

British & Commonwealth Military Knives. *Ron Flook*, Airlife Publishing Ltd, Shrewsbury. 1999.

Conclusion

The heyday of London cutlery passed many years ago. Some of the major retailers lingered on but production of knives in London was virtually restricted to Wilkinson Sword who has we have seen earlier ceased its sword and knife production in 2005.
However one private cutler did work during the 1960's to 1996 and has gone on to become a major force amongst US custom knife makers and that is Howard Hitchmough.

Howard Hitchmough was probably London's last independent knife maker. Howard began his career in the cutlery trade by serving an apprenticeship as a surgical instrument maker with A L Hawkings. He later moved to the medical division of Unilever. In 1961 Howard began making hunting knives on a part time basis for himself and friends. He carried out his work from a cramped garage workshop attached to his London flat. When Unilever closed its medical facility and he was made redundant Howard turned full time maker. However with the custom knife market being somewhat limited in the UK he emigrated to the USA in 1997. He is now resident there and the only English maker (though now a US citizen) of the Knifemakers' Guild. He continues to make fine knives.

It is difficult to gauge the number of knives Howard made from his garage workshop but his own rough estimate is approximately 2000 including around 70 for Purdy, the London gun maker. These knives not only bear the Purdy name but that of Howard Hitchmough.
He also made 5 for Rigsby and an unknown number for William Evans. His work is of very high quality and despite the 2000 piece output his London-made knives only very rarely appear on the open market.

The knives illustrated were made by Hitchmough in about 1983.

HITCHMOUGH
LONDON ENGLAND
HITCHMOUGH
LONDON ENGLAND

W C
FOUNDLING HOSPITAL
BRITISH MUSEUM
GRAYS INN GARDENS
NEW OXFORD STREET
HIGH HOLBORN
STRAND
VICTORIA EMBANKMENT